W9-ASJ-225

A12901 103168

ILLINOIS CENTRAL COLLEGE
HV7436.D38 1993
STACKS
Under fire :

A12901 103168

WITHDRAWN

HV 7436 .D38 1993

DAVIDSON, OSHA GRAY.

UNDER FIRE

83639

**Illinois Central College**
**Learning Resources Center**

GAYLORD

# UNDER FIRE

ALSO BY OSHA GRAY DAVIDSON

*Broken Heartland*
(Free Press, 1990)

# OSHA GRAY DAVIDSON

HENRY HOLT AND COMPANY / NEW YORK

# UNDER FIRE

## THE NRA AND
## THE BATTLE FOR GUN CONTROL

I.C.C. LIBRARY

83639

HV
7436
.D38
1993

Grateful acknowledgment is made to the National Rifle Association of America to reprint material that appears on pages 47–48 and 159–60. The text of the ads and the lyrics are copyright © by National Rifle Association of America.

Henry Holt and Company, Inc.
*Publishers since 1866*
115 West 18th Street
New York, New York 10011

Henry Holt® is a
registered trademark of
Henry Holt and Company, Inc.

Copyright © 1993 by Osha Gray Davidson
All rights reserved.
Published in Canada by Fitzhenry and Whiteside Limited,
91 Granton Drive, Richmond Hill, Ontario L4B 2N5.

Library of Congress Cataloging-in-Publication Data
Davidson, Osha Gray.
Under fire : the NRA and the battle for gun control / Osha Gray
Davidson.—1st ed.
p. cm.
Includes bibliographical references and index.
1. National Rifle Association of America. 2. Gun control—United
States. 3. Lobbying—United States. I. Title.
HV7436.D38 1993
363.3'3'06073—dc20 92-30814
ISBN 0-8050-1904-9 (alk. paper) CIP

First Edition—1993

Designed by Katy Riegel
Printed in the United States of America
All first editions are
printed on acid-free
paper. ∞

1 3 5 7 9 10 8 6 4 2

*For my parents,*
*Sol and Penny Davidson,*
*with love and respect.*

# CONTENTS

# ACKNOWLEDGMENTS

Many people helped to produce this book. Rather than list by name those individuals whose interviews appear on the following pages, I'll thank them all collectively here: Your cooperation was invaluable.

I'd also like to thank Ron and Cheryl Flax-Davidson and their daughters, Skylar and Devorah, for putting me up (as well as putting up with me) during my stay in Washington, D.C.

Thanks to the staff of the MedSTAR Trauma Unit, Washington Hospital Center in Washington, D.C., for allowing me to spend two eye-opening nights with them—and especially to Dr. Daniel Webster for arranging my visits.

At the National Rifle Association, I am indebted to Tom Wyld, Patrick G. O'Malley, and Amie Smith for arranging interviews and providing me with information and documents.

Thanks also to the many aides to members of both houses of Congress for offering a wealth of information and all-important details about the legislative process. Many are quoted by name in the following pages, but many others asked to remain anonymous.

I owe a special debt to William Strachan, my editor at Henry Holt, whose idea this book was. Thanks, too, to Gerard McCauley for getting us together.

To my wife, Mary, who suffered through every draft with me,

my thanks and, as always, my love and appreciation. Thanks to my daughters, Sarah and Sienna, for once again being understanding about the eccentric life-style of a writer.

For furnishing a variety of information and miscellaneous assistance, thanks to: Susan Whitmore, director of communications for Handgun Control, Inc.; James A. Mercy, Division of Injury Control, Center for Environmental Health and Injury, Centers for Disease Control; Karen Cottrell and Deborah E. Nauser of Ackerman McQueen; Edward C. Ezell, curator/supervisor of the Division of Armed Forces History, National Museum of American History, Smithsonian Institution; John D. Aquilino, editor-in-chief, *Insider Gun News*; Jerry M. Tinker, staff director, and Thurgood Marshall, Jr., counsel, Senate Subcommittee on Immigration and Refugee Affairs; Mike Dickerson, Federal Elections Commission; George Black, former associate editor of *The Nation*; and the staff of the Senate Periodical Press Gallery.

I am especially grateful to the many NRA members who, though wary of journalists in general, were always warm, friendly, and helpful to this journalist. One elderly couple in particular stands out. I shared an elevator ride with them at the 1991 NRA annual convention in San Antonio, Texas. Noticing the name card pinned to my breast pocket that identified me as a journalist, the woman—who couldn't have been five feet tall, including her snow-white beehive hairdo—wagged a bony finger in my face and said, "Now, you remember to say something nice about us."

"No," her husband corrected in a firm but friendly voice, pushing back his Stetson, "you just tell the *truth*."

That is what I've tried to do.

# PART I

# THE RISE
# OF THE NRA

# 1

# THE STOCKTON
# LESSON

*17 January*
*11:42 A.M.*

*AT LAST HE has them in his sights.*

*So many gooks swarm over the flat, broad field just fifty yards in front of him that he doesn't even need to sight. Just point and shoot. Eddie has the enemy trapped between himself and a low L-shaped building.*

*Look at all of them. There must be three, four hundred of them. And all of them caught beneath the warm, brilliant sun with nowhere to hide.*

*He's so close now that even through his earplugs he can hear the sound of their hated language. Fucking Vietnamese. Incomprehensible. Alien. Singsong. The language of the suppressors.*

*He plants his feet wide and bends his knees slightly. He steadies the wooden stock of his AK-47 assault rifle against his hip.*

*The "AK" weighs just under ten pounds but it still delivers a considerable kick. And Eddie's rifle is heavier than most by a good pound and a half—the weight of a fixed bayonet, a round "drum" magazine, and the seventy-five 7.62-mm bullets that it holds.*

*He is well prepared for his Mission. In the black ammo pouch*

3

*strapped to his waist are three steel "banana" clips. In each clip there are thirty rounds. He also has a new Taurus 9-mm semiautomatic pistol—never even been fired—tucked into a black canvas holster and hidden by his camouflage jacket and olive-drab flak vest.*

*For one last second he surveys the enemy scurrying here and there in front of him. This is the moment Patrick Edward "Eddie" Purdy has been waiting for all his life. Twenty-four years old, and at long last his Mission is about to be fulfilled. A good soldier, he doesn't let the emotions of the moment—even this moment! his moment!— overwhelm him. That could jeopardize the Mission. He doesn't scream or shout, like he did the time he was captured. He doesn't even smile.*

*He simply points the muzzle of his gun in the direction of the enemy, braces himself, and squeezes the trigger.*

When D. H. Lawrence wrote that "the essential American soul is hard, isolate, stoic, and a killer," he must have had someone like Patrick Edward Purdy in mind. Lawrence was, of course, writing of America at its worst, describing those bewildered (and bewildering) souls who live in a state of moral twilight, who transform their vast inner emotional pain into numerous acts of casual violence. If they're not stopped—either by jail, death, or redemption—that inner suffering can explode without warning in a final, ritualistic act of remarkable brutality.

Patrick "Eddie" Purdy was that kind of American. The kind the rest of us pray we, members of our family, and our friends will never meet. His life story—short, lonely, violent—reads so much like a textbook description of a psychotic that it is difficult to see him as an individual. For most, he remains simply a "classic" representative of a type: the American mass murderer. Afterward, the newspapers would identify Purdy as a "drifter." For once, that overused label was accurate. The twenty-four-year-old with tangled light-brown hair and hazel-gray eyes had drifted around the country, drifted from job to job, and drifted from one cheap motel to another ever since his mother kicked him out of the house when he was thirteen years old. In just the last six months of his life Purdy lived in several states across the country. He stayed with an aunt in Oregon for a while—until he was laid off at his job welding water tanks—then traveled to Dallas, where he had a line on another job. When that fell through, Purdy headed to Memphis. He managed to scratch up another job there, but quit within a week. As he complained to his aunt in a collect phone call, he "had to work with a bunch of niggers." He wandered up to Connecticut, where he worked for a month or so before quitting again. Finally, on December 27, 1988, Purdy moved to what was to be his last address: Room 104, the El Rancho Motel, Lodi, California.

But this last move was different. Purdy had not drifted to this suburb of Stockton, California. Far from it. His Mission had returned him to his childhood home.

Purdy had lived in Stockton for three years (from 1969 to 1972) and had attended the Cleveland Elementary School during that time, passing from kindergarten through second grade. He lived with his mother, Kathleen, stepfather, Albert Gulart, a sister, and a half brother in a modest tract home just a half mile from the school. His mother and natural father (Patrick Benjamin Purdy, who had earlier been forced out of the military for "petty criminality and psychotic instability") had separated when Purdy was just a toddler. Now, Purdy often had to stand helplessly by as his new stepfather beat his mother in front of him. In 1972, when Eddie Purdy was seven years old, his mother and stepfather separated and Kathleen Gulart moved her children to Sacramento the following year. This might have been a fresh start for the troubled family, but even without an abusive husband around, Eddie's mother showed little interest in child-rearing. She partied at night, and worked and slept during the day. After a neighbor notified the authorities that the children were being neglected, the state took them into temporary protective custody. But Eddie and his brother and sister were returned after Kathleen Gulart agreed to see a counselor.

It wasn't long before drugs and alcohol found their way into Purdy's life. He once told an acquaintance that his mother was an alcoholic, and he himself joined Alcoholics Anonymous. For years, Purdy was never sober for more than two or three days at a time, and he often blacked out after a particularly wild binge.

"He wouldn't stop drinking," an AA acquaintance said later. Purdy acted like he was "hurting inside," he recalled, adding that "sometimes when you hurt inside you want to hurt others."

Purdy had many reasons to feel wounded. He did poorly at school, he had no close friends, and life at home was chaotic and tense. In the summer of 1978, after a particularly severe fight, his mother kicked Purdy out of the house. Thirteen years old, he was shuttled between foster homes for a time. Eventually, he ended up living with his natural father in Lodi, California, outside of Stockton.

Never a good student, Purdy fell further behind over the years. (Years later, a police report would say he suffered from "mild mental retardation," but that was never substantiated.) A teacher at the Mt. Talac Continuation School—a high school for students with academic and disciplinary problems—remembers Eddie Purdy as a loner who "never hung around girls or other students. In fact, you never saw him with other human beings."

Purdy sat in class hiding inside an oversized military fatigue jacket, staring off into space, never volunteering answers. Even among a group of detached students, Purdy's withdrawal seemed so acute that his teachers suspected he was smoking pot or maybe even sniffing glue. They were right on both counts. He was also drinking a half gallon of cheap wine each day.

In 1981, while walking down a dark street at night, Patrick Purdy, Sr., was struck by a car and killed. Eddie Purdy was, at the age of sixteen, officially on his own.

What little stability his life possessed was now gone. He bounced among cheap motels in Stockton, Lodi, and nearby Modesto, living mostly off of the Social Security checks that arrived after his father's death. His run-ins with the law, which had begun even before his father died, became more frequent—and more serious. When Eddie was only fourteen, he had been arrested for extortion. Using a crude spear (a stick with a nail fixed to its end), Purdy had robbed two smaller boys of a grand total of nine cents. And so it went for years; his long police record is a recitation of botched petty crimes and miscellaneous offenses:

November 1979—Juvenile contact. Disposition unknown.

December 1979—Listed as a suspect in a juvenile case. Disposition unknown.

May 1980—Arrested for violating a court order.

June 1980—Listed as a suspect in a theft.

June 1980—Arrested for public intoxication.

August 1980—Arrested for solicitation of prostitution after offering to perform oral sex on an undercover policeman for $30.

November 1980—Listed as a suspect in a vandalism case.

January 1981—Arrested for violating a court order.

August 1982—Involved in fistfight with roommate. Police responding find four baggies of marijuana and arrest Purdy.

August 1982—Arrested after breaking into former apartment and causing $200 in damages.

January 1983—Arrested for driving under the influence of drugs/alcohol.

February 1983—Arrested for public intoxication.

May 1983—Arrested for possession of stolen property.

July 1983—Listed as suspect in vandalism case.

October 1984—Arrested on charge of attempted robbery. Charge reduced to being an accessory to a felony.

Another pattern became established during this period: a fascination with weapons of all kinds. While cruising a Beverly Hills street in 1983, a policeman noticed an outdated registration sticker on the license plate of the car ahead of him and pulled the car over. It was registered to the driver, who was, according to the license, a twenty-year-old Caucasian male, five feet eleven inches tall, by the name of Eddie Purdy West. His race was the only accurate information on the license. Purdy often used this alias, for no particular reason, and had also lied about his height, which was only five feet seven inches. The drifter with the long brown hair was actually born in 1964—not 1962, as he had told the California Department of Motor Vehicles (or 1960, the birth year he gave to Oregon officials).

As the policeman was looking over the registration, he glanced into the car's backseat and saw a pair of nunchaku sticks, a martial arts weapon illegal in California.

"What're you doing with those?" asked the cop.

Purdy shrugged. "They're just to mess around with."

He was arrested for possessing a dangerous weapon, sentenced for a misdemeanor, and received probation.

Over the next several years, Purdy's interest in arms went beyond Kung Fu–type novelties. He accumulated a small arsenal of weapons, mostly semiautomatic pistols, all of them bought legally. (Although it is illegal for a convicted felon to purchase a handgun in California, and although Purdy would be arrested for felonies, the charges were always plea-bargained down to misdemeanors. It *is* legal for those convicted of misdemeanors to purchase guns.) Neither are there any barriers on such purchases for those who are emotionally or mentally disturbed. If there were, they would certainly have applied to Purdy, whose already-fragile mental health was rapidly crumbling. As far back as 1979, a social worker had concluded that if Purdy didn't receive help he would "develop into a highly deceptive sociopathic character and be practically untreatable." Although in and out of treatment programs for years, Purdy was obviously not getting the help he needed. In late September 1986 Purdy stumbled into a Sacramento mental health center. He was crying and nearly incoherent. Purdy told workers there that he strongly identified with a postal worker who had recently shot several co-workers after hearing voices that told him "to do things." Purdy, too, complained of hallucinations and fantasizing about killing people. He was given Thorazine, a powerful tranquilizer, and told to come back for a follow-up visit. One week later he walked into a Sacramento gun shop and bought a Browning Hi-Power 9-mm semiautomatic pistol.

In April of 1987, Purdy had his most serious encounter with the law. Still coming down after ingesting a quantity of the notorious animal tranquilizer PCP and psychedelic mushrooms, Purdy and his half brother, Albert, threw some clothes and a couple of guns into the back of Eddie's car, bought some beer, and headed up to the mountains for a little fun. They drove to a place they had frequented when they lived at Lake Tahoe—a campground at the southern tip of the lake, in the El Dorado National Forest. The pair wandered into the woods with a few beers and their guns to get drunk and blast away at trees, rocks, squirrels, whatever. They both had 9-mm semiautomatic pistols and close to a hundred rounds of ammunition. They hadn't been shooting very long when a sheriff's deputy followed the sound of gunfire to their position at a thickly wooded spot. The deputy walked up from behind them and told them to put the guns away. Purdy was very drunk by this time.

"Listen, we can shoot here," Purdy told the man testily. "This is a national forest, public property. It's a citizen's right."

The deputy, named Phillips, silently confiscated their weapons and marched them over to his car on a nearby road. When the deputy placed the two under arrest, Purdy exploded.

He made a fist and assumed what Phillips later called "a fighting stance."

"Listen, fucker," Purdy screamed at the lawman, "I've been messed with a lot. It's my right to shoot here! It's my right to resist you fucking suppressors!"

Phillips grabbed Purdy and handcuffed him, throwing him, still screaming, into the backseat of the patrol car.

"I'm not going to be pushed around anymore," Purdy yelled, his face red with rage. "I'll kill anybody who tries to push me around!" He lay down on the seat and kicked the window with his combat boots, shattering the glass.

Purdy was thrown into the drunk tank of the local jail, where he tried to slit his wrists with the only "weapons" the police had left him: his own fingernails and toenails. That didn't work, so he attempted to hang himself with his T-shirt. He was discovered and cut down by a jailer. Purdy was tied down to a cot, naked and crying.

He was transferred to the El Dorado County Mental Health Hospital, halfway between Lake Tahoe and Sacramento, where he was held for observation for three days. The doctors there determined that Purdy was suffering from mixed substance abuse, the result of ingesting alcohol, a homemade concoction of nicotine sulfate, and the residual effects of the mushrooms and PCP. One doctor concluded: ". . . this writer would consider him a risk, albeit ambiguous, to harm himself. He does however appear to be a greater risk to others. That is, he would probably hurt someone else before he hurt himself."

Although initially classified "extremely dangerous," after a few days under observation, Purdy was ruled competent to stand trial on a variety of charges: unlawful discharge of a firearm, public intoxication, and resisting arrest. He pled guilty and was sentenced to forty-five days in jail.

Two and a half months after walking out of jail (and just days after a periodic disability report determined that Purdy was "getting worse as time goes by . . . he can't handle people at all") he bought an Ingram MAC-10 9-mm semiautomatic pistol.

Out on the streets, Purdy returned to his old habits of drifting and drugs. And hating. Anyone who knew him knew that inside Patrick Edward Purdy there burned an intense hatred, a loathing that began with himself and his family and that gradually extended outward to include the world at large. While seeking treatment for drug addiction, Purdy described his mother as a "bitch, liar, thief, asshole, witch, cruel, torturer, mean, low down, evil, black whore, child abuser, inflicter of cruel and unusual punishment" whose head he'd like to chop off. Purdy felt the world hated him, and he hated it back. One of his former co-workers recalled that Purdy "expressed hatred, anger, and bitterness at just about anybody who asked him to do anything. Every time you tried to explain something, he looked like he wanted to jump on you."

Eventually, racism provided Purdy with a focus for that hatred, a group to blame for his problems. And while all minorities were suspect, it was the many Southeast Asians who had settled in the San Joaquin Valley in the 1980s who earned his special enmity. Cambodians, Pakistanis, and especially Vietnamese refugees, young and old, male and female, were all demons in Purdy's eyes. He complained bitterly about the large number of "gooks" enrolled in the industrial arts course he was taking at the San Joaquin Delta Community College. "He didn't like the idea of jobs being taken away, and he didn't like having to compete with them in class," said a man who worked with Purdy at the time. Soon, Purdy would do something about that situation. For once in his life, *he* would be the actor, and others would be the victims.

No one can say when the idea for his Mission first began to grow in Purdy's tangled mind. Was it still inchoate when he walked into the Sandy Trading Post on August 3, 1988, and bought the Chinese-made version of the AK-47 assault rifle? (This was five months after he told a mental health worker that he was troubled by audio-hallucinations of his mother's voice calling to him. He also claimed he had "a mission to destroy property," and, in desperation, told the worker "I can't go on like this." He was given a drug, an appointment for a month later, and was shown to the door.)

Perhaps the Mission was what prompted him to buy the rotary magazine for the AK-47 at a Rhode Island gun shop in December of 1988. Surely, he had a general idea of what he was going to do, even if he hadn't yet selected the target, when he suddenly quit his well-paying welding job out east and moved into the $95-a-week room at the El Rancho Motel, with its faded yellow stucco walls and phony Spanish tile roof, in Lodi on the day after Christmas, 1988.

Two days after arriving in Lodi, Purdy put on a clean pair of slacks and a sport coat—for him, this was a disguise—and walked into Hunter Loan and Jewelry in Stockton. He looked over the store's selection of guns before settling on a Taurus 9-mm semiautomatic pistol.

"Are you twenty-one?" the salesman asked Purdy suspiciously.

Without a word, Purdy produced his driver's license and four $100 bills. He returned to the store after California's mandatory fifteen-day waiting period elapsed and picked up his new gun.

Four days before his Mission, Purdy spent some time at the trailer of his twenty-year-old half brother, Albert E. Gulart, Jr., outside of Modesto. The two got together sometimes, just to shoot the shit and fire some of their many guns. Like Eddie, Albert possessed a variety of firearms. At his trailer he kept an Ingram MAC-10 9-mm semiautomatic pistol, an M1 carbine, an arsenal of ammunition, assorted blasting caps, and even a box of two-and-one-half-inch artillery shells.

On a different night, not long before, they had been sitting around getting drunk and stoned when they hit on a plan to have some fun. Why not kill a cop? After all, the police were always "suppressing" them. It would be so easy. They figured they could just wait until a motorcycle cop came flying up over the Modesto Bridge, and—*blam*— they'd let him have it. The pair decided to wait until summer, when the heat in the San Joaquin Valley would force the cops to leave their bulletproof vests back at the station. It would be fun.

On this day, though, Purdy seemed a bit subdued, as if he had something on his mind. When he was getting ready to leave, Eddie turned to Albert and said simply but mysteriously: "You're going to be reading about me pretty soon."

On the morning of January 17, Eddie Purdy got dressed, smoked a cigarette, and drank a cup of coffee. It was the morning of his Mission. He was wearing his uniform: heavy combat boots, jeans, a brown camouflage jacket, and a flak vest. On the vest he had used a black felt-tip pen to write several words, including *Libya, PLO, Earthmans,* and, in a column on the right side of the vest: *Evil, Evil, Evil, Evil.*

He packed the three AK-47 banana clips into a small bag on which he had written the words *freedom, humanoids,* and *evil.* Carved into the stock of the rifle was *Hezbollah*, the name of a pro-Iranian terrorist group.

When detectives entered room 104 in search of evidence later that same day, they made what was, under the circumstances, a sickening discovery. Arranged in neat groups around the dingy motel room were dozens of plastic toy soldiers fighting mock battles. The twenty-four-year-old Purdy had perched a row of little plastic sharpshooters across a curtain rod; several toy infantrymen marched across the shower stall; inside the freezer in the room's tiny kitchen was a green toy soldier covered with a white patina of frost.

Purdy was putting the assault rifle, which he had wrapped in a blanket, into his battered Chevrolet Caprice Estate station wagon when another resident of the motel came up and tried to start a conversation with him. The man made a joke about the owners of the El Rancho, an East Indian family. Purdy didn't laugh. He just shook his head and uttered what would be his last sentence to another human being: "The damn Hindus and boat people own everything." Then he got in his car and headed for the Cleveland Elementary School, just a few miles away.


LORI MACKEY WAS the kind of teacher every child wants: bright and enthusiastic, young and caring. The thirty-year-old California native was devoted to her students at Cleveland Elementary. She felt especially close to the group she was teaching that January morning, a class of ten sixth graders, seven of them deaf or hearing-impaired.

And who wouldn't have felt sympathy for them? Life had been hard on these children. Most were refugees from the many wars in Southeast Asia; many still had nightmares about the violence they had left behind. The children had endured so much, first in their native lands, and then in transit to the United States. The squalor and disease of life in the refugee camps. The dangerous journey through pirate-infested waters on overcrowded, rickety boats. All had lost family along the way. Lori knew that the voyage to America was a turning point for these students and their families, and it gave her a sense of satisfaction to be a part—however small—of that quest for a new life.

Just as America transformed the lives of the immigrants, the new

Asian residents changed the communities to which they came. The change was sudden and dramatic for Stockton: In 1980, fewer than 1,000 Southeast Asian immigrants had settled in the entire San Joaquin Valley; by 1988, there were more than 30,000 in Stockton alone. Half were Cambodian, refugees from Pol Pot's genocidal war. A third of the immigrants were Vietnamese; the remainder were Laotian and Hmong.

Most of the immigrants planned to settle on small plots of land where they would farm as their ancestors had done for generations, but California land proved far too expensive. Few had been able to escape from Southeast Asia with anything more than their lives. The more fortunate among them opened small specialty stores that catered to the needs of other refugees. But most were penniless, unskilled in any trade needed in the United States, and unable even to speak English. They ended up on welfare, living in the crowded and seedy apartment complexes that filled Stockton's poorer areas.

In Or, a thirty-six-year-old Cambodian woman, was typical of the new immigrants. She fled her native country after her husband, a rebel soldier, had been killed by the Khmer Rouge. Asked why she had come to Stockton, the slight woman would answer simply that it was for Rathanar, her nine-year-old son, who was skinny and wore a perpetual impish smile. "I wanted to be in a place of peace and freedom," she'd say with a broad smile.

Most people in Stockton welcomed the new immigrants. Mayor Barbara Fass often bragged about how diverse and exotic her city had become. With genuine enthusiasm, she'd tell visitors how wonderful it was to be walking down a city street and suddenly detect the delicate scents of star anise or cardamom wafting out of a tiny restaurant.

"We're used to a very heterogeneous community," she'd boast. "We've always had large Filipino and Japanese communities—this is just another addition to the mix."

Of course, not everyone felt the way Mayor Fass and Lori Mackey did. Almost every new immigrant could tell stories about insults shouted by cowards from the safety of passing cars or muttered under the breath in a store or on the sidewalk: "This country isn't for you!" "Go back to where you belong!"

Lori was ashamed of how some Stockton residents treated the

Southeast Asians. With kind words (or, in the case of the deaf students, with hand signs), she let the students know that they were cherished—at least in *her* classroom.

By 11:30 on that warm January morning, the students had put away their language arts books and were moving on to math.

Uh-oh, thought Lori to herself, looking at her lesson plan. They were supposed to work on story problems this morning, a concept that several of the children hadn't quite grasped. Lori would have to be careful to go slow. She smiled to herself when she thought of the stereotype of Asian students—that they were all math "whiz kids." She knew better.

Lori stood at the front of the room, pointed to the hand-drawn rocket ship that was projected onto a screen, and began to sign out the story problem: "If it takes . . . two hours . . . for a rocket . . . to travel . . . one hundred miles . . ." She was interrupted by a loud popping noise coming from outside.

Firecrackers, was her first thought. Someone had lighted a string of firecrackers just outside her classroom.

The mini-explosions were so loud that they hurt Lori's ears. At least they wouldn't bother most of the kids in her class, she thought as she walked over to the door at the front of the room. Her usually cheerful brown eyes narrowed in irritation. She was going to give the troublemakers holy hell for lighting those things during school hours. They probably figured they could get away with it out here by the temporary classroom, the single-story aluminum structure separated from Cleveland Elementary's main L-shaped building by a large playground. She'd let them know that order reigned out here, too.

The door to the classroom was made of metal on the bottom and clear glass on the top. Lori was about to shove the door open when something on the other side of the window caught her attention. Slightly to her left and no more than five or six feet away was a man with long brown hair. He was dressed in combat fatigues and firing a rifle.

The scene didn't make any sense to her for a moment, perhaps because it was the last thing Lori had expected to see. The man was making wide, slow sweeping movements with the gun as he fired.

Left to right. Right to left.

Left to right. Right to left.

His expression was strangely blank, the face of a mannequin. Lori's gaze instinctively turned in the direction the man's rifle was pointed. The playground. Recess.

"Oh God," she said. The scene that met her gaze was one of utter chaos. Hundreds of children were scattering in all directions as they tried to escape from the barrage of bullets. She saw some children, hit by gunfire, tumble to the ground and lie there screaming. Others collapsed in small heaps and didn't move at all. She watched in horror as another teacher, a good friend, tried to shepherd children into the safety of the main classroom building. The teacher, too, was hit and went down.

Without thinking—if she thought, she'd be paralyzed with fear—Lori grabbed the phone hanging next to the door and dialed 911. The line clicked for what seemed like an eternity, paused, and then went dead.

Fighting off the panic that now crept up her limbs, she dialed the school's main office. An almost surreally pleasant voice answered. "Good morning, Cleveland Elementary."

"There's a man outside with a gun shooting," Lori whispered into the phone, afraid of drawing the gunman's attention. "Please, call the police!"

Silence. Followed, at last, by an incredulous "What?"

Afraid to talk any longer, Lori hung up.

She signed to the children to get down on the floor and crawl under a table in a far corner of the room. They needed to be very quiet, she signed, because there was a man outside with a gun.

She didn't need to worry about getting her students' attention. Although many of the children couldn't hear the gunfire, they were acutely sensitive to any visual stimulus, and all eyes had been on Lori from the moment she had started to the door. Now, as they huddled together under the table, their attention was riveted on the shadow of the solitary man as he stopped firing and walked past their room. A bank of frosted-glass windows ran the length of the classroom, and Lori and the children could follow his progress. He was in no hurry. He walked slowly to the east, his translucent shadow gliding from one pane of glass to another. Lori could hear the heavy footsteps made by his combat boots on the sidewalk just inches from her classroom.

She prayed that he wouldn't aim his fire through the flimsy aluminum walls. Did he know they were inside the room? she wondered. Maybe he thought they were all out at recess. Finally, the man's silhouette disappeared from the easternmost window.

The children whimpered as they crouched beneath the table surrounding Lori. Several of them remembered hiding from gunfire back in their homelands, and they now thought that a war had started here in America. Their parents had told them they had arrived in a safe land. In America, they wouldn't have to be afraid anymore. As they cowered under the table, the children thought their parents had been wrong: The war had found them. It had reached its terrible hand out across the ocean, and now it had them.

Lori saw the look of fear on her students' faces, and in turn she felt terror welling up inside of her. The thought formed before she could stop it: Maybe I'll never see these children again.

As calmly as she could, she signed that everything was going to be okay, that she could hear police sirens getting closer now. Everything was going to be just fine.

There were no sirens, but the children didn't know that. Suddenly, the silence was again broken by the roar of gunfire, this time coming from the east side of the building. Lori immediately jumped up, ran to the door, locked it, and raced back to her hiding place under the table.

After a minute or so the firing stopped. And once again Lori and the children watched in fear as the gunman's shadow reappeared on the frosted windows, this time heading back to his original position.

Again the firing began, lasting for a minute or so. And then it stopped and once again they watched as that dreadful shadow drifted across their windows from one pane to another, going from west to east. The shadow disappeared. Silence. Then one more shot—a single report—followed by stillness.

For twenty minutes Lori and the children remained under the table. They could only guess what was happening on the other side of the door. The quiet frightened Lori almost as much as the gunfire had. Was the gunman holding children hostage? Would he burst into their classroom at any second, his rifle blazing?

Soon Lori heard a new sound, the *whoosh-whoosh-whoosh* of a helicopter. Several helicopters. Then sirens filled the air. After a while, Lori couldn't endure the suspense any longer. She crawled to the clear window in the door and looked out.

The schoolyard was a war zone. The air was filled with dust kicked up by the wash of helicopter blades, and through the haze she could see paramedics and police scrambling here and there, tending the many small bodies that dotted the playground. Several children sat in a group, some crying silently, clutching yellow cards that identified their wounds. The paramedics had prioritized the casualties and were treating the most serious ones first.

Before long, a policeman came to escort the teacher and her class from the building. He told Lori that the police had at first thought there had been two gunmen, because Purdy had fired from two locations. But there had been just a single gunman, and he was now dead from a single self-inflicted pistol shot to the head, his lifeless body sprawled on the sidewalk beside the temporary classroom, already outlined by pale blue chalk.

The entire episode had lasted only a few minutes, but as Lori Mackey and her class were led across the playground to the main school building they were stunned by the carnage wrought in that short time. One hundred and five rounds had been fired—not including the single pistol bullet that ended Purdy's life. Thirty-three students and one teacher had been shot. Five of the students lay dead: four girls (three Cambodian and one Vietnamese), aged eight and six, and a nine-year-old Cambodian boy, Rathanar Or, In Or's son.

The entire town struggled to accept what had happened. Three days after the shootings, In Or and some hundred other mourners led by monks wearing saffron-colored robes gathered in a local funeral home and chanted traditional Buddhist prayers for their dead. Lori Mackey was part of a standing-room-only crowd that jammed into the Stockton Civic Auditorium three days later for a community-wide memorial service. Most of the mourners were dressed in white, the traditional color of death and loss in Asia. On a stage at the front of the auditorium were the children's simple wooden coffins flanked by hundreds of bouquets and wreaths and large photographs of the students who died on the schoolyard. At exactly 11:45, the moment of the attack, the crowd observed five minutes of silence for the five students, punctuated only by the ringing of a small bell as their names were read: Sokhim An. Thuy Tran. Oeun Lim. Ram Chun. Rathanar Or.

Across town, mourners gathered at the funeral service for six-year-old Thuy Tran at St. Luke's Catholic Church, where the little girl had been a member of the church youth choir.

"I don't know that we will ever understand why such a thing occurred," Father Aloys Gruber told the grieving congregation, echoing, while at the same time attempting to transform, their helplessness and confusion. "All we can do from here is go on and try to draw the community together so that there might be a healing process."

IT WAS BATTLE, and not healing, that was on James Jay Baker's mind as the thirty-five-year-old lobbyist sat in his office in a posh section of Washington, D.C. Just days after the Stockton massacre, Baker was preparing for his upcoming appearance before a congressional subcommittee hearing on a bill to virtually ban the type of rifle used by Eddie Purdy.

The Stockton incident was anything but inexplicable to him. He took a long drag on his Vantage filter cigarette, set it on his desk ashtray, and wrote: "The real lesson to be drawn from the Purdy crime is that Patrick Edward Purdy was a criminal who ought to have been in jail rather than left free to roam the streets. . . . It was the criminal justice system that failed those five schoolchildren."

According to Baker, this was the Stockton lesson: Our society is too soft on criminals.

At the opposite end of the Washington Mall, the long grassy strip that stretches from the Lincoln Memorial to the Capitol Building, in his spacious office in the Russell Senate Office Building, Senator Howard M. Metzenbaum also prepared for battle. Like Baker, the white-haired, three-term senator from Ohio was clear about the "real lesson" of the Stockton killings. His conclusions, however, were 180 degrees from Baker's.

"Assault weapons are designed for one purpose, and one purpose alone, for killing human beings," he read aloud, practicing his opening statement before the subcommittee he chaired. To attack the problem as he saw it—easy access to these guns of war—Metzenbaum was championing a bill that would make it difficult to buy these weapons.

"If such a procedure had been in effect last August," he continued, "the local police would not have allowed Patrick Edward Purdy to buy the AK-47 he used to massacre five children in a California schoolyard."

According to Metzenbaum, *this* was the Stockton lesson: Our society has too many guns that are too powerful and are too readily available.

What was taking place on either end of the Mall was a time-honored ritual of transformation. An act of particularly appalling violence—in this case, the massacre of five schoolchildren by a berserk loner—was being converted into ammunition for one of this country's most bitter and intractable political debates: the fight for and against gun control. There was nothing new about either the situation or the major players, or even about the debate itself. What *was* new was that the organization James Baker represented was on the defensive.

The National Rifle Association—widely regarded as the most powerful lobby in Washington, a group that had for decades held a reputation for targeting those few in Congress who dared to oppose it and picking them off as easily as Eddie Purdy had shot his victims in California—now found *itself* under lethal fire.

# 2

# THE EARLY YEARS

FIERCELY PATRIOTIC AND headstrong, articulate and ambitious, a sworn enemy of "Communists, Socialists and other outlaws," William Conant Church was a likely architect of the National Rifle Association. For Church, a product of rock-ribbed nineteenth-century Boston and the son of a prominent Baptist preacher, the military was a religion, to be revered and defended against all detractors.

Church came by his zealous militarism honestly—it was in his genes, inherited from his forebears along with his straight brown hair and broad nose. Church's maternal great-grandfather had fought in the American Revolutionary War; his father's father had served at Valley Forge with General Washington and his grandfather on his mother's side had commanded a company during the War of 1812. A journalist by trade, Church resigned his position as a *New York Times* war correspondent to join the Union Army in 1862. In the following year, at the age of twenty-seven, he left active service but continued to help the war effort by editing a pro-Union newspaper devoted to fighting "the enemies of the Government and the advocates of a disgraceful PEACE."

Despite his unwavering loyalty to his country and its military, Church was also a heretic. Like John the Baptist in the wilderness, Church spread the good news about a revolutionary military doctrine in the years following the Civil War; he preached the gospel of target practice.

Most establishment military experts at the time believed that target practice was not only unnecessary but actually harmful. Training in riflery would enhance a sense of individualism among the soldiers, they argued, and while independence might be a good quality in officers it was the *last* characteristic the military wanted to encourage in its enlisted men.

The debate over target practice was touched off by advances in technology. There was no need to hone riflery skills when the standard military weapon was a crude muzzleloader. These primitive guns hurled their ill-shaped bullets in merely the *general direction* of the target. Under the old rules of engagement this presented few problems. Soldiers advanced toward each other side by side in long straight lines, and while the musket balls might miss their *intended* targets, they stood a passable chance of striking *some* soldier in the vicinity.

But the breech-loading guns and their metal cartridge ammunition, introduced on a wide scale after the Civil War, fired with much greater accuracy, and younger military thinkers like Church realized what the Old Guard hadn't: Marksmanship would become one of the keys to modern warfare. If target practice bred individualism, well, the military would just have to find other ways to stamp out that noxious trait, Church editorialized in his newspaper, *The Army and Navy Journal and Gazette*. Riflery was simply too important.

Church was not the only preacher of this new gospel; several former Union officers also encouraged the army and the National Guard to add target practice to their training programs. Foremost among these military men was General George Wingate, a veteran of the Battle of the Potomac and, following the war, a lawyer in private practice and an officer in the New York National Guard. Wingate had written a manual on the subject of target shooting that was serialized in *The Army and Navy Journal*.

It was no coincidence that the push for riflery practice came at a time of increasing social unrest following the Civil War. Tens of thousands of demobilized soldiers could not find work. Labor discontent with low wages, long hours, and unsafe working conditions had remained submerged beneath the national consciousness during the war, but it now bubbled to the surface—often with violent results. Strikers clashed with police and, more and more frequently, with units of the National Guard.

The militia's concern about labor activism is seen in a half-page advertisement in *The Army and Navy Journal* from this period. The ad, placed by Schuyler, Hartley and Graham of New York City, agents for the Gatling gun (the first machine gun), featured a rather absurd-looking illustration of a horse with a gun the size of a small cannon mounted on its back. This was the new "camel gun"—in truth, little more than a Gatling gun grafted onto the back of any handy quadruped. "For militia use, in suppression of riots . . . it is the most effective of any known weapon," crowed the advertiser's copy.

It was against this backdrop of social upheaval that fifteen men crowded into the offices of *The Army and Navy Journal* at 192 Broadway in lower Manhattan on a stifling August afternoon in 1871 and discussed the formation of the National Rifle Association. The organizers of the meeting were William Church and George Wingate, and while General Ambrose Burnside was listed as the president of the organization born that day, the Civil War leader with the famous whiskers (sideburns were named for him) took little part in the group's activities and resigned a year later. From the start, Church and Wingate were the true leaders of the group.

The purpose of the NRA was—in Church's words—to turn "the Guard into sharpshooters." But while the group was centered around military life and included mostly members of the armed forces (all but one of the men attending the first meeting bore a military title), it was officially independent from the armed forces. As a result, the fledgling National Rifle Association had to look elsewhere for the money to finance its first major project: the construction of a state-of-the-art rifle range. Church and Wingate turned to a friend for help: New York State Assemblyman David W. Judd. With the aid of General Burnside's lobbying (his one great contribution to the NRA), Judd managed in 1872 to push legislation through the New York legislature appropriating $25,000 to buy a hundred acres on Long Island to be developed into a rifle range.

It was the beginning of an important and long-lasting pattern for the gun group. For much of its long history, the NRA's fortunes would rise and fall according to the largess of public institutions. Some might have considered the private organization's dependence on government funds ironic—especially given Church's virulent opposition to social-ism in any form—but that inconsistency was apparently lost on the NRA founder himself. Church felt that the NRA was merely doing what the government itself *should* have been doing: providing for military preparedness.

"The National Guard is today too slow in getting about this reform [instituting riflery practice]," Church wrote in *The Army and Navy Journal.* "Private enterprise must take up the matter and push it into life."

And if "private enterprise" occasionally needed government funds to continue its patriotic work, well, what of it? was Church's attitude.

The NRA quickly began sponsoring target shooting competitions at its Creedmoor, Long Island, range to publicize the group's work and provide its riflemen with an incentive to improve their skills. Marksmen competed for cash prizes and firearms donated by manufac-turers, including a gold-mounted Winchester rifle and a Gatling gun worth $1,500.

The first international shooting competition at the new Creedmoor rifle range was held in late September 1874. A team from the NRA's Amateur Rifle Club (made up of nonmilitary riflemen) took on the world champion Irish Rifle Association squad, and the scene on the barren fields of Long Island that day was part circus, part garden party. The tournament was one of the gala social events of the season for New Yorkers, who crowded into railroad cars by the thousands to make the thirteen-mile journey out to see the spectacle. By the time the 800-yard competition commenced at 10:30 A.M., nearly 8,000 spectators packed the viewing area. As the temperature climbed to eighty-five degrees, women protected themselves from the burning sun with multicolored parasols. Wearing top hats, bowlers, or pith helmets, the men drank warm bottles of ginger ale (the only beverage served at the range) or drifted off to the nearby Century Hotel, where they could gulp down a glass of cold ale or a shot of whiskey before hurrying back to the range. In keeping with the dignified air the sponsors were trying to maintain, the crowd was discouraged from cheering. Partisan spectators were free, however, to wave small flags—both American and Irish were everywhere—after each success-ful shot.

Some of the shooting positions assumed by the competitors seemed odd, if not ridiculous, to the inexperienced eye (which included nearly everybody but the contestants). A rifleman lay on his back, his knees slightly bent, legs crossed just above the ankles, with the rifle barrel resting at this juncture. Propped up on his right elbow, he pulled the trigger with his right hand, while steadying the rifle butt with the left hand, which was passed *behind* the head. While the position might have looked strange, it provided the shooter with surprising stability, absolutely necessary when aiming at the farthest targets—1,000 yards, over a half mile, away.

The contestants used guns that looked much like the standard rifles of their day but were vastly superior to normal firearms supplied by the military or carried by hunters. The Irish team used a muzzle-loading rifle designed a decade earlier by its best shooter, John Rigby—equipped with an adjustable rear sight and a wind gauge, the Rigby match rifle was considered the finest gun of its type in the world. Each country was required to use only domestically produced guns in international competitions, which created a problem for the Americans since no U.S. arms manufacturer made a gun accurate at competition distances. Luckily for the Americans, Church and Wingate convinced friends within the industry to make a gun especially for the match, and both Remington and Sharp produced match-grade breechloaders that were used by the American team at Creedmoor. (The Remington Long-Range Creedmoor Rolling Block Rifle proved so popular that the company soon began turning out a production model—selling for the then-unheard-of price of $100.)

While the crowd enthusiastically supported the American team, no one really expected it to offer much of a challenge to the world champion Irish. The U.S. team, after all, had only recently begun shooting at long distances. Just a year earlier, the army's crack sharp-shooters, told to fire at targets at the 500-yard mark, had thought the command was a joke. No one could hit a target at that distance, they complained. The Irish team, on the other hand, was made up of veterans of many international competitions for whom 1,000 yards was a standard shooting distance. And the American team was hardly a "national" body—members were all from the New York City area. An NRA historian compared the matchup to a baseball game pitting a "small-town sandlot baseball club" against the World Series champions.

So when the Americans led the Irish team by nine points after the conclusion of the 800-yard competition, most of those gathered at the Creedmoor range were surprised. And when the Americans were still ahead following the shooting at 900 yards (although their lead had been reduced to seven points) the excitement grew. So did the size of the crowd; each time match scores were telegraphed back to New York City more people decided to run out to Long Island and see what all the fuss was about.

By the time the last American lay down on the firing line to take the last shot of the day at 1,000 yards, the Irish team, which had finished firing first, was ahead by a score of 931 to 930. American Colonel John Bodine, a tall, middle-aged ex–Union infantryman, needed to fire a bull's-eye from a distance of ten football fields to win the match for his team. The crowd, which by this time extended the full length of the range, had, in its excitement, pushed in closer to the target, forming an immense human V and "leaving scarcely enough room to make it safe to shoot," recalled Wingate later.

Bodine adjusted his sights, waited for the wind to die down, and took aim at the six-foot-tall metal target with its yard-square bull's-eye—a mere speck at 1,000 yards. All sighting was done with the naked eye, since telescopic sights were banned from competition matches. Bodine's task was made even more difficult by the distorting heat waves that radiated up from the sun-warmed field. Finally, between wind gusts, Bodine slowly squeezed the trigger of his rifle, and a cloud of white smoke exploded from the end of his thirty-four-inch-long barrel as the bullet headed down the range. Traveling at a rate slightly below the speed of sound, the .44-caliber bullet took a full three seconds to reach the distant target. It took another three seconds for the bell-like sound of the projectile striking the metal target to return to the firing line. But Bodine needed a bull's-eye, not just a hit, to win the match, and several tense seconds ticked by before the crowd saw the large white disk held aloft on a pole over the target, signifying a bull's-eye. The cheering mob broke through the police cordon and enveloped the colonel.

As General Wingate fondly recalled in his memoirs some thirty years later: "Pandemonium broke loose, and the sky was darkened with the hats that were thrown into the air."

The NRA thrived for several years following that first match at

Creedmoor, training many National Guard units and hosting dozens of similar competitions (and winning the next four international championships); rifle clubs and ranges popped up at an astonishing rate across the country. But within a decade the NRA ran upon hard times, buffeted by a host of problems. First, the novelty of target shooting simply ran its course. Next, western states began to complain that the NRA was too allied with eastern interests, especially industrial ones. Besides designing and supplying guns for the 1874 international competition, the Sharp and Remington companies had paid the gun club's $1,000 tournament entry fee. Rumblings were heard in the sporting press that the NRA was a shill for arms manufacturers.

But the most devastating blow to the NRA was struck, ironically, by the military itself. From its creation, the NRA had struggled with an identity crisis: Was it a military organization or was it a civilian group? Its neither-nor status left the group open to constant political struggles. For Church and Wingate, the NRA was always primarily military-oriented, but the military hadn't fully accepted the notion that wars would be won by sharpshooters. Jealousies over turf also hampered the NRA's military recruiting mission, even among those in the army who recognized a need for target practice. In 1879, the Grand Army of the Republic formed its own organization for riflery. In the following year, the governor of New York informed Wingate that riflery was unnecessary since the world was entering a glorious age of peace.

"There will be no war in my time or in the time of my children," Governor Alonzo Cornell told Wingate in a tense meeting. "The only need for a National Guard is to show itself in parades and ceremonies." With that, Cornell withdrew state support for the competitions at Creedmoor. The action was devastating for the NRA, for the money the group had squeezed out of the New York State legislature in 1872 to build the rifle range at Creedmoor had been just the first of many such grants. Cut off from the public trough, the NRA collapsed.

"DOWN, BUT NOT Out" could be the NRA's motto. Despite its ignoble disintegration at the end of the nineteenth century, by the beginning of the twentieth the gun group was back again, and in a very short time it was more powerful than ever. The National Rifle Association owed its comeback to a war fought thousands of miles away and in which the United States did not even participate. The South African Boer War pitted the well-disciplined British army against a ragtag collection of South African farmers of Dutch extraction called Boers. Although the English finally won the war, the Boers gave them a run for their money, waging a devastating guerrilla campaign. A large part of the Boers' effectiveness was due to their superb marksmanship and their use of modern rifles, many equipped with telescopic sights. These facts were not lost on the British, who immediately made target shooting an important part of military training—perhaps the most important part.

The renewed interest in riflery spread quickly throughout the British Empire, eventually reaching the United States by way of Canada. In response to the growing clamor for "military preparedness" heard throughout the country, the National Rifle Association was reborn in 1901. Once again, however, it took aid from the government to get the group on its feet—and keep it there. Membership in the new NRA remained small at first and was limited, as before, mainly to the East Coast. But in 1903, at the NRA's recommendation, Congress created the National Board for the Promotion of Rifle Practice (NBPRP) to build ranges for civilian use and to promote them. Although the body was organized as a division of the War Department, the NRA was certain to have a large say in the NBPRP's activities since over one third of the board's officers were trustees of the National Rifle Association. It's not hard now to see the NRA's invisible hand at work behind the 1905 passage of Public Law 149, which authorized the sale of surplus military firearms and ammunition—at cost—to rifle clubs meeting the specifications drawn up by the NBPRP. One of those specifications was that the rifle club had to be sponsored by the National Rifle Association. Five years later the deal was sweetened considerably when the military began *giving away* surplus rifles and ammunition to NRA-sponsored clubs. In 1912, Congress began funding the annual NRA shooting matches, and, in the following year, sent 1,000 regular army troops to help out at the competitions.

These were clearly the best of times for the NRA. Thanks to the free and low-cost firearms supplied by the government, its membership roster swelled. While the supply of weapons was interrupted by World War I, the handouts began again as soon as the last shots were fired in Europe. Between the two world wars NRA members received—at cost—over 200,000 rifles, and according to a regulation enacted in 1924, *only* NRA members were allowed to receive the weapons. The group had carved out a lucrative monopoly for itself, although at least one NRA official had the temerity to gripe about "cheap-skates" who joined the rifle association just to grab up the cheap weapons and "then lost all interest in the shooting game and the Association which made it possible for them to get the gun in the first place."

The gun group received another boost following World War II as nine million demobilized servicemen returned to civilian life, many bringing with them a newly acquired interest in firearms. Thanks to these ex-soldiers, the NRA's membership tripled in the three years following the end of the war. The new members also caused an important shift in the NRA's priorities. Most of the former servicemen had little interest in shooting competitions (which, perhaps, reminded them too much of military life). The new members were much more captivated by hunting, and while the NRA didn't drop competitive shooting, it began to place a greater emphasis on programs that served hunters. The NRA made this shift, in part, to counter the bad image many of these returning G.I.s—few of whom were good shots—were giving hunters and hunting.

According to a 1949 article in the NRA's magazine *American Rifleman*:

Farmers and hunters are complaining bitterly about the risks they incur from wild flying buckshot. Where there is no big game, the carelessness of shotgun shooters and of .22 shooters arouses a storm of protest. Vandalism and "wise guy" stunts in breaking down fences and hedgerows, shooting out electric and phone lines, insulators and transformers, road signs and railroad crossing warnings are turning large segments of industry and the public against the shooting game. . . . Education and training is the primary need.

And so, gradually, almost imperceptibly, the National Rifle Association changed from a quasi-governmental league devoted to military preparedness to a truly national group catering to the needs of all sportsmen carrying guns. It is much more difficult to say with any certainty when the group became a lobby. From the beginning the

NRA was in the business of swaying legislation to benefit its members and itself. The group had moved its headquarters to Washington, D.C., in 1907, but that had been primarily to be closer to the military brass. Not that the gun group supported governmental controls on gun ownership. When calls for such legislation swept the urban East in 1911 the NRA denounced the trend in strong terms.

"A warning should be sounded to legislators against passing laws which on the face of them seem to make it impossible for a criminal to get a pistol, if the same laws would make it very difficult for an honest man and a good citizen to obtain them," wrote James Drain, the organization's president. "Such laws have the effect of arming the bad man and disarming the good one to the injury of the community."

But despite the NRA's powerful opposition to gun control, lobbying continued to be only a minor part of the association's work—mostly because such antigun legislation was itself still uncommon. The first major attempt at a federal gun-control policy came in the 1930s with the introduction of sweeping legislation to ban or regulate a wide variety of firearms. The NRA unleashed a massive letter-writing campaign, and the result was the National Firearms Act of 1934—which regulated the sale of machine guns and sawed-off shotguns and nothing else. Four years later Congress passed two more provisions: one prohibiting unlicensed dealers from selling guns across state lines and the other banning the sale of firearms to convicted felons and fugitives. The NRA had agreed to both regulations.

After this flurry of activity, Congress and the NRA went back to their respective corners and more or less left each other alone. Over the years, the NRA devoted more resources to nipping gun-control legislation in the bud, but its lobbying wing remained incidental to the organization's primary mission of serving hunters and target shooters.

By the mid-1950s, with its membership rolls pushing the 300,000 mark, the NRA's headquarters in Washington, D.C., could no longer accommodate the group's 140 employees. The organization's new eight-story building, with its sleek façade of black marble, and a basement rifle and pistol range, was seen by members as a fitting home for their thriving group. Affixed to the marble façade to the right of the building's main entrance were metal letters spelling out what were still the NRA's main objectives in 1958: FIREARMS SAFETY EDUCATION, MARKSMANSHIP TRAINING, SHOOTING FOR RECREATION.

And that's the way things might have remained—if it hadn't been for the man who took a fancy to an Italian army surplus rifle advertised in the pages of the NRA's *American Rifleman* and ordered himself one, equipped with a four-power telescopic sight (for just $19.95). Although he bought the gun under the alias "A. Hidell," the man's true name was Lee Harvey Oswald, and when he allegedly shot and killed President John F. Kennedy in Dallas in November of 1963 using his mail-order Mannlicher-Carcano bolt-action rifle, he set off a national outcry for gun control. The result was the Gun Control Act of 1968 (GCA), which, among other things, banned the mail-order sale of guns and ammunition.

The seat of real power in the NRA had shifted from the presidency to the office of the executive vice president by 1968. The man who occupied the commanding post at the time, retired General Franklin Orth, testified before Congress in favor of the GCA, saying, "We do not think that any sane American, who calls himself an American, can object to placing into this bill the instrument which killed the president of the United States."

But, in fact, a growing number of NRA members felt otherwise. This group of hard-core gun enthusiasts was adamantly opposed to the GCA, even though the bill had been watered down considerably in the five years it took sponsors to push it through Congress. Their objections didn't so much stem from opposition to any specific sections of the legislation; it was the concept of *gun control itself* that they disliked, even hated. Furious at Orth, the hard-liners tried to have him fired. They failed, but the executive vice president was effectively muzzled for the duration of his term.

And that was that—as far as most NRA members knew. The NRA hierarchy reported that any disagreements over the passage of the GCA had been ironed out, but that was merely wishful thinking. The 1968 dispute was, in fact, just the opening volley in what was to become an all-out war, one that would split the gun group wide open over the next decade. On one side were men like Orth, mostly older, avuncular types who thought the NRA should remain primarily a sportsmen's organization, devoted to teaching gun safety, organizing shooting competitions, and running clinics for hunters. On the other side were the hard-liners, Young Turks for the most part, who were convinced that the NRA was due for a sea change as dramatic as the one that followed World War II, when the gun group was transformed from a quasi-military organization to a sportsmen's league. According to this subgroup, the NRA needed to spend less time and energy shooting at paper targets and ducks and more blasting away at gun-control legislation.

In outward appearances, the old guard appeared to have the upper hand. They dominated the organization's leadership ranks; they had, at least at first, superior numbers in the membership, and tradition favored them. For years the NRA had been building a reputation as *the* representative body for hunters and target shooters. When Boy Scouts wanted to learn how to shoot, they turned to the NRA. When police departments from San Francisco to Long Island needed to train officers in handgun safety and use, they called the NRA. When the U.S. Olympic Committee organized a riflery team, it was placed under the auspices of the NRA. When people thought of organized shooting—in whatever form—they thought of the National Rifle Association.

But the sportsmen never had a chance, for the hard-liners had Harlon Carter on their side.

In the long history of the National Rifle Association, Harlon Bronson Carter looms as a singular, towering figure—at least as important as William Conant Church, and certainly more so to the modern gun group. Even macho hunters grow misty-eyed at the mere mention of his name. To the NRA faithful, Harlon Carter is Moses, George Washington, and John Wayne rolled into one.

Part of Carter's personal appeal was due to his striking physical appearance. Above piercing ice-blue eyes, he kept his bald head as polished as the nose cone of an ICBM. (His detractors sometimes referred to him as Ol' Bullet Head.) If he seemed taller than he actually was, perhaps that was because of his barrel chest and massive arms; Carter looked like a Rodin statue come to life.

His larger-than-life personal history lent itself to the kind of myth-making American traditionalists love. Born poor in a small Texas town in 1913, Carter had grown up with guns. A crack shot who held some forty-four national shooting records in his lifetime, he joined the NRA at the age of sixteen and was elected to its board of directors in 1951. But most of Carter's working life was devoted to serving the United States Border Patrol, an organization second only to the Texas Rangers in Old West mystique. Carter was following a family tradition; his father, Horace, was a lawman with the Border Patrol his entire life. But Harlon proved more ambitious than his father, and at thirty-seven he was appointed head of the entire organization. Later, he became a commissioner of the Border Patrol's governing agency, the Immigration and Naturalization Service.

Old West lawman, champion target shooter, world-class hunter— Harlon Carter was the embodiment of everything the NRA stood for. The only blemish on his heroic image was the fact that Harlon Carter was also a convicted murderer, although the leader of the NRA dissident faction had done a pretty good job of keeping that a secret.

On a hot March afternoon in 1931, when Carter was seventeen years old, Harlon had come home from school to find his mother distraught. The family was living in Laredo, Texas, a small town on the Mexican border, and the family car had been stolen three weeks earlier. Now, Mrs. Carter told her son, a group of Mexican kids had been standing outside the house all afternoon. Maybe they had something to do with the car theft.

The young Carter grabbed his shotgun and went out in search of the boys. He encountered the group of three young Mexicans as they were leaving a nearby swimming hole. Carter asked the boys to go with him back to his house so that Mrs. Carter could ask them some questions. Later at the trial, one of the boys, twelve-year-old Salvador Peña, testified that the eldest of the group, fifteen-year-old Ramón Casiano, refused, adding, "And you can't make us."

Casiano took out a knife; curses were exchanged.

According to Peña, Carter then aimed the shotgun at Casiano's chest, and the Mexican boy brushed the gun aside and laughed.

"You don't think I'd use it?" asked Carter. Before Casiano could respond, the gun went off. The fifteen-year-old fell to the ground with a gaping wound on the right side of his chest. He died within minutes.

At his trial, Carter told a slightly different version of the events of that fateful day. When Casiano threatened him with the knife, said Carter, he fired in self-defense, meaning only to wound the boy in the arm. According to his own story, the crack shot who would go on to win twoscore national shooting titles just aimed poorly that day.

The jury deliberated for an hour and a half before finding Carter guilty of murder without malice aforethought. The judge sentenced him to a jail term of not more than three years. If that were how the story ended, Carter's career with the Border Patrol would have been over before it started. But the case was overturned on appeal later that same year, on the grounds that the presiding judge had failed to instruct the jury adequately on the laws governing self-defense. The charges were later dropped.

Even with the dismissal the affair would have tarnished Carter's otherwise flawless image, so the future NRA leader covered up the incident. When a reporter later got wind of the episode and asked him about it, Carter said it was a case of mistaken identity. The other Carter spelled *his* first name Harl*a*n, the ex–Border Patrol agent pointed out, whereas he spelled his own name Harl*o*n. "It's on my birth certificate," Carter said. "I spelled it Harlon from earliest beginnings."

But John Crewdson, a conscientious reporter with *The New York Times*, checked Texas courthouse records and found that the NRA leader had been born Harl*a*n Carter and had changed the spelling of his name two years after the murder. (Years later, on the occasion of his retirement from the NRA, the organization's PR department put together a half-hour video, *Tribute to Harlon Carter*, which was shown at a testimonial dinner. At one point, the camera focuses on an extreme close-up of Carter's original NRA membership card, from when he joined at the age of sixteen—one year before the killing. The typewritten name on the card reads "Harlon Carter," but beneath the *o* in the first name a ghostly *a* is visible.)

When confronted with the evidence of his name change, a flustered Carter refused to talk about the matter further, insisting that he was "not going to rehash that case or any other that does not relate to the National Rifle Association at this time."

Apparently, Carter needn't have bothered with his cover-up. When the story of his past was made public, NRA members didn't bat an eye. If anything, the fact that somewhere in the dim past, and way out west, Carter had once killed a man, possibly in self-defense, only added to his mythic reputation. The matter was dropped.

If there was one thing Harlon Carter could not stand, it was gun control. The very idea of the government coming between a law-abiding citizen and his or her choice of firearms sent Carter into fits. Sweat would break out on his already glossy dome, and his face would turn as red as freshly butchered game.

*You don't stop crime by attacking guns*—he'd thunder, his blue eyes ablaze—*you stop crime by stopping criminals!*

It was bad enough when East Coast liberals talked such foolishness. You couldn't expect any better from them. But when Orth, a military man *and the head of the NRA for chrissake,* started spouting that drivel, that was heresy!

After 1968, things continued to go downhill as far as Carter was concerned. The NRA leadership steered the group further away from legislative issues and back toward hunting and conservation. In 1975 all responsibility for lobbying was handed over to a new, quasi-independent wing (it was on a longer leash, at any rate) called the Institute for Legislative Action (ILA), with Harlon Carter at the helm. Carter was continually complaining that he wasn't given the resources to do the job necessary. In point of fact, the organization was becoming more and more polarized on the issue of exactly how much of a job *was* necessary.

If Carter and his faction of hard-liners were upset by the leadership's penny-pinching when it came to lobbying, they were infuriated when they learned what else the old guard had planned for their beloved NRA.

The new controversy centered around the NRA's annual shooting competition, which had been moved from Creedmoor, Long Island, to Camp Perry, Ohio, some years earlier. In the late 1960s, the tournaments were still being paid for by U.S. tax dollars funneled through the army's Division of Civilian Marksmanship (DCM). The matches, which now cost $3 million a year and required the aid of 5,000 army troops, seemed like a colossal waste of resources to Senator Edward Kennedy (who was, admittedly, no friend of the NRA)—especially at a time when the Vietnam War was gobbling up the nation's treasury. Kennedy moved to have the military drop the program.

Although he wasn't immediately successful, the leaders of the NRA saw the handwriting on the wall and decided it would be prudent to begin looking for an alternative site, should they be denied access to Camp Perry at some time in the future. A search committee was formed, and eventually it selected a suitable location in a beautiful and wild section of northern New Mexico. The NRA bought 37,000 acres of land there.

There was some grumbling among the hard-liners about the decision to spend a lot of money for a new rifle range when the ILA was still trying to scrimp by, but the matter wasn't seen as being too important. At least not until the hard-liners learned that the old guard had bigger plans for the National Shooting Center outside of Raton, New Mexico. It wouldn't just be a place to shoot. With so many acres at their disposal it made good sense to add some other, related, activities like camping and wilderness survival training; conservation education; environmental awareness. The NRA could teach all types of outdoor skills there. That being the case—mused the old guard— why call it a National *Shooting* Center at all? Maybe just the National *Outdoor* Center.

This was treason. To the hard-liners, the name change was a bullet aimed at the very soul of the gun organization. Maybe they could hold *bird-watching* classes, the hard-liners sneered. National *Outdoor* Center? Why stop there? Hell, why not just change the name from the National Rifle Association to the National Outdoor Association? Immediately, a rumor swept through the hard-liner ranks that at least one powerful board member was considering just such a proposal.

Harlon Carter had heard enough. Always a man of action, he now decided that the time had come to do something. He was in the midst of plotting a palace coup when, late one afternoon in November 1976, the old guard got the drop on the former Border Patrol agent and fired seventy-four NRA employees—most of them members of Carter's hard-liner group. The firings, which came on a Saturday, would be forever remembered by NRA veterans as the "Weekend Massacre."

Although Carter himself was too powerful a figure to terminate, he resigned in protest over the mass firings. The members of the old guard breathed a sigh of relief. With Carter and his foot soldiers gone they could get back to their work of making the NRA into the nation's preeminent outdoors organization. In furtherance of this goal, they announced plans to sell the headquarters building in Washington, D.C., and move all operations to Colorado Springs, not far from the National Outdoor Center. That might make the task of lobbying Congress more difficult, but then legislative action was no longer an NRA priority.

Six months later, the NRA's executive vice president (and leader of the old guard), General Maxwell Rich, stood on a stage at the Cincinnati Convention-Exposition Center and welcomed members to the group's annual meeting. This was to be a time of healing, hoped Rich—of pulling together, of forgetting the fights of the past few years and getting on with the business of building a stronger NRA.

Harlon Carter and his brigade of hard-liners had other plans for the meeting, however. Like the marines hitting the beach at Anzio, the group of hard-liners—calling themselves the Federation for NRA—took over the meeting, using parliamentary procedure as their heavy artillery. Coordinating their moves by means of walkie-talkies, the men introduced several changes in the group's bylaws that would diminish the power in the hands of the elected officials and give the membership more say in the organization's affairs.

The old guard never knew what hit them. The membership overwhelmingly voted for the changes. Plans to move the group's headquarters to Colorado Springs were put on hold, as were those for the hated National Outdoor Center. And then the members overwhelmingly voted against nearly every top NRA official, one by one. When the smoke cleared, leaders of the Federation for NRA occupied every position of power.

Minutes before his elevation to the supreme post of executive vice president, the commander of the federation forces mounted the podium at the front of the hall and addressed the cheering crowd below. "Beginning in this place and at this hour, this period in NRA history is finished," Harlon Carter proclaimed.

Carter was right. The Cincinnati Revolt (as the episode became known) changed forever the face of the NRA. Under Carter's robust leadership, and with the help of his chief lieutenant, Neal Knox (who took over as head of the ILA), the NRA became more than a rifle club. It became the Gun Lobby. Forget about hunting clinics, forget target shooting; those activities were now sideshows, mere extras. The new NRA would be devoted single-mindedly—and proud of the fact—to the proposition that Americans and their guns must never, *never* be parted.

Testifying before Congress in a calm but steel-edged voice, his blue eyes fixed directly on the committee chairman, Carter gave his enemies fair warning.

"We are," he told them, "in this game for keeps."

# 3

# ONE OF THE GREAT
# RELIGIONS OF THE WORLD

ALMOST SIX YEARS to the day after Harlon Carter led the group of dissidents to its stunning victory in Cincinnati, the grand old man of the NRA stood quietly smiling, waiting to ascend to the stage at yet another NRA annual convention. Carter had good reason to be happy. The past years had been a period of unparalleled growth for the National Rifle Association. Carter himself, now sixty-nine years old, was at the peak of his considerable powers within the organization he loved. All 4,000 seats in the Phoenix, Arizona, Civic Center were filled—and an additional 1,000 members were jammed into a nearby room to watch the proceedings on closed-circuit TV.

Although Carter was as popular as ever with the membership, most of the people in the auditorium weren't there to see him. They had come hoping to catch a glimpse of the special guest who now stood beside the NRA leader.

The hubbub in the cavernous auditorium subsided as the conductor of the army band raised his baton. The baton fell and the familiar strains of "Hail to the Chief" filled the hall. Then, over the public-address system came the words NRA members had been waiting to hear since they had first arrived in town.

"Ladies and gentlemen," intoned a deep baritone voice, "the President of the United States, and Harlon Carter."

Ronald Reagan and Harlon Carter together climbed the steps to the podium, where they stood and waved to the adoring and cheering crowd. Reagan was the first sitting president in U.S. history to come before an NRA gathering, and his presence on the stage in Phoenix reflected the new level of power and prestige of the organization Carter had led since 1977.

It was Harlon Carter's finest moment, one that vindicated the in-your-face, never-give-an-inch path the brawny Texan had marched the NRA down since his ascension to power. President Reagan's words bore out the success of that approach again and again in his half-hour keynote address. Standing beneath a giant NRA emblem (a screaming eagle clutching a rifle in its talons, superimposed on a red-white-and-blue shield), the conservative president told the members: "You live by Lincoln's words, 'Important principles may and must be inflexible.' Your philosophy puts its trust in people. So you insist individuals be held accountable for their actions. The NRA believes America's laws were made to be obeyed and that our constitutional liberties are just as important today as two hundred years ago."

The president's eyes sparkled as he prepared to deliver his next line. "And by the way," he added, as if the thought had just occurred to him, "the Constitution does not say government shall *decree* the right to keep and bear arms. The Constitution says 'the right of the people to keep and bear arms shall not be infringed.' "

The crowd roared its approval. The sound of scores of pairs of cowboy boots stamping on the Civic Center floor in a show of western-style support reverberated through the auditorium. Now *here* was a president who had his head on straight. Reagan's short address was interrupted by applause some thirty times, and Harlon Carter's grin grew larger with every round of clapping and stamping.

The president went on to compliment, by name, virtually all NRA programs. He praised the organization's hunter safety training efforts, its support for police, its wildlife and conservation programs, its calls for more prisons and mandatory sentencing of armed criminals. Adding that he "always felt a special bond with members of your group," Reagan solemnly promised to work on behalf of NRA-backed legislation and to stand shoulder-to-shoulder with the gun group in opposing antigun measures.

"We will never disarm any American who seeks to protect his or her family from fear or harm," the president promised, bringing the crowd to its feet again. "Good organizations don't just happen," Reagan reminded the group. "They take root in a body of shared beliefs. They flow from strong leadership with vision, initiative, and determination to reach great goals. . . . May I just say we have great respect for your fine, effective leaders in Washington: Harlon Carter, Warren Cassidy [who had recently replaced Neal Knox as head of the ILA], and your Institute for Legislative Action."

The crowd applauded. Harlon Carter beamed.

Carter and the ILA had indeed been effective, and they were becoming more influential every day, both in Congress and in state-houses across the country. "Few lobbies have so mastered the marble halls and concrete canyons of Washington," *The Washington Post* admitted begrudgingly in an editorial. A piece in *The New York Times* referred to the gun lobby as "the most persistent and resourceful of all single-issue groups."

Harlon Carter's takeover at Cincinnati was the beginning of the group's new Golden Age, a time when its myth of invincibility came the closest to reality. Never had the NRA's base of support been so broad; members were joining the group in record numbers. When Carter and his lieutenants ousted the old guard in 1977 the organiza-tion had slightly over 1 million members. By 1983, NRA member-ship had more than doubled to over 2.6 million individuals—and it was still growing at the phenomenal rate of 3,000 members each week.

No federal antigun legislation had been passed since 1968, and the future looked just as bright—perhaps even brighter, for the group's lobbyists now planned to go on the offensive, pushing Congress to roll back previous gun-control measures. It was an ebullient Harlon Carter—yet realistically so—who shared his vision of the NRA's future with members following President Reagan's address: "I see a period, the most magnificent, the most resplendent, in the NRA's history," he said in his booming voice, the hint of a Texas twang mellowing the words only slightly. "I see a National Rifle Association by the summer of 1984 or the early fall, of three million members. . . . I see an NRA with wealth and political strength and vigor, led by [the] ILA, an NRA . . . so strong and so dedicated that no politician in America, mindful of his political career, would want to challenge our legitimate goals."

By 1986, Carter's vision of the NRA's future would be proved remarkably prescient.

The rise of the NRA's fortunes was intertwined with those of their guest that day in Phoenix. Just as Ronald Reagan was the first sitting president to address an NRA gathering, so the NRA's endorsement of Reagan in the 1980 presidential campaign marked the first time in the gun organization's 109-year history that it had backed a candidate for the nation's top office.

The National Rifle Association had stopped just short of endorsing then-president Gerald Ford over Jimmy Carter in 1976 after Ford had promised the gun group that if elected he would "oppose any attempt to deprive law-abiding citizens of their traditional freedom to own firearms." In a letter to the editor of *American Rifleman*, Ford wrote:

> I believe in punishing only those who commit crimes. I am unalterably opposed to the federal registration of guns or the licensing of gun owners. It has been my long-held belief that these measures would be futile in attempting to stop the criminal. Instead they would treat law-abiding citizens as potential criminals. Those who intend to use guns for criminal purposes will never conform to legal requirements of any sort. In short, it is my intention to preserve for future generations the time-honored traditional freedoms that we and our forefathers have enjoyed throughout our 200-year history.

Jimmy Carter, an avid hunter and outdoorsman, also made many of the right noises about guns. In a press release, candidate Carter agreed with Ford and the NRA about the need to protect the rights of the "vast majority of hunters and other gun sportsmen [who] use their firearms respectfully and responsibly. We should not be penalized," he continued (the *We* indicating which side of the debate Carter wanted to be identified with), "because criminals use firearms, particularly handguns, to commit crimes."

But Carter was saddled with a Democratic platform that called for unspecified federal action to control the manufacture, sale, and possession of handguns. Worse, as far as the NRA was concerned, was the platform's support for a national ban on cheap handguns—Saturday Night Specials. And Carter himself had indicated he would support both registration of handguns and a national waiting period for their purchase.

Still, the NRA didn't formally support President For
preferring instead to remain on the sidelines, hoping that t
vice president (who had assumed the office of chief executiv
Watergate scandal) would be elected. But Ford lost, and ιυυι years
later a very different NRA, operating in a radically changed political
environment, enthusiastically endorsed challenger Ronald Reagan
over the incumbent Jimmy Carter.

With a rhetorical overkill that was fast becoming a defining characteristic of the gun lobby, the NRA complained: "The litany of Jimmy
Carter's affront on our Second Amendment rights and upon hunting
is endless." According to the gun group, President Carter had allowed
the Federal Bureau of Alcohol, Tobacco and Firearms (ATF) to conduct
"a campaign of harassment, of physical abuse, and persecution" of gun
owners. He had tried to eliminate one of the National Rifle Association's pet projects—the government-funded Department of Civilian
Marksmanship (the former National Board for the Promotion of Rifle
Practice). Carter's Interior Department had angered hunters by closing parts of Alaska's wilderness areas to hunting, and Carter himself
had further alienated the NRA by appointing a pro-gun-control congressman to the United States Court of Appeals. Members of Carter's
inner circle also failed to pass the NRA's litmus test. "Jimmy Carter's
list of close aides . . . is literally the 'Who's Who' of the antigun
movement," Harlon Carter once growled. The group particularly disliked Carter's chief of staff, Hamilton Jordan. In the opening days of
the administration, the brash young aide had allegedly told reporters,
"Carter will really go on gun control and really be tough. We're going
to get those bastards."

On the other hand, Ronald Reagan promised to be the best friend
the National Rifle Association had had in the White House since
Ulysses S. Grant served as titular head of the group back in the waning
years of the nineteenth century. Reagan's credentials as a staunch
supporter of gun owners' rights were well established: a lifetime member of the NRA, Reagan had received the California Rifle and Pistol
Association's top honor, the Outstanding Public Service Award, when
he was governor of that state.

As in all political alliances, the relationship owed much to mutual
back-scratching. Reagan opposed gun-control legislation and the NRA
threw its considerable weight behind him at election time. But in the

case of the NRA and Ronald Reagan something far more powerful was at work. The two were linked by their common identification with certain myths and images of America—aspects that were finding great appeal with the majority of Americans in the 1980s. Reagan and the National Rifle Association were (in their own worldview) the true-blue defenders of the "traditional American values" that had been eroding since the 1960s.

In his book *Magnum Force Lobby*, Edward Leddy, a leading intellectual of the progun movement, wrote in heroic terms about the mythic image with which the NRA identifies itself:

> If the National Rifle Association were to portray itself as a symbolic person, he would be a pioneer heading west with a rifle. He is self-reliant, morally strong, and competent. He is also peaceful by preference, but ready to defend himself from attack. He believes in personal rather than collective responsibility. He is not against government but sees its role as subordinate and supplementary to individual personal efforts. He opposes arbitrary abuse of government power but is openly patriotic.

This potent image also fit the public persona of Ronald Reagan. As a Hollywood actor, Reagan often played the part of the slow-to-anger-but-willing-to-fight gun-toting pioneer. His screen characters, in fact, helped to create—or at least to reinforce—the legend of an American West settled by "self-reliant, morally strong, and competent" individuals. And because Hollywood westerns did so much to popularize this view of an idealized West, Ronald Reagan was the perfect person to ride into Washington and clean out the various varmints who were undermining the American way of life.

When Reagan-the-screen-cowboy became Reagan-the-conservative-politician in the 1960s, the transformation was mostly one of wardrobe. He traded in his chaps, white hat, and fringe vest for the obligatory dark power suit. Otherwise, the man and his message remained much the same. No matter what the costume, Ronald Reagan, on screen and off, stood for the primacy of the lone God-fearing man over dark "un-American forces."

To both the NRA and Ronald Reagan the battle lines were clearly drawn, compromise unthinkable, and the outcome of the fight all-important to the future of this country. The NRA's Leddy labeled the enemy the "adversary culture," or the "new class" (borrowing the term from Lionel Trilling), which he described as "a large and influential group which rejects the frontier ideals of the National Rifle Association."

The new class made even traditional liberals look good, argued Leddy, by advocating the wholesale rejection of "American values." True liberals (of the New Deal variety) charged that America wasn't living up to its image, but the goal of the new class was nothing less than the wholesale replacement of "traditional middle-class" values by a new constellation of elitist values and social priorities. Leddy explained:

> What the National Rifle Association and much of America sees as virtuous—self-reliance, courage, strength, independence, and patriotism—the new adversary culture sees as faults: an outmoded and offensive male image, violence, chauvinism and anti-intellectualism. The adversary culture is guided by different principles and admires different virtues.

The Reagan camp shared the NRA's concern. Jeane Kirkpatrick, who was to become the United States' ambassador to the United Nations, and who would also serve in the unofficial position of Reagan administration chief intellectual, echoed the NRA fears:

> The political temptation of the new class lies in believing that their intelligence and exemplary motive equip them to reorder the institutions, the lives and even the characters of almost everyone—that is the totalitarian temptation. This is also the reason that a politics featuring large roles for intellectuals is especially dangerous to human liberty . . . a society that cherishes liberty will do well to protect itself from the excesses of the new class.

And the first line of protection from the new class, according to the NRA, was to be drawn around the issue of guns.

Why guns? Because, to NRA members, guns are the fundamental symbol of what makes this country great. For these Americans, generally but not exclusively rural people who grew up hunting, firearms represent all the original frontier values of rugged individualism, a love of the "great outdoors," and independence from illegitimate authority.

"The gun . . . is a symbol of freedom to these people," a former NRA executive told a congressional committee in 1981. "It has a lot more significance to people than a job."

Indeed, it may be helpful in understanding the depth of feeling provoked by even the mildest gun-control measures to think of firearms as totems mystically linking owners to their ancestors, and even more important, to our collective American forefathers. Former Oregon governor Victor Atiyeh, an NRA member since 1946, once said he collects guns in large part because of this spiritual link to early Americans.

"I look at the eighty guns in my collection and wonder 'Who owned them?' 'Who shot them?' " he stated in an advertisement for the NRA that appeared in *Reader's Digest* in 1983. "They kind of hook me up with history and make the days of George Washington, Lincoln and the pioneers much more real than the pages of a history book ever could."

Of course the link between the gun owner and a parent is more immediate and identifiable. The gun-owning tradition—and often the guns themselves—is passed down from one generation to the next. A major study of firearms ownership concluded that the single best predictor of whether an individual owns a gun or not is whether his or her father owned one.

The NRA's Warren Cassidy was correct, at least from a psychological perspective, when he claimed: "You would get a far better understanding if you approached us as if you were approaching one of the great religions of the world." That, in part, explains why the fight over *any* gun-control measure immediately takes on the quality of a holy war for firearms owners. (One writer had in mind this view of the NRA as a religious organization when he observed that "the first gun at puberty is the bar mitzvah of the rural WASP.")

But the religious fervor of many gun owners when it comes to firearms restrictions also has its roots in a less mystical and more pragmatic concern: the fear that all gun-control laws lead inexorably to the complete confiscation of all firearms.

Call it the "Potato Chip Theory of Gun Control." As Harlon Carter testified before Congress in 1975:

[I]t is kind of like the old Bert Lahr commercial that used to be on television. He used to eat a potato chip and say "I'll bet you can't eat just one." And I have no doubt at all that if it is a good thing to be in favor of a fourteen-day waiting period, next year ATF [the Bureau of Alcohol, Tobacco and Firearms] is going to be back and say we cannot do it in fourteen days. We will have to take ninety. Frankly, I can see where that leads, knowing how bureaucracies work. It is a little nibble first, and I'll bet you can't eat just one.

And after the longer waiting period doesn't stop crime, warns the NRA, the supporters of gun control will begin to nibble away at *other* areas of gun ownership: registering weapons, banning first a narrow class of firearms and then broadening the ban to include more and more weapons, until one day *all* weapons are outlawed.

"What the opposition *really* wants is a total ban on the private ownership of all firearms," maintains Richard Gardiner, director of state and local affairs for the ILA. "I have no doubt whatsoever."

When we talked at the NRA headquarters in mid-1991, the fortyish legislative director was nattily dressed in a light beige suit and yellow tie. With thinning blond hair, tortoiseshell glasses, and brown wing tips, Gardiner looked more like a corporate lawyer than a bulldog NRA lobbyist. In fact, the Pennsylvania native is a lawyer by training— although he has spent all his professional life working at the NRA— and allows that he has never been hunting, never even owned a gun. As a law student, Gardiner was simply taking a stroll by the NRA headquarters one beautiful spring day in 1976 ("I really *should* have been studying") when he spotted the sign NATIONAL FIREARMS MU-SEUM over a side entrance door. Intrigued, he went in to see what was inside. Gardiner asked a receptionist there if the organization needed a part-time law clerk and she referred him to the NRA's general counsel. The man hired Gardiner on the spot. Since that time, Gardi-ner has risen through the ranks, becoming assistant general counsel for the ILA in 1979, and taking over the reins of the state and local affairs division in 1989. From his D.C. office, Gardiner directs a staff of eight full-time lobbyists who coordinate the NRA's work on state and local gun legislation across the country.

Despite his mild looks, Gardiner is one tough customer. Smart, energetic, and happily combative, the self-described libertarian (he is an active member of the American Civil Liberties Union) is a fierce defender of the right to keep and bear arms.

"Once you've accepted the notion that you can succeed in reducing crime by regulating law-abiding people you're going to have to keep going, because it isn't going to work," Gardiner says. "And when phase one doesn't work and crime gets worse, you say, 'Well, let's go to phase two.' That's what they keep doing. I've never, ever, ever, *ever* heard anyone say: 'Well, *that* didn't work, let's go *back*.' "

And it is but one short step from the confiscation of weapons to the total subjugation of a people, warns the NRA in its magazines, promotional literature, and print and TV advertisements.

"Mark this well," cautioned Harlon Carter in a typical editorial on this theme in 1980. "Without a single exception in the history of all peoples, those who are oppressed never—repeat, *never*—have arms. Thus, the NRA is the protector of an indispensable mark of free men."

In the NRA perspective, *any* gun law is just the first step down a slippery slope that ends in virtual slavery at the hands of a totalitarian regime.

"Gun prohibition is the inevitable harbinger of oppression," argued Carter. "It can only be pursued by 'no-knock' laws under which jack-booted minions of government invade the homes of citizens; by 'stop-and-frisk' laws under which the person of citizens can be searched on the streets at the whim and suspicion of authority . . ."

While this "police state" scenario may strike many people—especially non–gun owners—as farfetched, the NRA insists that the potential for political repression should never be discounted. The private ownership of guns *must* be protected at all costs, it says, because the armed citizen will always remain the last line of defense against such an eventuality, however unlikely it may appear at present.

But in sounding the alarm about the dangers of authoritarianism, the NRA had created an image problem for itself. Phrases like "jack-booted minions" and simplistic bumper sticker argumentation (GUNS DON'T KILL PEOPLE; PEOPLE KILL PEOPLE) rub many people the wrong way—even many who are sympathetic to the group's legislative agenda. The NRA's rhetorical overkill helped to create an image that would haunt it time and again: that of the Gun Nut.

The NRA leadership publicly blames that image entirely on the machinations of its enemy: the new class, and especially members of the press. Yet, for years, the gun group clearly was shooting itself in the foot with its own bombast, playing squarely into the hands of those wanting to make the NRA look like a bunch of gun-toting kooks.

In January 1982, however, the NRA, under the guidance of Harlon Carter, unleashed an advertising campaign to counter that image. The opening blast in this war of images came in the form of a smiling eight-year-old, blond-haired, blue-eyed boy, photographed cradling a BB gun.

In the advertising copy accompanying the photo, the towheaded second-grader explains that he likes football and his dog—and his new BB gun. It is the gun, of course, that dominates the remainder of the ad.

The boy describes how excited he was to get the rifle and how he wanted to go out and start shooting right away. But his father explained that first he had to learn the rules of safe shooting. Someday (after he's had plenty of practice and has learned more safety rules), the boy says he's looking forward to going hunting with his grandfather.

In boldface type, above the Norman Rockwell–like picture, are the words that formed the basis of the advertising campaign: "I'm the NRA."

It was, quite literally, a textbook example of successful advertising; the ad was reprinted in college texts.

Other ads soon followed. Over the next eight years the NRA used thirty-eight different advertisements featuring a cross section of smiling Americans—men and women, black and white, famous and plebeian, and at least one sitting in a wheelchair—all holding guns. And positioned above every color portrait were the big, bold words "I'm the NRA."

"When Harlon Carter started, he wanted to get the message out that the NRA membership was diverse," says an employee at Acker-man McQueen, the agency that designed the campaign. "That was the primary purpose of these ads."

In this case, diverse means normal, friendly, and, most important, nonthreatening.

"Guns are threatening objects," acknowledged agency executive Marvin McQueen in a 1984 interview. "They're always pictured smoking or being pointed at Bambi. The whole idea here was to associate their image with something nonthreatening."

Many celebrities with squeaky clean images were used in the campaign, always linking their celebrity status to some aspect of firearms use.

Astronaut Wally Schirra: "I've been in space three times and it always made me think about how good the Earth is. I guess that's why I never spend a day in the field when I don't think about the beauty of our country. . . . Sometimes I get so absorbed with the environment I forget all about hunting."

Test pilot Chuck Yeager: "My good aim came in handy . . . as a test pilot. Even in the X-1 I'd look down on some mountain from 30,000 feet and think, 'I bet there's some great hunting down there.' "

Former Dallas Cowboys cheerleader and Ladies National Pistol champion Jo Anne Hall: "I enjoy competition. That's why I worked so hard to become a Dallas Cowboys Cheerleader. . . . I've become involved in competitive shooting as a hobby. . . . Women should know there's wholesome recreation connected with guns. It's something you can have fun with, besides having it for self-protection."

The advertisements all end with the celebrities praising the National Rifle Association, as Life Member Roy Rogers did in the one featuring him. After stating that he doesn't let just anyone use his name in a commercial, Rogers declares that he is proud to be identified with the NRA.

But the advertisements more commonly featured a carefully selected variety of more typical Americans: a pediatrician ("I've never treated a child for a gunshot wound, but I've lost count of those injured by bicycles, kitchen knives, poisons . . ."); a pastor ("For those who have the ears to hear, and eyes to see, there's pleasure in the pathless woods and thrills in the ways of the wilds"); a "wife, mother, businesswoman" ("My husband and I hunt almost every weekend during the season. It brings us closer together"). And in an obvious effort to counteract the image of NRA members as a collection of lawless gun nuts, a large number of the ads focused on law enforcement officers.

But the advertising campaign that NRA executives regarded as clever but innocuous caused a stir in the publishing world. Editors hotly debated whether or not they should run advertisements that showed guns. Several magazines rejected the ads outright. According to the NRA, these included *Better Homes and Gardens, Modern Maturity, Audubon,* and *McCall's.* Others (such as *Reader's Digest* and *Southern Living*) ran the advertisements as long as they limited photographs to long guns—rifles and shotguns. When the NRA sent them ads showing people holding *handguns,* the magazines refused to run them, even when the individuals pictured were law officers holding their service revolvers.

These rejections particularly galled the NRA because a great deal of effort had gone into designing ads that both advocated and depicted *responsible* gun use. When possible, guns were shown with their chambers open to show they held no rounds of ammunition. And in virtually every advertisement, the text included admonitions about the need for gun safety training.

Despite the several rejections, the "I'm the NRA" advertisements ran for 540 insertions in forty-five different magazines, from *U.S. News & World Report* to *Field and Stream* to *Smithsonian,* reaching a potential audience of a half billion people in eight years. And the ads appeared to work. Although no study was conducted to determine if public attitudes toward the NRA were shaped because of the campaign, it *is* known that the rise in the group's fortunes and the advertising campaign occurred simultaneously. Of course many things were happening at that same time; the advertising campaign was just one part of an all-out NRA effort to boost membership.

"Harlon saw that power is in numbers: money, PAC influence, letters, everything," says John Aquilino, director of public information for the National Rifle Association for almost ten years. "He put almost his complete attention toward this."

There were other factors as well. The NRA had an ideological soul mate in the White House. The internal wounds caused by the Cincinnati Revolt had apparently healed. And Americans were, by and large, becoming more conservative politically; the values the NRA had long preached were fashionable again. It was probably due to a convergence of factors, rather than a single element such as the "I'm the NRA" ad campaign, that the 1980s promised to be a splendid decade for the NRA.

This is despite the fact that the group slipped coming out of the gate in 1981, committing a serious blunder that threatened to poison its relationship with the Reagan administration just as it was getting started. The gaffe concerned one of the NRA's favorite whipping boys—the Bureau of Alcohol, Tobacco and Firearms, the government agency charged with enforcing federal gun laws.

When Congressman John Dingell told a reporter, "Occasionally, I'm going to have to do ugly things," the conservative Democrat and NRA board member might well have been describing his performance in a 1981 NRA-produced "documentary" about the ATF.

In the thirty-minute film, *It Can Happen Here*, Dingell compared ATF agents to Nazis: "If I were to select a jackbooted group of fascists who are perhaps as large a danger to American society as I could pick today, I would pick ATF."

The gun lobby attacks on the ATF dated back to the passage of the Gun Control Act of 1968, when the bureau's forerunner (the Alcohol and Tobacco Division) was charged with enforcing the new gun laws. Rex Davis, who joined the division as a field agent in 1949 and rose through the ranks to serve as director from 1970 to 1978, became an old hand at repelling NRA offensives.

"The relationship between the ATF and the NRA was already poor when I became director," he says today. "I wanted to improve things with better communication, but they weren't interested."

The NRA charged that ATF agents were harassing and abusing legitimate gun owners, often over what the gun group considered mere "technical violations." ATF agents should have been pursuing felons instead of conducting "a brutal crusade against the civil liberties of firearms owners," the NRA charged. The ATF responded that they were simply doing the job that Congress had charged them with. "[The NRA's] favorite tactic was to attack the agency charged with upholding the law, to reduce the agency's effectiveness," maintains Davis.

And the NRA attacks were withering.

On the floor of the House of Representatives, Republican John Ashbrook of Ohio—also an NRA board member—said: "I can honestly say that if I were to put into the [*Congressional*] *Record* the abuses of the Bureau of Alcohol, Tobacco and Firearms, I would have to ask leave to insert it at a cost of more than five hundred thousand dollars because I could fill five hundred pages of this *Record* with reckless abuse."

Gun Owners of America, a firearms lobby with links to the NRA (it was founded in 1975 by a man who would later become a board member of the NRA), fired off a particularly scathing members' mailing protesting the ATF's Honorary Junior Special Agent Program, in which children who toured the bureau's headquarters were given an ID identifying them as special agents.

> Your gun rights won't be worth a red cent if Federal agents recruit your neighbor's children to spy on you. The ATF recently offered to make our American youngsters "Junior Special Agents."
>
> Sounds harmless enough, doesn't it? But what will these Junior Special Agents be doing? There's no doubt in my mind that ATF is encouraging them to spy on their parents and neighbors. Tomorrow while you're at work these kids could be sneaking around your property. You can expect them to be peeking in the windows of your house or car trying to find out more about your hunting rifle or gun collection.
>
> Then, for an impressionable youngster, the most important part of all—sending a SECRET report to the Government. That is when you can expect the senior ATF agents to take over from the kids. And that is when you start becoming the "hunted instead of the hunter."
>
> All because an unsuspecting youngster has been duped into joining an organization that looks suspiciously like the "Hitler Youth." Is it any wonder that the ATF has been called "an American Gestapo"?

In defending its record, the ATF pointed out that 67 percent of cases they recommended for prosecution involved people with prior criminal records, and 45 percent involved convicted felons. But still the attacks came. Under the Carter administration, the ATF and the NRA were at a virtual standoff. But the situation changed dramatically when Ronald Reagan entered the picture, promising to eliminate the ATF's "abuse of power." With Ronald Reagan in the White House, the ATF's main defense, the support of the executive branch, was removed and the agency was left vulnerable. The NRA moved in for the kill, stepping up its propaganda campaign with the made-for-TV "documentary," attacks from the floor of Congress, and a blizzard of member mailings.

The group was, however, a bit too successful for its own good.

In early 1981, soon after Reagan took office, conventional wisdom in Washington was that the ATF would be abolished. The agency was slated for elimination in the spring round of Reagan budget cuts, but managed to survive with reduced funding, reportedly due to the intervention of Treasury Secretary Donald Regan (the ATF is under the jurisdiction of the Treasury Department). It was just a matter of time before the bureau's number was up, however. In September 1981, President Reagan unveiled his plans for the ATF at a meeting of the International Chiefs of Police in New Orleans. The agency would be dissolved and most of the special agents working on gun law enforcement would be fired. The NRA had won.

But Reagan hadn't taken into account the reaction to the news by the law enforcement crowd he was addressing. The chiefs of police were incensed over the planned massive layoffs of ATF special agents, so Reagan's advisers came up with what they later called a "very artful compromise."

The ATF would still be abolished, but rather than firing the special agents, they—and their duties—would be transferred to the Secret Service. It seemed perfect. The NRA would see the end of the "American Gestapo," the law enforcement community would see transfers rather than pink slips, and the budget cutters would see some savings from the consolidation of bureaucracies.

And at first everyone (except, of course, ATF executives) *was* happy about the compromise. It took a while, but soon it dawned on the NRA that if this plan went through, its goose was cooked. Enforcement of gun laws would no longer be in the hands of the low-profile—and low-prestige—Bureau of Alcohol, Tobacco and Firearms. Instead, the NRA would have to contend with the superstars of law enforcement: the Secret Service. The NRA realized that it wouldn't be able to call Secret Service agents "jackbooted fascists" and get away with it. Overnight, issuing from the NRA's black granite headquarters at 1600 Rhode Island Avenue came the sound of furious backpedaling.

The NRA and its supporters suddenly had a dozen reasons why the plan they had so recently supported was "unworkable" and "ill-advised." The ATF agents would contaminate the Secret Service. "Mix dirty water with clean water . . . and you get dirty water every time," offered Representative Dingell. Others warned that "those big Honeywell computers over there" at the Secret Service offices would be used for "backdoor gun registration." And then there was the simple fact that Senator Ted Kennedy supported the plan.

"Anything Teddy Kennedy backs, I think the honest citizens of this country should take a fast leap to the other side," cautioned an NRA spokesman.

In the end, a new compromise was hammered out, with the ATF still in charge of gun law enforcement, albeit with its budget and staff slashed. The NRA got its way, but in the process antagonized several Reagan administration members, including Attorney General Ed Meese. Fortunately for the gun group, Ronald Reagan himself stayed loyal to the cause and the rift soon healed.

In 1983, with its membership at an all-time high and its image improving, the NRA board and the leaders at the ILA decided it was time to spend some capital—both political and fiscal. While the group had successfully fought off all recent major gun-control legislation, there remained on the books a federal law that was a constant thorn in its side. The legislation barred mail-order and interstate shipment of firearms and ammunition and instituted a wide range of restrictions and regulations that frustrated gun owners and dealers. The NRA set its sights on the Gun Control Act of 1968.


THERE IS A truism little known outside the grand marble halls of Congress but well understood by all successful politicians: Three quarters of effective lawmaking is in "law busting." Crafting bills—what we are taught in civics class is the true business of Congress—is less important than demolishing them.

There are two reasons for this. First, legislative obstructionists can prevent what they consider bad bills from becoming bad laws. Second, by maintaining a credible threat that you intend to block someone else's legislation, you stand a far better chance of making a deal that results in *your* bill's passage.

Connoisseurs of obstructionism have developed a profusion of tricks and maneuvers designed to frustrate their opponents. A master can take a bill universally predicted to sail through a committee and stall it deader than a beached rowboat—and all the time appear to be supporting the legislation. Or he can allow the bill to make it to the floor, be debated, and then weight it down with so many amendments (all of them unreasonable) that the bill sinks and is never seen again. There are a million ways to stop a bill and only a few to get one passed.

We read little about such shenanigans. Generally speaking, bills that pass make news, those that don't, don't. But the lack of attention to this detail of parliamentary life shouldn't obscure its importance to the legislative process, especially in the case of gun control.

A group of legislators had for several years stymied the NRA's best attempts to repeal the Gun Control Act of 1968 (GCA) by using some of the most creative tricks of obstructionism. In the Senate, for example, Ted Kennedy and his staff perfected a highly effective gambit called the "Disappearing Quorum" that prevented the Judiciary Committee from considering any modification of the 1968 act.

This is how the maneuver worked: In order to transact any business on Capitol Hill, a minimum number of members—a quorum—must be present. In the House and Senate, a quorum is a simple majority of members, that is, 218 representatives and 51 senators (when all seats are filled). If a quorum isn't present, no business can be conducted and the body adjourns.

As chairman of the Senate Judiciary Committee in the 1970s, Kennedy was able to bury any assaults on the GCA without even getting his hair mussed. But the situation changed in 1981 when the Republicans swept into power in the Senate and Strom Thurmond of South Carolina took control of the Judiciary Committee. Kennedy then had to become more creative in his efforts to block anti-gun-control legislation.

At that time, nine members constituted a quorum on the Judiciary Committee. When a committee member was planning to discuss an NRA-backed attempt to gut the 1968 gun act, Kennedy would show up for the meeting lugging a briefing book the size of a desk encyclopedia. After the meeting was called to order, Kennedy would say, "Since this is such an important issue, I think we ought to go into it in some detail," and, much to the dismay of his colleagues, he'd open the huge volume to the first page and begin reading.

"It was pretty amazing to watch," recalls longtime Kennedy aide Jerry Tinker. In the briefing book were literally hundreds of state gun statutes. "Kennedy would say, 'Do you know what all the implications are for all the fifty states?' And then he'd begin reading all the state laws. Eyes would glaze over and one by one members would disappear and we'd lose the quorum."

Then Kennedy would look around the near-empty room, innocently note that it appeared the committee lacked a quorum, and the chair would have no choice but to adjourn the meeting. For one six-week period, Kennedy used the Disappearing Quorum repeatedly to fend off any consideration of the NRA's gun bill.

Of course, Kennedy had help in his efforts over the years. Before the Senate changed hands, supporters of an NRA-backed bill managed to get their legislation voted out of the Senate Judiciary Committee only to watch it wither away, blocked from consideration by the full Senate by the Majority Leader.

In the House, another obstructionist, Democrat Peter Rodino from New Jersey, routinely strangled the NRA's bills in the House Judiciary Committee, which he had chaired from 1973. Rodino was a typical gun-control advocate, having lived all his life in urban areas. To Rodino, guns were synonymous with crime. He was born and raised in Newark and then moved to Washington, D.C., after his election to the House of Representatives in 1950. And like Ted Kennedy, who lost two brothers to gun violence, Rodino was marked by an early experience with guns. While a student at the University of Newark (now Rutgers) Law School in the late 1930s, Rodino heard scuffling outside his dorm window one night. He looked out and saw two men fighting in the street below. The scuffle broke up quickly, but fifteen minutes later the men returned and faced each other. While Rodino looked on, one man drew a revolver out of his pocket and shot the other man dead.

Since that night, Rodino was a staunch advocate of gun control, which made him a leading enemy of the NRA—and, more important, of Harold Volkmer.

Democratic representative Howard L. Volkmer was everything Peter Rodino was not. Where Rodino was not only urban but urbane, suave, and distinguished-looking with his lion's mane of silver-gray hair, Volkmer was pure unpolished country. Born in Jefferson City, Missouri, Volkmer was known in the House for his curt voice and abrupt—some say surly—manner. While Volkmer denies that charge, saying that he's simply straightforward and forthright, he does allow that perhaps he isn't always "diplomatic" enough for some people. "I guess there are times in debate when I can be a little sarcastic to people, but I think there's an appropriate place for that," Volkmer says.

A lifelong hunter, Volkmer swore to overturn the GCA one year after coming to Congress in 1977. And, in fact, from 1978 on, the brusque Volkmer devoted himself to that end, soon earning himself the reputation of being the NRA's "point man" on Capitol Hill. Volkmer was so close to the gun group that his principal aide on firearms issues, Kenneth Schloman, eventually went to work for the National Rifle Association. The relationship between Volkmer and the NRA remains especially close; the Missouri Democrat's chief legislative assistant is Cherry Schloman—Kenneth Schloman's wife.

Volkmer and Rodino tangled over the gun issue many times when Volkmer served on the House Judiciary Committee between 1977 and 1980. In January of 1978, Volkmer began drafting a bill to roll back key provisions of the GCA. Over the next few years, Volkmer tried many times to get his bill to be considered, but Rodino kept the legislation bottled up in committee, even though eventually 171 representatives—almost 40 percent of the entire House—had signed on as co-sponsors. The gun bill wasn't the only legislation to meet that fate, however. The liberal Rodino was so effective as an obstructionist that angry conservatives began calling his Judiciary Committee the "legislative mortuary."

At the same time, over on the north end of the Capitol, Republican senator James McClure of Idaho took up the battle to reform the 1968 act. In their personalities, McClure and Volkmer had little in common. Amiable, if a bit quiet, McClure was well liked by virtually all his colleagues, especially by conservative Democrats who shared a similar worldview with the former county prosecutor from western Idaho.

Despite their differences in temperament, McClure and Volkmer were two ideological peas in a pod when it came to gun issues, a fact that was partly attributable to geography. Legislators from southern and western states generally take a progun position, as do House members who represent rural districts. Both McClure and Volkmer were elected by constituencies for whom "gun control" means how steady your shooting hand is. It was McClure's bill that Ted Kennedy had managed to keep bottled up in committee for weeks using the Disappearing Quorum act. In 1982, Kennedy added an amendment to McClure's anti-gun-control bill that would have mandated a fourteen-day waiting period for the purchase of handguns, but the bill never went anywhere.

In the spring of 1984, the tide began to turn in favor of the decontrollers. A bill, which came to be called the McClure-Volkmer Act,

had begun to wend its way through the labyrinth the obstruc
had managed to erect in both houses. Although the bill we
rewritten, modified, and amended many times during its jour
its earliest form McClure-Volkmer amounted to a wish list of changes
dreamed of by sportsmen and other gun owners, arms dealers, and,
of course, the National Rifle Association.

Major provisions of McClure-Volkmer included:

- Dropping the existing ban on the interstate sale of firearms.
- Allowing convicted felons to own firearms if their crimes
  only involved the regulation of business practices. Under
  the GCA *all* felons were prohibited from owning firearms.
- Exempting dealers from record-keeping obligations for ammunition sales.
- Prohibiting the government from barring the importation of
  guns determined to be "suitable for sporting purposes."
- Allowing gun dealers to transfer a gun from business inventory to a private collection and then sell it without recording
  the sale.
- Requiring ATF agents to have "reasonable cause" before
  inspecting a dealer's records, and then only after giving the
  dealer prior notice of the inspection.

In April 1984, the Senate Judiciary Committee took up its version
of McClure-Volkmer. This time, the committee defeated Kennedy's
waiting period amendment (by a vote of eleven to three), and it also
rejected an amendment retaining the ban on the interstate sale of
handguns. This last vote was the most alarming to gun-control advocates. The prohibition on selling handguns across state lines was considered by many to be a centerpiece of the GCA. If support for *that*
section was eroding, then the entire act was up for grabs.

Reacting quickly to the rapidly changing scene, both sides met to
negotiate. The bill's sponsors, Senators McClure and Orrin Hatch
(another Republican, from Utah), wanted to remove the GCA's ban
on interstate sales of *any* guns, but they also were well acquainted with
Kennedy's skill at keeping legislation bottled up. Kennedy weighed in
with a tempting offer: If the other side would agree to maintain the
existing ban on cross-border sales of *small handguns*—the so-called

Saturday Night Specials, or "snubbies"—he would agree to remove the embargo from all other firearms. For the next twenty minutes the small group loudly debated the compromise.

McClure, who was in the room at the time (although he wasn't a member of the committee), at first responded to Kennedy's proposal with misgivings. "Well, you know, Ted," he argued, "people go rabbit hunting with that sort of gun."

But that argument didn't hold up well even with his own side. "Oh, come on," said an exasperated Senator Paul Laxalt, a supporter of McClure-Volkmer. Finally, the compromise was accepted by all sides and voted out of committee.

"This is too good a deal to pass up," declared Kennedy.

Some gun-control advocates were surprised that Kennedy would accept such a deal—let alone deem it "too good to pass up." But the senator from Massachusetts had never been the unbending foe of gun owners that the National Rifle Association had made him out to be. Kennedy's position had long been that he was willing to loosen up restrictions on long guns—rifles and shotguns—as long as handguns continued to be strictly regulated, if not banned altogether. Even Kennedy aide Jerry Tinker was surprised by the senator's views on gun control.

"I had been working for Kennedy for ten years and hadn't really followed what his position on gun control was," recalls Tinker. "When I picked up this issue in 1981, I was astonished at how moderate his proposals were."

In fact, both sides had been close to compromising on a gun bill for some time. Strom Thurmond and Robert Dole, both powerful members of the Judiciary Committee, had earlier considered agreeing to Kennedy's tack, but they were cautioned by the NRA that any compromise was too much. The two backed off.

The McClure-Volkmer bill made it out of committee, but it didn't get much further. It was offered as an amendment to a civil rights bill, but was later removed. Still, an important threshold had been crossed in 1984 and both sides realized it. They upped the ante for the inevitable shootout over gun decontrol in the next Congress. The NRA declared McClure-Volkmer a "bill of rights for America's gun owners," and cranked up its PR machinery. Michael Beard, the head of the

National Coalition to Ban Handguns (NCBH), decri(
a senseless move in the wrong direction.

> Only a madman could look at the problem we have
> because of easy availability of handguns, and the re:
> injuries and fear of handgun crime, and then say that wh
> needs is to weaken our handgun control laws. But a:
> that may sound to the majority of Americans, the NRA will go all-out
> in this Congress to muscle through this outrageous piece of legislation.

The problem of handgun deaths in America during the time of the
debate on McClure-Volkmer was extremely complex and not given to
easy solutions—although that was all either side offered. While the
handgun murder rate had more than doubled in this country between
1966 and 1974 (jumping from 2.5 murders per 100,000 people to 5.3
murders), that number dropped over the next few years before rising
again to end up in 1980 at a point slightly below the 1974 level (5.1
handgun murders for every 100,000 people). Still, the gruesome fact
that in 1980 some 14,287 people were murdered by firearms—11,520
of them by handguns—alarmed most Americans and they demanded
that something be done. But while even the NRA denounced gun
violence, there was no consensus on exactly what should be done to
curb the bloodshed.

There were two basic views on the issue. The advocates of gun
control painted an appealingly simple picture, directly linking—in the
words of NCBH's Michael Beard—the "easy availability of handguns,
and the resulting deaths, injuries and fear of handgun crime." Get rid
of handguns and gun deaths will drop dramatically. Peter Rodino
reflected this viewpoint when he summed up the killing he had witnessed outside his dorm window in law school. "If he hadn't been able
to get his hands on a gun," Rodino said of the gunman, "it wouldn't
have happened."

On the other side of the debate, the National Rifle Association and
its backers claimed that there was no link between the availability of
firearms and the crime rate. GUN CONTROL ISN'T CRIME CONTROL,
NRA bumper stickers proclaimed. Neal Knox, one of the leaders of the
1977 Cincinnati Revolt, colorfully articulated this position in an exchange with Peter Rodino before the House Subcommittee on Crime.

"You control the criminal, not the means," Knox told Rodino. "[It's] very simple, sir. You recall when Moses came down from Mount Sinai the command was, 'Thou shalt not steal.' It did not say, 'Thou shalt not carry a rock with which to steal.' Now, what you are trying to do here is to control the rocks."

Although the NRA was coming at the problem from the opposite direction, its solution to crime was as simple (or simplistic) as that of its opponents': Toss anyone who criminally misuses a gun into jail and throw away the key. Get rid of plea-bargaining. Forget early-release programs and easy parole. Prosecute accused criminals to the full extent of the law, give them harsher sentences, and build more prisons to accommodate them. But *don't*—they emphasized—restrict the rights of gun owners in general.

The stage was set for the fight's final round in the Senate when James McClure introduced his bill on January 3, 1985—the first day of the 99th Congress. Rather than again haggle over the bill in committee, Majority Leader Bob Dole used the power of his office to have McClure-Volkmer posted directly on the Senate calendar, meaning that there would be no public hearing on the bill, other than floor debate, before it was put to a vote. Opponents of the bill were enraged, but there was little they could do. It was their turn to fume while the majority party ran the rules according to its own game plan.

And there the bill remained during the early months of 1985 as the Senate attended to other business. Then, on Thursday, June 13, Kennedy's staff called Handgun Control, Inc. (the main lobbying group opposing McClure-Volkmer), with some bad news: Senator Dole had just announced that the Senate would vote on the gun bill on the following Monday. Panic struck the gun-control lobby. Overnight, they put together and distributed notebooks to senators detailing what they considered the drawbacks of McClure-Volkmer. They also lined up senators to filibuster if McClure-Volkmer came up on Monday.

The two sides convened to try to avoid a procedural confrontation. At the meeting (over which Dole presided) were Senators Ted Kennedy, James McClure, Orrin Hatch, Howard Metzenbaum (a strong advocate of gun control), and representatives from both the National Rifle Association and Handgun Control, Inc. The negotiations went on for days; finally, a tentative deal was arranged. Opponents of McClure-Volkmer would agree not to filibuster in exchange for a two-week delay before the vote and the inclusion of several amendments considered key by the gun-control advocates. Howard Metzenbaum was the lone holdout. On June 24, the group adopted an amendment that would bar the importation of parts for Saturday Night Specials, and Senator Metzenbaum agreed to let the bill go ahead. Full floor debate was set for July 9.

When the sergeant at arms called the Senate to session on the morning of July 9, there was little doubt about the outcome of the historic vote. The bill had fifty-two co-sponsors, representing more than enough votes for passage. Still, given the fierce rhetoric coming from both sides, an observer sitting in the Senate gallery that day could be forgiven for thinking that what was occurring below was a pitched battle.

"The Gun Control Act of 1968 is snake oil," pronounced McClure. "It is medicine that does not solve the ill of violent firearms abuse. It is about time we changed the dose."

"This legislation," countered Connecticut Democrat Christopher Dodd, speaking against McClure-Volkmer, "turns back the clock of federal protection against handgun crime. . . ." (Senator Dodd's disappointment was all the more understandable because his father, Thomas Dodd, was one of the key architects of the GCA.)

Though the bill was expected to pass, the National Rifle Association wasn't taking any chances. The organization's computers had been busily churning out letters beseeching members to contact their senators about McClure-Volkmer. "This could be your last chance," they warned.

As usual, the members came through. By 9:00 A.M. on the day of the vote, one Senate office had already received eighty phone calls in support of McClure-Volkmer. As the voting began and the dimensions of the rout became apparent, one Senate aide groaned, "This place is marching in lockstep with the NRA."

Finally, the tally was official: The United States Senate had passed its first gun legislation in seventeen years—and by a commanding vote of seventy-nine to fifteen.

While some basked in the warm glow of success, at the headquarters of the NRA there was little celebration. The support in the Senate, while welcome, was expected. But now all eyes turned to the House of Representatives—which was still controlled by the Democrats and where a far more difficult battle remained. The fate of McClure-Volkmer lay, as it had for years, in the hands of Peter Rodino, the chairman of the House Judiciary Committee. For those naive enough to wonder how McClure-Volkmer would fare in his committee, Senator Rodino had a straightforward reply: "That bill will be dead on arrival," the silver-haired senator told a reporter.

Rodino would come to regret his cocky pronouncement.

ON JANUARY 26, 1985, an aging and ailing Harlon Carter stepped down from the helm of the National Rifle Association to be replaced by G. Ray Arnett, a blustery, tobacco-chewing former Interior Department official who had headed the California Fish and Game Department when Ronald Reagan was governor of that state. Like Harlon Carter, Arnett had grown up around guns—he, in fact, was born on a military base some sixty years earlier. But much of the NRA's real power was now based at the organization's lobbying wing, the ILA, where Warren Cassidy was the man in charge.

In some respects, Cassidy was an anomaly at the NRA. A former insurance company executive and ex-mayor of Lynn, Massachusetts, Cassidy had smoother edges than either Carter or Arnett. For example, when asked to justify the group's opposition to handgun laws given the fact that 44 percent of all murders in 1983 had been committed with handguns, Arnett just waved the question away. "I don't play the statistics game," he said. "Statistics are like a bikini bathing suit. They reveal what is interesting but they hide what is vital."

It would have been hard to imagine the polished Cassidy using that kind of "good ol' boy" analogy. Where the beefy Arnett always looked ill at ease in a suit and tie, as if he had been stuffed at gunpoint into the clothes, the trim and debonair head of the ILA looked as if he had been born in a power suit.

But Cassidy was just as passionate as Arnett when it came to guns. There are two types of NRA lobbyists: those who use the job to make contacts and then move on, and the true believers. In Warren Cassidy's case, beneath the manicured exterior beat the heart of a true believer. In fact, the former marine was accustomed to packing a pistol whenever he was in Boston at night, and was more than a little upset when, after moving to Washington, D.C., to head the ILA, he was denied permission by a local judge to continue the practice of going armed.

Although it normally didn't take much to get Harold Volkmer's blood boiling, Peter Rodino's claim that Volkmer's gun bill would be "dead on arrival" made the Missouri congressman laugh out loud.

"When I heard that, I knew Rodino was driving a nail in his own coffin," says Volkmer today. "I already knew he wasn't going to report the bill out of committee—or even give us a hearing."

Rodino's statement just confirmed Volkmer's charge that he wasn't being treated fairly. The question was, how could Volkmer capitalize on Rodino's assertion?

The answer was found in a little-known procedure called a discharge motion. Volkmer's good friend (and fellow NRA board member) Representative John Dingell once said, "If you let me write procedure and I let you write substance, I'll screw you every time." Volkmer would use procedure to get Rodino. If successful, the discharge motion would force Volkmer's bill to the floor—and a vote—without having to go through Rodino's committee. It was a simple plan, but to carry it off Volkmer needed a majority of House members to sign his petition. That meant he had to convince 218 representatives to bypass standard procedure, something most of them were normally loath to do. The majority of pundits didn't give Volkmer much of a chance of succeeding, pointing out that the last time such a motion had carried was in 1983. Volkmer himself didn't give a good goddamn about such predictions.

"Those experts didn't know that we had the momentum working for us, or that Peter Rodino was helping us," Volkmer says. "Even some members of the Judiciary Committee resented what he was doing. And, remember, it wasn't just my bill; he had bottled up a lot of other bills over the years. He was recognized as a person who used his personal opinions to strangle legislation."

By September of 1985, it dawned on Rodino that something was wrong. Several representatives were grumbling about his treatment of Volkmer—the "DOA" statement was mentioned frequently as a source of that displeasure—and were signing Volkmer's discharge petition. And there was talk about the fact that McClure-Volkmer had sailed through the Senate and should have a hearing in the House. Rodino, a master obstructionist, decided to head Volkmer off at the pass. He and William Hughes, the Democratic chairman of the House Subcommittee on Crime, put together a competing gun bill and announced hearings on their legislation to begin in October. Like McClure-Volkmer, the Hughes-Rodino bill would once again allow interstate sales of guns. Unlike McClure-Volkmer, however, their bill would continue the ban on such sales for handguns.

But Rodino and Hughes had misjudged the ground swell of support that was building for Volkmer's position. By late October, 95 representatives had signed the discharge motion, with more coming over every day. And although Rodino told the press that *he* had commitments from 160 members *not* to back Volkmer's petition, Rodino knew the tide was getting away from him.

Then Hughes made another mistake. He scheduled the hearings in New York City and in San Francisco, two cities known as "pro-gun-control" territory. Just when he and Rodino needed to bend over backwards to show that they were being fair to the other side, they instead provided Volkmer with high-powered ammunition to support his charge of bias. Many in the House sympathized with California State Senator (and NRA board member) Bill Richardson, who, when invited to testify at the hearing, refused, saying, "This hearing is nothing more than a circus. I gave up attending circuses as a little boy."

On December 20, when the House adjourned for the year, Harold Volkmer had 150 signatures on his discharge petition.


WHEN ADVOCATES OF gun control quote their opponents, they invariably use what can only be called the Gun Voice: "Theze an-*tie*-gunners ah try'n a take away yer rights! Stan' up and knock 'em out o' Congress!" That's how one congressional insider imitated the opposition in an interview.

The Gun Voice is immediately recognizable: macho, gruff, with a heavy southern accent and the unmistakable edge of madness, or, at the very least, of menace. While the Gun Voice represents a clear attempt to "demonize" the opposition, it does reveal certain important truths about members of the NRA, and about all those for whom "gun rights" are the most sacred rights Americans have.

They are overwhelmingly male, a fact clearly reflected in the makeup of the NRA's hierarchy. Its eight top officers are male, just one woman sits on the group's executive council (which has eleven seats), and women account for only 8 percent of the NRA's seventy-five-member board of directors. This is not surprising given that gun ownership and sporting use have historically been far higher among men than women.

The southern twang in the Gun Voice also has its roots in the real world. Men raised below the Mason-Dixon Line *are* more likely to own and use guns than those raised in the North.

But the last facet of the Gun Voice—the hard edge—is the most controversial.

"I have never gotten so many vituperative calls on any issue that we've ever dealt with as with the gun issue," says a Senate aide. "Violent, violent calls. People calling up threatening me, threatening the senator. Death threats. All that crap. The one thing you learn about this issue is that the most active people for gun rights are also the most violent people, the people you don't want to have guns."

The NRA simultaneously decries and promotes that image, walking a fine line between cultivating its menacing reputation ("You cross us and you're dead meat") while all the while insisting that it is *not* a collection of kooks.

Certainly, the facts are on the NRA's side when it argues that the overwhelming majority of gun owners are responsible individuals who commit no crimes with their firearms. Despite the opposition's many attempts to blame gun owners in general for crime, that is not the case.

The stereotype of gun owners as being uneducated and mostly from lower socioeconomic classes (a stereotype also hinted at in the Gun Voice) is likewise inaccurate. The typical gun owner in America is a reasonably well-educated member of the middle class.

But there is no denying that the passion displayed by many gun owners sometimes crosses the line of "spirited debate" and strays into the realm of extremism.

"You can tick off in our body politic at most ten single issues that really do galvanize people," says Jerry Tinker, aide to Senator Ted Kennedy. "Issues like abortion and gun control, where people are really *possessed* with that single issue and use that as a litmus test. In particular regions of the country it is *the* overarching concern. The National Rifle Association is one of the first of the single-issue political groups, and there are very few single issues out there that motivate people to take the kind of determined stand that the NRA does."

The NRA likes to call its members' passionate response to perceived threats "democracy in action." Its detractors—anyone who has ever been on the receiving end of an NRA campaign—call it "politics by intimidation." Whichever term one prefers, it's clear that it is the group's ability to make life quickly miserable for legislators who cross it—to crank up the Hassle Factor—that endows the NRA with much of its power. To better motivate and direct gun owners' energy, the NRA pioneered the use of direct-mail techniques in politics. When the gun group put out a mass mailing to its nearly three million members during the McClure-Volkmer debate, the response was immediate. A deluge of letters, phone messages, and telegrams, with varying degrees of outrage, poured into the offices of elected officials.

Constituent communications have a powerful effect on politicians. "This place gets twenty letters and we think there's a national trend," says the legislative assistant to a California representative. "Have you ever seen what a stack of one thousand letters looks like?" He leans forward in his chair while holding his arm out from his side to indicate the stack's height. "It's impressive." Even William Hughes spoke with begrudging admiration for the influence of his foe. "[The NRA] can put fifteen thousand letters in your district overnight and have people in your town hall meetings interrupting you," he said.

Although the day would come when it would work against it, in 1986 the Hassle Factor provided by irate gun owners was still the NRA's chief asset, and in the House fight for McClure-Volkmer, the NRA relied heavily on it. In his monthly column in the January 1986 issue of *American Rifleman*, NRA Executive Vice President Ray Arnett sounded the alarm: "It is urgent that all firearm owners and dealers contact their representatives and ask them to sign the discharge petition so that the right to keep and bear arms for all law-abiding citizens can be protected."

The opposition issued a similar battle cry in its newsletter: "To counter the NRA's campaign, [we] must activate those hundreds of thousands of supporters who want stronger, not weaker, federal handgun laws. . . . Only with your support can we stop the NRA's discharge drive."

As part of its hardball campaign, the NRA sent letters to members whose legislators hadn't yet signed Volkmer's petition, questioning the loyalty of those representatives. Tennessee Democrat Jim Cooper was particularly upset by the four-page letter the NRA mailed to members in his district.

The letter informed gun owners: "If your congressman doesn't sign the discharge petition on the Firearms Owners Protection Act [the official name for the McClure-Volkmer bill], he's not working for gun and hunting rights in America. It's that plain and simple. . . . This is the litmus test on where your congressman stands on gun and hunting rights—either he is for us or he is against us."

The letter clearly illustrates two of the NRA's most important grass roots lobbying tactics: portraying every fight over gun legislation as *the final showdown* between gun owners and "gun grabbers"; and dividing the world into two mutually exclusive factions: "with us" and "against us."

The letter deeply offended Congressman Cooper because he supported, not opposed, McClure-Volkmer. He was also angry about the NRA's inference that he had voted for other discharge motions in the past but now refused to sign this one, which was not the case.

"What the NRA has already done is damage my reputation throughout my district before they even bothered to get in touch with me," Cooper complained. "I don't feel like I've been treated fairly."

But the same tactics that were making some legislators uncomfortable were paying big dividends in votes. More and more representatives were signing Volkmer's discharge petition—due to the Hassle Factor, widespread dissatisfaction with Rodino's obstructionism, or because they genuinely believed in the bill.

The NRA still faced another important problem, however: The Justice Department was putting out mixed signals about the legislation. The gun lobby considered it critical to have the nation's top law enforcement agency solidly behind McClure-Volkmer, because the opposition would use any doubts coming from the Justice Department to paint the legislation as "antipolice." The conflict stemmed from chance remarks made by Attorney General Edwin Meese at a meeting of the conservative group the 721 Club. This little-known clique was made up of lawmakers and representatives from victims' rights organizations and law enforcement agencies, who met informally every few weeks to discuss the Comprehensive Crime Control Act, which was being debated at that time in Congress. During one of these meetings, Richard Gardiner, then the NRA's assistant general counsel, asked for Attorney General Meese's opinion of McClure-Volkmer. Gardiner was hoping, and fully expecting, that Mr. Meese would give the bill his unconditional support.

But according to an internal Justice Department memo: "[T]he Attorney General surprised the NRA members present when he stated that he had problems with the bill [and] that the bill was no longer necessary since the Administration had solved the problems that gave rise to the bill in the first place"—a reference to alleged ATF abuses of gun dealers during the Carter administration.

At 3:15 on the afternoon of January 22, 1986, a tense meeting took place at the Justice Department in which the NRA hoped to iron out its differences with the agency. The department's delegation was led by John Bolton, Assistant Attorney General for Legislative and Intergovernmental Affairs, and included several attorneys on his staff. The NRA contingent consisted of Warren Cassidy, Richard Gardiner, ILA lobbyists Wayne LaPierre and James Jay Baker, and an outside lobbyist—representing the NRA—Tom Korologos.

Korologos was a familiar figure in the Beltway game of power politics during the Reagan years. A personal friend of the president, Korologos had left the White House to work for Timmons and Company, one of the most powerful Republican lobbying firms in Washington. Korologos's presence at the meeting was the NRA's way of letting the Justice Department know just how important this issue was to it—and, potentially, to the president.

The two groups went back and forth on various interpretations of sections of the bill for some time, disagreeing, as well, on the necessity of the legislation as a whole. Neither side was fully able to satisfy the other. When someone from the NRA reminded Mr. Bolton that Attorney General Meese had already written a short letter supporting McClure-Volkmer (while he was still serving in the White House), a Justice Department representative countered that the letter "simply expressed the administration's agreement in principle with the bill, but did not expressly approve it in every detail."

Finally, toward the end of the meeting, Warren Cassidy introduced one of the primary political reasons for the NRA's concern. It was important, he stated, that McClure-Volkmer pass in the House in the same form as the Senate had already approved. Normally any differences in bills passed by both houses are worked out in a "conference committee." But that was precisely the problem, Cassidy reminded the group. House members of the conference committee would be appointed by the Speaker of the House, Tip O'Neill, an advocate of gun control. Whatever had been done on the floor of both chambers to reform the GCA could be easily *undone* in a conference committee stacked by O'Neill. The Justice Department officials just shrugged. They weren't about to give up their objections to the bill just to make life easier for the NRA. They held to their position of generally supporting the bill, but with several caveats.

(Later, gun-control advocates did focus on this disagreement, just as the NRA had feared. During one of the hearings on the Hughes-Rodino bill, Democratic congressman Lawrence Smith introduced an internal memo written by the director of the ATF, Stephen Higgins, in which the director weighed the positive and negative features of McClure-Volkmer.

After reminding the committee members that the administration had said it "supported" the bill, Smith remarked, "According to this memo, there are thirteen negative points and six positive points." He added dryly, "I certainly wouldn't want them on my team for developing the preponderance of evidence in a civil case.")

About the disagreement, Harold Volkmer says, "They [the Justice Department] had their viewpoint about what should be in there and we had ours. But it didn't bother us. We had the momentum."

That momentum had been built by a carefully coordinated campaign planned by the National Rifle Association and the progun legislators. Soon after the Senate vote in July of 1985, Volkmer had called together a group of sympathetic representatives and formed a task force to map out each move.

"We met in my office several times," Volkmer recalls. "First, we concentrated on the members we knew we were going to get. Then we went after the others. We divided up names so everybody knew who they were supposed to contact. We knew exactly how it was going at all times: who was signing up, who wasn't, and *why* they weren't."

Volkmer adds that the task force shared its lists with the National Rifle Association. "So that they could get to work on them back home," he explains.

On February 27, the fight for a discharge motion entered the home stretch. Volkmer had obtained 190 signatures on his petition and needed just 28 more. The day before, Attorney General Meese had told reporters that the administration, while generally supporting McClure-Volkmer, still felt that there were "things in the bill that could be improved." Volkmer didn't care. His attention was focused solely on getting those last few names on his petition.

That's exactly where Peter Rodino's attention was focused as well: on Harold Volkmer's discharge motion. Rodino tried one last gambit, making personal appeals to those representatives who had already signed on with Volkmer to withdraw their names. Rodino, who had been in the House for over three decades, had made many friends over those years and had many favors owed him; he was now calling in his chits. But as Harold Volkmer likes to say, the momentum was on *his* side. Only one representative asked to have his name removed following Rodino's appeal.

Inside the legislative pressure cooker of the House, tempers were beginning to boil. During a hearing on the Hughes-Rodino bill, the following exchange took place between Representative Hughes and the NRA's Warren Cassidy and Richard Gardiner:

HUGHES: My question to you is: Is it important for us to be able to determine whether or not a terrorist group in this country is distributing weapons to their members? Is that important for us to keep records of those transactions?

CASSIDY: Assuming that is a rhetorical question, and you want a yes answer, how would you do that?

HUGHES: You would do that, first of all, by requiring them to complete the application, if they are purchasing it through legitimate means.

CASSIDY: A terrorist group?

[Gardiner makes some unrecorded action or comment]

HUGHES: You have a problem, Mr. Gardiner?

GARDINER: Yes, excuse me, Mr. Hughes, I think that is so absurd.

HUGHES: You know something, I find your conduct here today absolutely reprehensible, *reprehensible*. I understand you are representing a special interest group, and it is your job to represent them to the best of your ability, but your conduct is anything except what I would expect from a member of my profession.

In early March, while Rodino and Hughes were still planning to hold more hearings on their bill, Speaker of the House Tip O'Neill warned them that if they wanted to offer a bill, they had better dispense with hearings and get something, *anything*, to the floor immediately. The word was that Volkmer needed just a few more signatures on his petition. If he got those before the Judiciary Committee passed a bill, the battle was over: The House would debate and vote on McClure-Volkmer immediately.

In a desperate attempt to head off Volkmer, Rodino managed to ram his own bill through the Judiciary Committee, thirty-five to zero, on March 11. Volkmer needed to file his petition as soon as possible, before the House took up the Hughes-Rodino bill.

The next day, March 12, Volkmer was only one signature shy of the magic number, 218. The House met late into the evening that night and Volkmer missed his flight back to Saint Louis. Finally, after the last vote of the day, Volkmer rushed out to catch the final United flight to Chicago, where he'd transfer to a shuttle bound for Saint Louis. The weary legislator had just sat down on the jet when Vin Weber, a Republican congressman from Minnesota, dropped into the seat next to him.

"Guess what?" said Weber, a large grin spreading across his face. "Roy Dyson just signed your petition. You've got your two hundred eighteen!"

Larry Craig, a conservative representative from Idaho who, like Volkmer, served on the National Rifle Association's board of directors, had enlisted Dyson, a Maryland Democrat, just as the House was adjourning. Volkmer was elated. It was a moment of personal, as well as political, triumph. He had worked for almost eight years to get his bill before Congress, and now he was assured a vote, having pulled off a historic end run around one of Congress's master obstructionists.

Two hours later, bleary-eyed travelers at a lounge in O'Hare Air-

port watched as two equally tired United States representatives raised
their beer mugs into the air and offered a toast to "Larry Craig and
the two hundred and eighteen signatories."

ALTHOUGH THE JUDICIARY Committee's passage of the Hughes-Rodino
bill superseded his discharge motion, Harold Volkmer was in an excellent strategic position with the Rules Committee, which was responsible for fashioning the rules under which the two gun bills would now
be debated. The 218 signatures on his petition represented a majority
of the House and told committee members that Volkmer could win
any floor vote over contested rules.

On March 19, the committee issued its rules, and as expected they
worked in favor of McClure-Volkmer. Volkmer would be allowed to
offer his bill as a substitute to the Hughes-Rodino bill; if McClure-
Volkmer won that vote, the House would not get to vote on Rodino's
bill at all. Only five hours of debate would be allowed, including time
taken for roll call votes. With so little time allowed for debate, gun-
control advocates would be able to offer few amendments to McClure-
Volkmer. Action was to begin the very next day, March 20.

But after waiting eight years to get to this point, Harold Volkmer
was going to have to wait a little longer. The House spent ten hours
that day debating and eventually voting down President Reagan's
request to send increased aid to the Nicaraguan Contras. When that
issue was at last laid to rest, and as Harold Volkmer was preparing to
do battle with the antigun faction, the Democratic leadership suddenly
yanked the gun bills from the floor, saying that members were too
tired to begin debate on such a major issue after having just finished
another debilitating disputation.

A strained twenty-minute meeting between both sides ended with
the understanding that the bill would at last be debated three weeks
later, on April 9. Volkmer grumbled about "stalling tactics" but gave
in when O'Neill agreed to a specific date. The delay was, as Volkmer
charged, due more to political considerations than to any concerns
about the stamina of individual members. The opposition needed time
to regroup, to work out a strategy to stop the seemingly inexorable
tide to adopt McClure-Volkmer. It is also likely that O'Neill figured
that many representatives who had crossed the president once that

day on a major piece of legislation would be tempted to "even things out" by voting with Reagan on McClure-Volkmer. A few weeks' delay would help separate the two votes in members' minds.

While the legislative contest waited, the battle shifted to the public arena. A little more than a week before Congress was to take up the rival gun bills, Peter Rodino made a last-ditch effort to sway public opinion. In a *New York Times* opinion editorial, Rodino reminded Americans that some 10,000 citizens were being killed by handguns every year. He concluded:

> [T]he NRA is turning up the heat on every member of Congress in order to peel away votes from the Judiciary Committee bill in favor of an NRA substitute that would emasculate the minimal gun control laws now on the books. If the NRA gets its way, it would be easier for anyone—criminals, drug addicts, mental incompetents—to buy a handgun. . . . Let us hope that it won't take another John Hinckley [who had shot President Reagan in 1981] or Sirhan Sirhan [Robert Kennedy's assassin] to bring us back to our senses.

Finally, on the afternoon of April 9, Harold Volkmer stepped up to the microphone on the floor of the House of Representatives and began speaking: "We are here today to discuss and debate reform in this nation's firearms legislation. . . . [I]t has been a long time coming. This legislation represents the second most important step in the history of American gun owners. The first was the Second Amendment to the U.S. Constitution."

During the course of the debate, the strategy of the Rodino forces became apparent. Realizing that McClure-Volkmer had overwhelming support in the House (as evidenced by the discharge motion), the gun-control advocates tried to minimize the damage done to the Gun Control Act of 1968 by attempting to tack as many amendments as possible onto Volkmer's bill. William Hughes, co-sponsor of the Hughes-Rodino bill, first offered a package of amendments that included a ban on the interstate transportation of handguns, a ban on the interstate sale of handguns, and tighter record-keeping requirements for gun dealers. The package went down in flames—176 for; 248 opposed. Then Hughes tried offering the amendments separately. The ban on interstate transportation of handguns also fell—177 to 242.

At about 6:30 P.M., Hughes was about to offer the ban on interstate sales of handguns when Speaker of the House Tip O'Neill intervened. Saying, "We have got to start watching pennies around here," O'Neill pointed out that in a few minutes Capitol employees would have to be paid overtime, and the body was adjourned until the next day.

Volkmer threw up his hands. Another delay! "It was politically motivated," he says of the adjournment, but there was little he could do but what he had been doing for years: wait.

On April 10, at 10:00 A.M., the House chaplain, the Reverend James David Ford, strode to the clerk's lectern at the front of the House chamber and offered a prayer:

> Gracious God, as we seek to learn how to walk the way of righteousness, help us to discern the transient from the eternal. May our actions be tempered by the things that bring lasting benefit and goodwill among people and may we resist the temptation to gain personal advantage. Fill our spirits with thoughts and feelings of gracefulness that we will be the people You would have us be. Amen.

Five minutes later the House of Representatives took up consideration of the two gun bills with just a single hour remaining for debating amendments to the bills. As Harold Volkmer told a reporter, "It's now or never."

The momentum that had been building for so long now rushed through the House. After a short debate, the first vote taken was on Hughes's amendment to ban the interstate sale of handguns. This time, Hughes was victorious: The vote was 233 for, 184 against.

Volkmer would later attempt to put that vote in the best possible light. "I wouldn't say it was a major defeat for me," he explains today. "It *was* something I had worked on ever since I started this, something I wanted very badly, something I didn't get. But the way I look at legislation is: You get everything you can, and if it's still better than what you've got now, go with it. That bill was a lot better than what we had. So, if I had to lose on one, that's fine."

After the vote on the Hughes handgun amendment, only four minutes remained for debate before the vote on whether to substitute Volkmer's bill for Hughes-Rodino. Volkmer was elated. Several representatives, however, were upset by the limited amount of debate time and complained to the chair, New York Democrat Charles Rangel.

"Mr. Chairman," said Representative Buddy Roemer, clearly annoyed, "explain to me under the rules of the House and under this debate for amendments not able to be discussed within the next two hundred and forty seconds, what happens to those amendments? Do we have a chance to vote yes or no?"

Rangel explained that under the rules developed by the Rules Committee, any amendments not voted on when the allotted time ran out simply died. There could be no chance for a vote.

Immediately, William Hughes rose and asked if Volkmer would agree to extend debate time for an additional hour.

Harold Volkmer just smiled as Chairman Rangel explained that changes were not allowed under the rules. Volkmer had limited the amount of time allowed for debate for this very reason: to prevent Hughes and his supporters from tacking diluting amendments onto his bill. Now, with the clock ticking the last seconds away, Volkmer was confident that his plan had worked. He waited for Rangel to recognize Representative Bill McCollum, who was going to offer a final amendment banning silencers. Although the NRA objected to such a restriction on the basis that it amounted to "gun control," Volkmer had agreed to support McCollum's amendment because McCollum had generally backed the Volkmer bill.

But the smile on Volkmer's face disappeared as Rangel, instead of recognizing McCollum, gave the nod to William Hughes.

"Mr. Chairman," called out Hughes, "I offer an amendment to the amendment to the amendment offered as a substitute for the committee amendment in the nature of a substitute."

It might have sounded like gobbledygook to John or Jane Q. Public, but Volkmer knew exactly what it meant, and he was furious. Hughes was going to try to offer one more amendment. The Missouri Democrat was incensed. If he had known Hughes was going to be recognized instead of McCollum, Volkmer would have used up the last few minutes of debate time on the previous amendment. The only reason he hadn't was as a favor to McCollum.

The hotheaded Missourian jumped to his feet.

"Mr. Chairman, I have a parliamentary inquiry," he thundered.

"The gentleman will state it," said Rangel.

Volkmer, desperately searching for some technical impropriety that would derail Hughes, asked if the new amendment had been printed in advance in the *Congressional Record* as required.

It had.

Had Mr. Hughes himself printed the amendment in the *Record*? asked Volkmer.

That's not required, answered Rangel, who then instructed the clerk to read the amendment.

Hughes's amendment would ban machine guns. These weapons, which fire a stream of bullets as long as the trigger is kept depressed, had been strictly regulated since 1934, but Hughes's bill would fully outlaw the manufacture and sale of these automatic firearms— although those who already owned machine guns would be allowed to keep them.

House rules stipulate that an amendment must be read out loud before the chamber can vote on it, but this is rarely done. What usually happens is that the clerk begins reading the amendment and someone asks for the body's permission to suspend the reading and begin debate. If a single legislator objects, the reading must continue, but this rarely happens.

With precious time running out, Hughes asked that the reading of his amendment be suspended. Republican Robert Walker of Pennsylvania immediately objected.

The reading continued.

Hughes rose again, pleading that the reading be suspended.

"I ask my colleagues, in all fairness and rationality—we only have three minutes left—to give me an opportunity to explain why machine guns should be banned."

Hughes's words didn't move Walker, who again objected.

The clerk continued reading.

His eyes on the clock, Hughes asked again that the House agree to dispense with the reading.

This time a different Republican, F. James Sensenbrenner, Jr., of Wisconsin, objected.

The reading continued.

A red-faced Hughes was immediately on his feet, repeating his request and adding, "I do not know why anyone would object to the banning of machine guns!"

Sensenbrenner repeated his objection.

As the clerk finished the reading, and with only seconds left, Hughes tried one last tack. He moved that the Committee of the Whole rise.

The Committee of the Whole is a parliamentary device used to speed up consideration of bills and amendments. When the House is meeting "in the committee," only 100 representatives are required to be present. The Speaker of the House steps down at the beginning of this committee hearing, after appointing a chairman (in this case, Charles Rangel). After amendments are debated, the committee "rises"—or ends—the Speaker returns to the podium, and the House debates or votes on the final bill.

Hughes was moving that the committee end its session so that he could then ask the Rules Committee to allow more time for debate. But Hughes's attempt failed. His motion was soundly defeated, 124 to 298.

At precisely 11:30, Rangel announced that time had run out for debating Hughes's amendment—which, of course, had not been debated at all.

Hughes rose to request unanimous consent that debate time be extended another five minutes. Sensenbrenner once again objected and this time Hughes sat down, defeated. A vote on his amendment to ban machine guns was called. What happened next would be a point of contention—and contempt—for years to come.

Charles Rangel, still sitting as chairman of the Committee of the Whole, called for a voice vote on Hughes's amendment. All those in favor of the amendment called out "Aye"; those opposed yelled "No."

Rangel declared that Hughes's ban on machine guns had passed.

NRA officials and their supporters in the House charged that Rangel simply declared Hughes the winner, even though the noes had actually carried the vote. They also accused Rangel of ignoring repeated calls for a recorded vote.

One of Hughes's aides today admits that he was troubled by what he witnessed in the House that day. "There was this enormously panicked feeling on the floor," recalls Eric Sterling, at that time the majority counsel for the Crime Subcommittee chaired by Hughes. "I do think the amendment passed on the voice vote, and I don't recall hearing people clamoring for a recorded vote, but there probably were such members. A member in the chair who was more cautious, and friendlier to the NRA, might have called for a recorded vote. But sometimes when time is running out the parliamentary niceties are dispensed with."

After a pause, Sterling adds: "It was not the *most* flagrant abuse of power of the chair that I've seen on the floor. It wasn't a steal. But it wasn't the fairest way it could have been handled, either."

Volkmer fumed, but there was nothing he could do.

Immediately, Rangel turned to the larger question of McClure-Volkmer. The question before the House was, Should the Hughes-Rodino bill be replaced by Volkmer's bill? A voice vote was called. The ayes and nays were shouted out and Rangel announced that the noes had it. The McClure-Volkmer bill had been defeated.

This time Volkmer jumped to his feet and, in a voice that could not be ignored, demanded a recorded vote. He needn't have worried. Rangel had no intention of ignoring him and risking the undying enmity of a majority of the House for using a trick to defeat the legislation as a whole. The recorded vote was taken.

Harold Volkmer inserted his plastic identification card into an electronic console, about the size of a cigar box, which was mounted to the chair back in front of him. He waited for the computer, located across Independence Avenue in the Rayburn House Office Building, to send a "ready" signal: a blue light illuminated on the console. When the light came on, Volkmer didn't hesitate. He jabbed the yea button, which lit up green, to signal that his vote was locked in. Volkmer looked up at one of the four electronic tally boards mounted above and behind the Speaker's rostrum. A green yea light blinked on next to his name.

As the minutes went by, Volkmer watched with growing satisfaction as more and more green lights flashed on. He figured that the green lights outnumbered the red nay ones by at least two to one.

Finally, the vote was announced. The U.S. House of Representatives had voted to toss out the Hughes-Rodino bill and replace it with the McClure-Volkmer bill. The vote was 292 in favor of the move, 130 against it. Harold Volkmer and the National Rifle Association had, at long last, won their battle.

IMMEDIATELY, AND PREDICTABLY, the spin doctors on both sides went to work. Standard operating procedure in Washington dictates that no matter how a vote turns out, politicians must always show up at the ensuing press conference grinning from ear to ear and declaring victory. Reactions to the passage of McClure-Volkmer proved no exception to that rule.

NRA lobbyist Wayne LaPierre, smiling, called the vote "a major advancement." A representative of Handgun Control, Inc., also beaming, told reporters, "I'm calling it a victory and I'm happy." Two weeks later, at the NRA annual convention, an organization officer told the delegates that McClure-Volkmer was "the greatest legislative milestone in the history of the National Rifle Association." Michael Beard, head of the National Coalition to Ban Handguns, termed McClure-Volkmer "the NRA's first major defeat," adding that "anybody who really followed that battle knows they got creamed. Going from reinstating interstate sale of guns, down to making it a little more difficult to get handguns and banning machine guns."

But when all the "interpretations" and "clarifications" are peeled away it is hard to see McClure-Volkmer as anything but an NRA victory—and a major one at that. A gun-control expert with the Congressional Research Service just chuckles at the suggestion that McClure-Volkmer represented a defeat for the NRA. He calls the bill "a setback for people who generally espouse strong controls," and adds that "there were certainly some things that happened to the bill that weren't all that pleasing to those who pushed that bill, but it would be very difficult to claim that overall it was a victory for the procontrol people."

Exactly *how* that victory was managed is still open to debate. The NRA says that the bill won on its own merits. McClure-Volkmer, they say, was just good law, and legislators recognized that fact.

There were, however, undoubtedly other factors at work as well.

The day after McClure-Volkmer passed in the House, an editorial in *The Washington Post* credited the victory to the NRA's "paid army of House members," raising, once again, the specter of the National Rifle Association as the nation's preeminent influence-buying lobby. (The paper had made a similar charge concerning the signers of Volkmer's discharge petition back in March, alleging that the NRA had "done a bang-up job of buying support in Congress.")

One week after the House vote, the *Post* ran a story in which it attempted to document its charge. Using data compiled by the legislative watchdog group Common Cause, the paper revealed that 80 percent of those legislators who voted with the NRA (that is, against the Hughes amendment) had received campaign contributions from the gun group, while 80 percent of those who voted against the NRA's position had not received any NRA support. But this "cause and effect" explanation is too simplistic; it is misleading to credit the NRA's Political Action Committee's contributions for the 1986 victory.

"To speak of the NRA is to speak simultaneously of a powerful lobby, an affluent PAC, and a potent grass roots organization," points out political scientist Frank Sorauf. "It is also to speak of a group of voters with such intense feelings about gun control that they are the prototypical 'single issue' voters—voters for whom a single issue overrides all others."

In other words: When gauging the power of the National Rifle Association, don't overlook the Hassle Factor. Dennis Burke, an aide to Democratic senator Dennis DeConcini, agrees with this assessment.

"You always hear these arguments: It's the NRA money; these guys are bought," he says. "I don't think these guys care about the contributions they get from the NRA. They care about the piles of mail, these nasty calls, and people picketing their state offices. Politicians are risk adverse. They get no real pounding from anybody if they vote *with* the NRA. The pundits and the Op-Eds may nail them, but so what?"

By its own account, the NRA spent an estimated $1.6 million working to overturn the GCA—a figure that doesn't include campaign contributions. The money was spent in a variety of ways: on member mailings, advertisements, and various lobbying expenses. According to Federal Election Commission records, the NRA PAC (officially called the PVF, or Political Victory Fund) spent a total of $1.7 million on U.S. House and Senate races in 1986. The money was almost equally divided between contributions to candidates and "independent expenditures"—funds spent for or against a candidate outside his or her campaign organizations. While this is indeed a lot of money, it isn't unusually large by Washington standards.

One Democratic representative admitted, anonymously, that it was a combination of the Hassle Factor and the threat of losing the votes of gun owners back home that convinced him to vote for

McClure-Volkmer. The congressman told a *Washington Post* reporter that he was not alone in this action, estimating that he was one of thirty House members to vote against their better judgment. If a priest had been on the floor of the House when the bill was voted on, he said, an awful lot of representatives would have been asking for absolution.

> We made the hard political calculus, "Do I want to spend the next five months debating one crummy vote on gun control? The NRA's got the network, the head counts, they know who's wavering. . . . It's the kind of issue that could defeat me when nothing else could."

But whatever the reasons for the outcome of the vote, McClure-Volkmer represented a signal victory for the NRA. And certainly for Harold Volkmer the bill was more than just a legislative victory. "It is one of my major accomplishments," he says, and then adds after a moment's hesitation, "To be honest, it is *the* major accomplishment of my career. Yes, it was my high water mark."

The bill's passage also represents the National Rifle Association's high water mark as an organization. It was sitting on assets of well over $80 million; total annual income was put at around $66 million. The organization boasted some three million members—400,000 more than when Harlon Carter had shared the limelight with President Reagan in Phoenix in 1983. His words on that glorious day had now been borne out by the success of McClure-Volkmer.

"I see an NRA," Carter had told the crowd, "with wealth and political strength and vigor, led by [the] ILA, an NRA . . . so strong and so dedicated that no politician in America, mindful of his political career, would want to challenge our legitimate goals."

Just three years later, the NRA had fulfilled that prediction. It had a reputation—backed by a towering legislative achievement—as the most powerful single-issue organization in the nation's capital.

# PART II

# CRACKS
# IN THE EMPIRE

# 4

# THE BULLET AND
# THE BADGE

FOR THE NATIONAL Rifle Association, as for Adam and Eve, the problems first began with an apple. In the case of the NRA it was not a real apple that caused the difficulties, but a bullet nicknamed the "apple green" for the light green coating of Teflon fused to its tip. Apple greens—or, as they were properly known, KTW bullets—were not new when they became a cause célèbre in the early 1980s. They had been around since an Ohio county coroner and his two policeman friends came up with the idea in a home workshop in 1970.

The coroner, Dr. Paul Kopsch, and his partners were upset by the fact that in shootouts with police, criminals often fired from the relative shelter of an automobile, the metal body providing an effective armor against police bullets.

"We wanted to develop a load which in an ordinary thirty-eight special [the standard police handgun] would get police bullets *into* cars and get the people in the cars *out*," says Kopsch. What they needed was a bullet that would easily go through metal. There were several ways to accomplish this feat, but each had its own drawback. A larger amount of gunpowder could be used to hurl the bullet at its target with greater force, but that would require the use of a larger gun. Not many departments would be willing to switch to a new

85

firearm, the Ohio men realized. If the length of the gun's muzzle were increased, the same bullet would have a greater velocity and so pack a greater punch, but again, that involved using a different, or at least modified, handgun.

The trio decided that the best and easiest way to increase a bullet's ability to penetrate hard material was to change its metallic composition. Most ammunition is made of lead, a soft metal that will spread out, or "mushroom," when it strikes its target. That effect is desirable for law officers—and hunters—because the mushroomed bullet will cause a larger, more devastating wound. But mushrooming also *decreases* the ability of a bullet to penetrate hard materials, because its force is spread out over a larger area. Dr. Kopsch and his partners decided to make their bullet out of bronze, a very hard metal that retains its shape when meeting resistance.

But the three were still not satisfied, even though tests showed that the new bronze rounds could penetrate metal 50 percent better than those made of lead. They wanted to make their bullets even more effective.

"We knew that when you're cutting metal with a lathe tool or milling machine, it does better if the tools are constantly lubricated," says Kopsch, now retired. "But we also knew any oil or grease would be whirled off by the centrifugal force of the bullet." So the men looked into the various solid lubricants then becoming popular, and quickly narrowed their focus to two candidates: silicon and Teflon. Silicon added a slight boost to the bullet's penetrating power—something on the order of 7 to 10 percent, Kopsch estimated—but the men wanted their bullet to have more power.

In the course of his research, Kopsch discovered that Germany, the United States, and England had all tried coating artillery shells with Teflon to reduce the friction generated inside cannons when shells were fired. All three had terminated the practice after discovering that small bits of the Teflon coating flaked off the shells and gummed up the barrel, making the velocity of the projectiles unpredictable. Kopsch and friends hit on the idea of covering only the *front part* of each bullet with Teflon; the trailing bare-metal end would clean out any bits of Teflon each time the gun was fired. Their idea worked as well on the firing range as it did on the drawing board. The Teflon covering increased the bullet's penetrating ability by another 20 percent. The men decided on the distinctive apple-green coloring for the Teflon to make their powerful bullets look less threatening. "We thought it kind of reminded you of a nice spring day," Kopsch says.

Soon, the apple greens were rolling off the assembly line at the North American Ordnance Corporation plant in Pontiac, Michigan. (Kopsch and his partners had no interest in manufacturing. "The fun," he says, "is in the developing of this stuff.")

At first, the KTWs—named after the inventors, Kopsch, police lieutenant Daniel Turcus, Jr., and investigator Donald Ward—worked better than the men had expected. They were snapped up by police departments across the country; trade magazines soon dubbed the ammunition the "Super Bullet." But an unexpected problem developed. The Super Bullet was a bit *too* super. It went through a car door as promised, but the rounds continued on through the door on the *other* side of the car, striking whoever happened to be passing by. The bullets also ricocheted wildly. They held their shape so well that the bronze projectiles bounced around with lethal velocity after missing, or passing through, their original target. One by one police departments dropped the apple greens, deemed too dangerous to use, and state legislatures banned their sale.

And there the story of the bullet that was supposed to "remind you of a nice spring day" and slammed through metal like a miniature antitank round would have likely ended—had it not been for a 1981 NBC news segment in which it was reported that the bullets could also pierce the lightweight body armor worn by law enforcement agents across the country. The apple greens, or Super Bullets, instantly acquired a new nickname: "cop-killers."

The development of soft body armor in the early 1970s had been a giant leap forward in protecting the lives of America's law enforcement officers. Made of a tough but lightweight fiber called Kevlar (which was developed, ironically, by Du Pont, the same company that sold the apple-green Teflon to Kopsch and friends), the armor was credited with saving the lives of over 400 officers between 1975, when the Kevlar vests were first distributed on a large scale, and 1980. While bulletproof vests had been around for years, the old-style protection was extremely heavy, bulky, and hot. Because they were so uncomfortable, police only wore them on especially dangerous assignments. But vests made of Kevlar were light and cool enough to be worn by officers on the beat. News that the armor-piercing rounds could breach these vests sent tremors through the law enforcement community.

Acting on this concern, the New York Patrolmen's Benevolent Association—a police union—contacted Democratic congressman Mario Biaggi asking for his help in introducing legislation that would ban the bullets. Biaggi was the logical choice for the job. A twenty-three-year police veteran, the New York congressman knew firsthand the dangers of firearms: He had been shot ten times in his career in law enforcement. Biaggi sponsored a bill calling on the secretary of the Treasury (who oversaw the Bureau of Alcohol, Tobacco and Firearms) to draft legislation banning bullets capable of penetrating the Kevlar vests. In the meantime, more states rushed into the legislative void and banned the manufacture, sale, or possession of the ammunition.

The furor over the KTW bullets was a tempest in a teapot to the NRA—a "nonissue," they would call it later. As far as anyone knew, no law enforcement officers had been killed by these bullets penetrating soft body armor. Furthermore, since they had been deemed too dangerous for police work, and since they were originally marketed primarily to the police, few of the bullets were still around.

But why not just allow these admittedly dangerous bullets to be banned, if just to mollify the police? Because, the NRA calculated, such legislation would set a bad precedent. If the apple greens could be prohibited, couldn't the "gun-grabbers" next outlaw Saturday Night Specials, claiming that the cheap handguns posed a special threat to law officers and citizens? Next thing you know, they'll be banning *all* handguns, and then shotguns and rifles. Harlon Carter's Potato Chip Theory of gun control necessitated that the group take a hard line from the beginning. "There is no such thing as a good or bad bullet," said an NRA spokesman while explaining the group's opposition to the ban on apple greens.

Before the NRA had issued a public statement on the issue, Michael Beard, the director of the National Coalition to Ban Handguns, wrote the NRA's Harlon Carter to see if their two groups could work together on a bill banning the armor-piercing rounds. Wayne LaPierre, the NRA's fiery young lobbyist, wrote Beard back, telling him to forget about any cooperation on the issue. "[A ban] on those bullets found to penetrate soft body armor would undoubtedly impact on bullets used by sportsmen," claimed LaPierre.

Beard told a reporter that he was "astounded that the NRA, which claims to be a friend of law enforcement officers, wants to stop a bill aimed at saving lives of those who protect our own."

The NRA knew its opposition to the ban would anger some law officers, but it was betting that the damage would be minimal. The police were, after all, bureaucratically disorganized, split between management and the rank and file, and legislatively inexperienced. Their unions were used to dealing with issues like pay raises—not gun control. Besides, over the years the NRA had forged an iron bond with law enforcement, one that would hardly be threatened by an issue as small as this. Not only was the gun group seen in police quarters as a supporter of tough law-and-order measures, but the NRA had for decades provided firearms instruction to the nation's cops.

"The NRA and police were tight," says one twenty-seven-year police veteran and firearms instructor. "If you asked someone, 'Where do I go to learn first aid?' they'd send you to the Red Cross. There's no place else. If you asked somebody, 'Where do I go to learn how to shoot?' there was just no other place: It was the NRA."

In addition to training the police, the NRA also sponsored hundreds of shooting matches for law enforcement officers each year. Their shared affinity for guns of all kinds provided a solid foundation on which to build their relationship. The NRA emphasized this alliance in publications with titles such as *NRA and Law Enforcement: America's Anti-crime Team.*

Still, Neal Knox (at that time still the director of the ILA) was sufficiently concerned about the threat to police relations posed by the flap over the KTW bullets that he asked the board of directors to decide what the official position on the matter should be. On February 26, 1982, the board's legislative policy committee decided that the ban, whether at a national or state level, should be opposed, but the committee left the decision on how hard to go after the ban up to the ILA's staff.

Although the NRA presented a unified public front on the issue, there were some insiders who disagreed with this stand. In fact, the head of the group's PR department later complained that the NRA's California field representative (a man named Dick Cox) helped "launch" the issue by cooperating in NBC's original exposé and then urging the board of directors to support the ban. But in the end the hard-liners prevailed and the group fought any prohibition on the bullets.

At a congressional hearing in mid-1982 and on the House floor in January of 1983, the fight picked up steam. "These bullets are not used for legitimate purposes," Congressman Biaggi told his colleagues, "but they have been used by criminals to shoot and kill police officers. My bill would outlaw these bullets but would in no way limit the availability of ammunition used by law-abiding citizens."

While it was true that armor-piercing bullets had killed police officers, the deaths had not occurred in the manner Biaggi implied. The victims had not been wearing body armor when they had been shot, and one of them had been shot in the head. He would have died even if he had been wearing the armor—and even if he had been shot by a non-armor-piercing bullet.

But there was an even more serious flaw to Biaggi's argument. Biaggi and others supporting the bill cried that the NRA was being unreasonable for not backing a measure that would outlaw only armor-piercing rounds. When the NRA responded that the bill would also outlaw other far more common types of ammunition, backers of the legislation merely snickered.

"They'll say anything," recalls Baltimore chief of police Neil Behan, who actively sought the bill's passage. "It's not so. The bill wasn't that broad." The NRA was using this specious argument to subvert a fair and important piece of legislation, the critics charged.

But in fact, the bill *would* have banned a lot of hunting and sporting ammunition. "This is a case where the NRA was right," says Eric Sterling. "The bill *was* too broad."

Sterling should know. As assistant counsel to the House Crime Subcommittee from 1981 to 1989, Sterling wrote much of the pro-gun-control legislation coming from that body during the decade, including parts of the armor-piercing-bullet bill. A Treasury Department study of the legislation confirms the NRA's contention. Associate Attorney General Rudolph Giuliani found that the bill, as written, would prohibit several types of ammunition, and concluded: "We cannot justify legislation banning all ammunition capable of penetrating the type of soft body armor worn by law enforcement officers."

Another Treasury official, Deputy Assistant Robert Powis, told

Congress: "Many sporting rifle cartridges would end up being re-stricted by this bill. This is a factual statement. It is not something that we have dreamed up. . . . This bill goes too far. It does not just ban true armor-piercing ammunition, it bans a considerable amount of sporting ammunition which is available in much greater quantity."

Biaggi, unfazed by the NRA's claims—or the Treasury Depart-ment's studies—continued to dismiss the gun lobby's opposition as "nothing but a knee-jerk reaction based more on paranoia than on any semblance of reason."

In truth, the NRA's opposition to the legislation was based on about equal parts of each. The bill *was* overly broad, but had the legislative restrictions been more narrowly defined, the NRA would have still likely opposed it on the grounds that the bill opened the door to other gun-control measures. The group's concern about definitional problems was both a reason and an excuse.

The NRA took a drubbing for its opposition, especially after the pro-gun-control group Handgun Control, Inc., ran an advertisement in police trade magazines with the headline HELP STOP THE COP-KILLERS.

The strategy was effective. Across the country police groups re-acted in outrage. Newspaper editorials and television commentators asked how the National Rifle Association could be defending "cop-killers."

The NRA realized that it now had a major problem on its hands. Even some members were now admitting doubts about the group's position. Jerry Kenney of *The New York Daily News*—an NRA sup-porter—expressed the views of many people both inside the organiza-tion and out when he condemned the NRA's opposition to the bill.

"Hunters and target shooters have traditionally been known as sportsmen and most of them are members of the N.R.A.," he wrote. "They stand by the organization in most of its decisions, particularly in the campaign against gun control. But the stand the N.R.A. is taking in the name of its many millions of members to allow the production and sale of ammunition that has no logical use except to penetrate armor and bulletproof vests is an outrage."

The NRA sought to dampen the outcry by mailing the membership an informational call to arms:

Mark my words, the so-called "cop-killer" bullet issue is a Trojan Horse waiting outside gun owners' doors. If the anti-gunners have their way, this highly publicized and emotionalized issue will be used to enact a backdoor, national gun control scheme. . . . You must write your Senator and Congressman and you must write today. . . . Never has an issue been more distorted or downright lied about than the armor-piercing bullet issue. The anti-gun forces will go to any lengths to void your right to keep and bear arms. It's time we set them straight! I am asking you—each and every NRA member and your friends—to flood the United States Congress with your letters. . . . Anti-gun groups are well aware of our activities with law enforcement and have been looking for an issue to drive a wedge between America's gun owners and our nation's law enforcement.

A variety of police groups issued formal denunciations of the NRA for opposing the legislation. There were, however, a few muted voices of dissent. For example, the chairman of the Firearms and Explosives Subcommittee of the International Association of Chiefs of Police sent a letter to the organization's director complaining about what appeared to him to be a rush to judgment on the matter:

Partial information, faulty logic and emotionalism were found to exist in public discussions, in statements within the law enforcement community, and in congressional deliberations. We urge you as president of the International Association of Chiefs of Police to suspend any official Association activities and withhold all public statements regarding "cop-killer bullets" until a rational and informed study of the problem has been conducted. This subcommittee believes that this is necessary to avoid potentially damaging legislative overreactions.

Both sides squared off again in hearings before the House Crime Subcommittee during May 1984 (held, not coincidentally, during National Police Week).

The NRA's Wayne LaPierre lashed out at Biaggi's bill, testifying that it was "riddled with technical inaccuracies, unenforceable provisions and the legislation is drafted in response to a nonproblem."

"The NRA may be willing to wait and see how many police officers die from the cop-killer bullets," responded a huffy Congressman Biaggi, "but I am not."

Neither side was willing to give an inch and nonaligned committee members complained that they were caught in the middle of a complicated, technical, and bitterly disputed grudge match, one that presented no easy—that is, politically safe—solution.

And so the standoff continued.

Then, in early June 1984, the Reagan administration invited the leaders of several different police groups to the White House. At that meeting, the police were told—politely but firmly—that the Treasury Department had come up with a bill to deal with the problem of the armor-piercing rounds. The bill restricted the manufacture and importation of bullets made out of seven hard metals capable of penetrating Kevlar vests when fired from standard handguns (tungsten alloy, steel-iron, bronze, beryllium, copper, brass, and depleted uranium). The administration told the police that this was the only approach it would accept: There would be no compromises; no amendments would be allowed. And, the administration said, the police needed to approve the bill (giving it full public support) as soon as they left the room. If the police didn't agree to these terms the administration would drop the matter and the standoff would continue. The police had little choice—they left the meeting praising the new bill.

What the police were not told was that the NRA had helped draft the legislation. James Jay Baker, the young NRA lobbyist, had sat down with officials from Justice and Treasury and explained what the NRA would and would not accept in the bill. The fact that the group would take this action proved two points. First, it meant that the gun lobby was concerned about the breach in police-NRA relations and wanted to end the controversy quickly, even if it meant agreeing to a "gun-control" bill. But second was the fact that they could sit down and draft legislation as the administration's partner—legislation that would then be presented to the other side in a take-it-or-leave-it fashion—which pointed to the NRA's growing political power.

The bill (which was, of course, supported by the NRA) was quickly introduced in the Senate. Even Senator Patrick Moynihan, one of the early sponsors of the original disputed legislation, became a co-sponsor. "I will take what we can get," he explained with a shrug. "We were about to get nothing two months ago."

Overnight, the complexion of the issue had changed. What had before seemed an intractable, insoluble legislative problem was now deemed "a sure thing" by the pundits. The legislation was on track.

The NRA was happy. The police, if not exactly happy, were at least amenable to the bill, and had given it their support.

And then the "sure thing" proceeded to fall apart like the jerry-built contraption it was. Both sides would later point accusing fingers at the other, trying to affix blame for the breakdown. Cries of "Sellout!" and "Double-crosser!" were traded at hastily called press conferences. The NRA accused the opposition of backing out of a deal. The police accused the gun lobby of quibbling over technicalities while police officers faced cop-killer bullets. But the true culprit was far simpler and much more human than political duplicity or disagreement over technical data. The breakdown was caused by a few—albeit large—bruised egos.

When the Reagan administration sent out invitations to its June White House meeting, it neglected to invite the congressmen who were sponsoring the legislation. Particularly miffed were Representatives Biaggi and William Hughes.

Eric Sterling, counsel to Representative Hughes's Crime Subcommittee, remembers the hurt feelings caused by the perceived White House snub. "There was this feeling: 'Wait a minute. I thought it was the job of the *Congress* to write the law. How come you didn't consult with any of us?' Suddenly everybody was scrambling. Biaggi introduced a bill, 'on behalf of cops.' [Democratic representative Jack] Brooks and [Republican Hamilton] Fish introduced theirs. Brooks on behalf of the NRA; Fish on behalf of the administration. Those of us who weren't beholden to the compromise looked at it and said, 'Look at all these things wrong with it. We're coming up with our own new bill.' "

Biaggi and Hughes added a few restricting amendments to the bill and the fight was back on. Then, on September 26, 1984, just when debate on the armor-piercing-bullet legislation was about to begin in the House, Speaker Tip O'Neill yanked the legislation off the floor, saying "We have enough controversy" without adding the armor-piercing-bullet issue. O'Neill's explanation was a not-too-veiled reference to the upcoming November elections. The Speaker wanted to spare fellow Democrats the chore of having to take on either the NRA or swarms of angry police officers just before facing the voters.

Although the move outraged Hughes (who blamed "the self-centeredness of the NRA and the shortsightedness of the administration" for O'Neill's action), it was popular with a majority of representatives, and the bill was effectively killed for the rest of the legislative year.

During 1985, a revised armor-piercing-bullet bill ran the congressional gauntlet, passing through committees in both the House and Senate with little controversy. The relative lack of interest in an issue that had recently generated so much heat was due to the fact that the fight over gun control had now shifted to the McClure-Volkmer bill, which was also working its way through Congress. The NRA wanted the support of the police on that bill (or lacking that, to blunt their opposition), and so the gun group officially took no position on the ammunition legislation, even though it contained provisions the NRA had originally fought. With little fanfare, the bill passed the House, by a vote of 400 to 21, in December of 1985. It passed in the Senate by a similarly wide margin in the following August, and was signed into law by President Reagan on August 28, 1986.

ILA director Warren Cassidy recounted the NRA's battle tactics in a column in the association's magazine: "[The] ILA would try to kill the issue outright in as many states as possible; if resisted we would attempt to substitute the NRA-supported language for mandatory penalty for misuse; if the substitution wouldn't fly, we would lobby for the most narrow definition of 'AP' ammo."

But Cassidy admitted that the negative publicity about "cop-killer bullets" took its toll: "Under this barrage many of our best friends in the Congress, with A+ ratings and unimpeachable progun credentials, advised us that they would have to vote for a 'reasonable bill.'

"Regardless of what you may have read or heard from our critics, a worse bill would surely have passed into law if we had not hammered out a less damaging alternative. As events clearly show, we outfought, outthought, and outflanked our foes. We redefined the rules of the debate in a manner so as to protect the rights of all law-abiding citizens. A proud achievement!"

While the NRA could legitimately boast of its success in drafting an ammunition bill that protected its constituency, that goal had been achieved at the expense of its close relationship with many in law enforcement. It was clearly fence-mending time for the NRA. So in the summer, NRA head G. Ray Arnett wrote the police groups, trying to explain the gun lobby's position.

"Legislation that is unenforceable and generated solely to gain headlines or to make 'political points' is bad legislation," he reasoned. "It offers no protection to law enforcement or the public."

Although the response to Arnett's letter was lukewarm, the NRA hoped that the situation was now in hand, that the long-standing good feelings between the NRA and law enforcement were once again growing. The fight, the NRA leadership believed, was behind them. As it turned out, it was just the first round. No sooner had the battle over the armor-piercing bullets died down and ruffled feathers begun to be smoothed than a new point of contention appeared on the horizon: the plastic gun.

In fact, the controversy over a gun with the unlikely name of Glock 17 arose even before the armor-piercing-bullet legislation had been signed into law, although it took some time before the issue drew much attention. In a series of three columns, starting in January of 1986, syndicated columnist Jack Anderson reported that a new 9-mm semiautomatic pistol—the Glock 17—could pass through airport security systems undetected thanks to the fact that key components of the gun were made of plastic.

To make matters worse, Anderson wrote, "Libyan dictator Muammar Qaddafi [is] dickering to buy 100 to 300 of the Glock 17 pistols on the black market."

The reports alarmed many Americans, who imagined Libyan hit squads, packing undetectable plastic pistols in their carry-on luggage, boarding scores of doomed domestic flights. Such a scenario seemed quite possible given that, as Anderson reported, a "Pentagon security expert had succeeded twice in carrying a dismantled Glock 17 through the human and mechanical weapons detectors at Washington's National Airport."

Anderson followed with another column in which he quoted a cable reportedly sent on March 27 by the U.S. ambassador to West Germany, Richard Burt, to Secretary of State George Shultz. Burt forwarded a "rough translation" of a high-level German ministry report on the Glock, which was manufactured in Austria.

"The tests showed that the completely assembled weapon is extremely hard to recognize on the X-ray screen," claimed the report. "Disassembled, the weapon was X-rayed together with a camera in a camera bag. In this condition only the barrel could be detected as a thick black line. The plastic parts could not be detected."

Police groups were quick to pick up on the new threat, calling for legislation to ban plastic guns. The NRA tried to head off what it saw as a new attack on guns in general.

"Make no mistake about it, 'plastic' guns represent a clear and present danger to the security of the American people," wrote the NRA's James Jay Baker in an *American Rifleman* article. "The danger, however, is not posed by foreign terrorists brandishing non-metal firearms aboard jet airliners. No, the threat is much nearer to home. Some U.S. politicians are playing on the fear of terrorism to mask their anti-gun agendas."

The "plastic gun" causing the ruckus, the Glock 17, actually contained nineteen ounces of steel, and experts were divided—to say the least—on the threat it posed to airline security. A letter to Congressman Biaggi from a representative of the company that manufactured nearly all the X-ray units used in American airports downplayed the security problems associated with the Glock.

"Fully assembled, the Glock 17 looks exactly like any other automatic pistol when viewed on the television monitor of our Linescan airport X-Ray security machine," wrote John Battema, vice president of marketing for the Astrophysics Research Corporation, Long Beach, California.

> Further, it causes our Mark 100 Metal Detector to alarm at the normal setting just as any other pistol does. When the Glock 17 is broken down into its three basic components (metal barrel, metal ammunition clip and plastic frame), all three components are still visible and identifiable on the television monitor of the X-Ray system by a trained security operator. In all tests, the Glock 17 was X-Rayed while inside a standard briefcase with a normal amount of paper (approximately 1″ thick) and other items usually found in a briefcase. Even the plastic frame shows as clearly as a toy plastic gun which, incidentally, is one of the most common items identified by airport security personell [*sic*]. . . . In my estimation, it would be as difficult to pass a Glock 17 pistol through an X-Ray security checkpoint as it would be to pass any other real pistol through the same checkpoint.

As in the case of the armor-piercing bullets, the NRA opposed legislation aimed at the "plastic guns" for two reasons, one practical, the other political. While the ban on these guns would do nothing to make U.S. air travel any more secure, the NRA argued, such legislation would outlaw many small firearms. But the NRA feared even more the possibility that a bill banning one type of gun would, as they had so often warned, "open the door" to other gun-control bills—and ultimately to the confiscation of *all* firearms. The NRA's battle plan in this fight was the same as the one outlined by ILA director Warren Cassidy during the armor-piercing-bullet dispute: total opposition when possible, compromise only when confronted with defeat.

But unlike that earlier battle, the NRA was forced to fight on two fronts this time: The plastic gun debate was peaking just as the McClure-Volkmer bill was coming to the floor of Congress. And this time the police were better organized—partly in reaction to the NRA's campaign for McClure-Volkmer.

"The [police] organizations thought it was a good idea to get together to protect ourselves from being misrepresented by the NRA," says Baltimore police chief Neil Behan.

According to Behan, only days before the Senate voted on McClure-Volkmer he learned that the NRA, while declaring support for the legislation, claimed it represented law enforcement. Behan was appalled. Most cops he knew were dead-set against McClure-Volkmer. After comparing notes with the leaders of several police groups, Behan found no one who had told the NRA that police favored the bill. Behan concluded that the gun lobby was misrepresenting the police stand and so, together with several other police officers, he went to Washington to tell legislators what law enforcement really thought of McClure-Volkmer.

As senators filed into the chamber on the day of the vote, they had to pass uniformed policemen standing at attention before each chamber entrance—a silent reminder to "do the right thing" for the men and women in blue. Behan was shocked when the Senate passed the bill by a wide margin.

The leader of one law enforcement organization said later that after the vote several politicians admitted to him that they agreed with his stand, but politics dictated their vote. "You guys will forgive and forget," said one senator. "They [the NRA] *never* do."

"It was at that point," Behan recalls, "that we realized we had to organize in some fashion, to be able to present ourselves as a large organized group to the legislators—to offset the tremendous lobbying capability of the NRA."

Behan was the right man for the job, with impeccable law enforcement credentials and the feisty temperament required to stand up to the NRA. He had served in several positions in the New York Police Department for thirty-one years. He had started on the force as a patrolman and risen to the rank of captain. Later he had done stints as head of planning, chief of personnel, area commander (of Brooklyn South), and commanding officer of the police academy. When he left New York he was chief of patrol for the city. Since that time, Behan had served as the police chief of Baltimore County, Maryland.

In October of 1985, Behan put together a coalition of police groups called the Law Enforcement Steering Committee (LESC). (The umbrella organization included the Fraternal Order of Police, the Federal Law Enforcement Officers Association, the National Troopers Coalition, the Police Executive Research Forum, the National Sheriffs Association, the National Organization of Black Law Enforcement Executives, the International Brotherhood of Police Officers, and the National Association of Police Organizations.)

The lobbying organization gave the heads of law enforcement something they had never had before: institutional support—and cover—for their views. While many police chiefs had been in favor of some gun-control measures over the years (their friendly ties to the NRA notwithstanding), they had rarely gone public with these views for fear of losing their jobs. The position of police chief is far more political than is generally realized—which accounts for the fact that the average length of time American chiefs serve in each job is just three years.

"Chiefs don't need new enemies," says the chief of a large western city. "You have enough in your job. Chiefs feel more comfortable doing this as part of an organization, rather than as individuals."

The NRA had to respond in some way to law enforcement's newfound assertiveness. Although the gun lobby didn't realize it at the time, it was at a crossroads and its future as an organization would be determined in large part by how it treated this challenge. In a very real sense, however, the NRA had no choice. It was driven by an institutional culture that knew only one response to opposition: Strike back hard with everything you've got. Within the marble halls of the NRA, compromise was a dirty word. The Cincinnati Revolt stood as a constant reminder of the fate awaiting any NRA official who dared to use the dreaded "C" word favorably.

Besides, the NRA's hardball tactics were working. Hadn't the group frustrated gun-control advocates for years? And hadn't the membership rolls swelled (and the group's coffers filled) precisely *because* the NRA was now known as a group you cross at your own risk? No, the police would be dealt with just like any other opposition group: swiftly and harshly.

The NRA went after the leaders of the police groups with a vengeance, claiming that chiefs like Behan were "out of touch" with rank-and-file cops who, the NRA maintained, were against gun-control measures of any kind. The law enforcement leaders were stooges of antigun organizations, according to the NRA.

One of the first to feel the heat from the NRA campaign was Jerald Vaughn, director of the International Association of Chiefs of Police. In a letter to NRA head G. Ray Arnett in February of 1985, Vaughn had criticized the gun lobby's behavior during the debate on McClure-Volkmer.

"Your tactics," he wrote, "have included taking the liberty of imporperly [*sic*] acting as a spokesman for law enforcement in this country. You have misrepresented our position, you have attempted to discredit and undermine the leadership of our professional law enforcement associations and have blatantly insulted our intelligence by implying that we are the dupes of the anti-gun lobby. You have disorted [*sic*] facts to suit your purposes and have attempted to suppress free and open debate on perhaps the most critical public safety issue to come about in recent memory.

"The purpose of this letter is to clearly state to you that the continuation of such tactics on your part, will seriously jeopardize the future relationship between the NRA and law enforcement. . . . I would implore you to consider the issues I have brought to your attention and ponder the implications for the future."

That same warning was echoed, in a less confrontational manner, by an open letter from the organization's president, John Norton, that appeared in the IACP magazine in April 1985:

"While I have been proud to be a member of the NRA and support firearms sportsmenship [sic], education and training efforts, my sacred sworn obligation in law enforcement is to protect the public, and this obligation is paramount, as is my right of free speech. Hopefully, when the emotions surrounding these issues [various gun-control measures] subside, the NRA and law enforcement will again engage in a partnership beneficial to the public safety needs and the requirements of all Americans."

Norton was prompted to write this letter after a Pennsylvania gun group affiliated with the National Rifle Association passed a resolution in January of that year calling for Norton's expulsion from the NRA.

But the NRA saved its most vitriolic rhetoric for one of the superstars of the law enforcement world: Joseph D. McNamara, then chief of police for San Jose, California. It was a decision the group would later have cause to regret.

The Manhattan-born son of an Irish cop, McNamara joined the New York force at the age of twenty-one, and then spent a decade on rough beats that included Harlem and the Bronx. Bright as well as tough, McNamara earned a bachelor's degree by attending night classes at John Jay College and went on to receive a Ph.D. in public administration from Harvard in 1973. He became the nation's youngest chief of police when he took that post in Kansas City, Missouri, and left after three years to become chief of police in San Jose, a position he would hold for the next fifteen years (the longest tenure of any major city's police chief in the country). So successful was McNamara in California that he was once considered a likely candidate for the directorship of the FBI. McNamara's problems with the NRA began when he came out early and publicly for what he felt were very modest gun-control measures, including the ban on armor-piercing bullets and on assault weapons.

"The NRA is an excellent lobbying organization," McNamara says today.

They did a lot of police training and police shooting matches, and generally projected an image of the good ol' boy, superpatriot, law-and-order group. I found by my own experience that that was a false image. They were very anti–law enforcement in my opinion. It might have started out as a legitimate patriotic kind of organization, representing mostly sportsmen. But then it turned into a kind of shill for the gun manufacturers and gun dealers. They seem to oppose any legislation on firearms. As I began to expose this they tried to dismiss me as just a maverick, an oddball chief. When, in fact, I did represent the mainstream of American police.

What particularly bothered the NRA was that this handsome, articulate cop, chief of a major city (and the author of a best-selling crime novel), was taking such a public stand against them—something that had never happened before. Because of his telegenic appeal, McNamara was invited to appear on talk shows regularly—invitations he rarely turned down—and once on television, McNamara didn't just advocate some specific pieces of gun-control legislation (although that would have been bad enough). The pugnacious McNamara berated the National Rifle Association by name, criticizing the group for working against the interests of law enforcement and on behalf of arms manufacturers.

The gun lobby fired back. An NRA lawyer dashed off a letter to McNamara warning that if the police chief dared to repeat his charges in public one more time it "would result in the immediate initiation of litigation."

McNamara's response to the NRA was short and Irish-cop sweet: "I told them to go to hell." McNamara continued to press for gun-control legislation and persisted in characterizing the NRA as a captive of special interests. Rather than filing a suit against him as threatened, the NRA opted to take its fight to the court of public opinion. The gun group took the unprecedented step of placing full-page anti-McNamara advertisements in *Time, Newsweek,* and *USA Today.*

A photograph of McNamara ran with the headline SO YOU WANT LEGALIZED DRUGS IN AMERICA? SORRY ABOUT THAT, CHIEF. The text ran as follows:

Pictured and quoted in recent national news media, San Jose Police Chief Joseph McNamara wants to legalize drugs, marijuana, cocaine, heroin, crack. The cruel cripplers invading our neighborhoods and shattering our families.

So why does one man's opinion cause the National Rifle Association to run this message?

Because we care about American kids and families, about the future of this country and its freedoms. And because it is also Joseph McNamara who is leading Handgun Control, Inc. on its march to deprive Americans of lawful firearms ownership.

It's ironic that a police chief—an entrusted model of moral behavior for our youth—wants to make illegal drugs legal but lawful guns unlawful. Such nonsense says nothing about real solutions to drugs and crime, but much about McNamara's lost confidence in his ability to enforce the law. And tough law enforcement is part of the answer.

That's why McNamara should chase drug pushers, not headlines. McNamara should attack repeat offenders, not millions of law-abiding firearms owners. McNamara should support constitutional freedom, not drug freedom.

As long as Chief McNamara wants to make criminals of the law-abiding and law-abiding of criminals, we think he will hear a resounding response: Sorry about that, Chief.

The advertisement was vintage NRA. It was clever, caustic, and it sought to position the group as a friend of "American kids and families" that defended "the future of this country and its freedoms."

There was only one thing wrong with the advertisement: It was based on a lie. McNamara had never supported legalizing drugs.

The NRA's charge was based on statements made by McNamara on the Oprah Winfrey show. According to a transcript of that show, Winfrey had said to McNamara, "You say, Police Chief McNamara, it's time to legalize?"

McNamara's response was quite unequivocal about the issue: "No, I haven't [said that]. What I said is, it's time to consider this in an unemotional way. We must find a way to take the profit out of drugs."

Today, McNamara amplifies that response, saying, "I *am* very critical of some of the stupidities of the so-called war on drugs, but that doesn't necessarily mean I'm for legalization. In fact, I've *opposed* it."

According to McNamara, the only effect the advertisement had on him was "to make me feel important for a couple of days." After all, the gun group had spent around $150,000 just to give a local police chief a bad name. But the anti-McNamara campaign had two other important effects. It gave the police chief greater visibility with the media, and so more forums from which to spread his pro-gun-control, anti-NRA message. And, even more important, the advertisements also increased the law enforcement/NRA schism.

"Those ads," says McNamara, "were one of the great strategic mistakes that the NRA made."

A similar conclusion was reached by former NRA spokesperson John Aquilino, who criticized the NRA's advertising agency/public relations firm, Ackerman, Hood, & McQueen, in his newsletter *Insider Gun News*. Aquilino told his readers that the biggest threat to NRA/law enforcement relations was the advertising firm's "continued inability to . . . tell the unvarnished truth."

Aquilino's charges against AH&M are, however, misplaced (perhaps the result of sour grapes, since AH&M took over Aquilino's position at the NRA). The ads were, after all, just part of a larger campaign to attack any police chief possessing the temerity to disagree with the NRA on gun issues. The advertisements were merely the outgrowth of a corporate culture dedicated to the principle that the best defense is a brutal, no-holds-barred offense. And that principle, far from being dreamed up in the offices of AH&M, shined like a beacon from the executive suite on the eighth floor of the NRA headquarters.

For one brief moment in October of 1986, following the passage of McClure-Volkmer a few months before, there was one faint glimmer of hope that what had threatened to become all-out war between law enforcement and the National Rifle Association could be averted.

Jerald Vaughn, head of the International Association of Chiefs of Police, telephoned the NRA's Warren Cassidy, suggesting that the two get together for a private lunch to talk over their differences. Cassidy agreed to meet Vaughn at a chic private Republican club on Capitol Hill. Over expensive dishes of nouvelle cuisine, the patrician, silver-haired former mayor of Lynn, Massachusetts, and the short ex–police chief of Largo, Florida, held a mini peace conference.

The meeting began with understandable tension; the two men represented groups that had recently been at each other's throats. But as the lunch continued, Vaughn and Cassidy warmed to each other as they found important common ground: Both said that they were committed to ending the warfare that was hurting their groups.

Vaughn confronted Cassidy with four main complaints. The NRA, he said, had tried to undermine the leadership of police organizations;

it had distorted the facts about the McClure-Volkmer bill; it had claimed to speak for law enforcement when in fact it did not; and it called the IACP "antigun," a charge Vaughn vigorously denied.

Although Cassidy didn't specifically back down from any NRA positions or tactics, Vaughn says the NRA chief did indicate that his group was now turning its attention to state legislative issues and would not attack the views of individual chiefs of police—or of the IACP. Vaughn was satisfied that something like a rapprochement had been achieved at the lunch, and remembers leaving the club feeling exuberant.

"Quite frankly, I thought that meeting was quite productive," says Vaughn. "We had what I believed to be an agreement. I felt it was possible that we had formed the basis of a very positive future, a working relationship."

But a scant two weeks later, that dream was crushed when a reporter for *The Los Angeles Times* called Vaughn for the police executive's reaction to a new NRA attack on Joe McNamara.

Vaughn hung up and dialed Warren Cassidy.

"Hey, what gives?" demanded an irate Vaughn. "I thought this wasn't going to happen anymore."

"Well, this is different," replied Cassidy. "We believe McNamara represents a threat to our people."

Vaughn was livid.

"So what you're saying is we only have a selective agreement. When you choose to abide by it, that's okay, but when you choose not to I'm supposed to say that's okay, too?"

"We felt we had to speak out against McNamara," Cassidy argued.

"Fine," said Vaughn, and hung up.

The two-week truce—if that's what the lull was—was over. The NRA continued attacking police chiefs who spoke out for gun control and the rift between law enforcement and the gun lobby continued to grow. The IACP retaliated by rejecting the NRA's application to set up an exhibit booth at the police group's 1987 annual conference in Nashville, Tennessee. Police chiefs charge that the NRA next undertook a campaign to have chiefs it didn't like fired from their positions and also attempted to block the hiring of these chiefs when they were applying for new positions.

The NRA, either directly or through members of affiliated local gun clubs, unleashed its characteristic mail and telephone barrages against several chiefs. One target was Keith Bergstrom, the chief of police in Oak Park, Illinois, who had applied for that same position in Tarpon Springs, Florida, in 1987. Bergstrom had earned a position on the NRA hit list by enforcing an antihandgun ordinance passed by the Oak Park city council in 1984. After Bergstrom applied for the post in Florida, 400 NRA members in Tarpon Springs received mailings from the group's headquarters insisting they contact the city council demanding that Bergstrom not be hired. Bergstrom was given the job despite the campaign.

The NRA was apparently more successful in the case of Minneapolis chief of police Anthony Bouza. Bouza's transgression was even more blatant than Bergstrom's: The Minneapolis chief had appeared in a pro-gun-control video produced by the group Handgun Control, Inc. In retaliation, NRA members sent 1,000 anti-Bouza letters and made 1,200 angry phone calls to officials in Suffolk County, New York, where the Minneapolis policeman had applied for a job as police chief. County officials later admitted the calls and letters "played a role" in their decision not to select Bouza.

Joe Casey, president of the IACP and police chief for Nashville, Tennessee, felt the wrath of the NRA when he articulated the police organization's stand in support of a waiting period for the purchase of handguns.

Casey is no "antigunner." Like most law enforcement officials, he was, in fact, an enthusiastic supporter of the right of private citizens to own and use firearms during his thirty-seven years with the Nashville Police Department. But like the majority of police officers, Casey felt that some restrictions on that right were essential to maintaining law and order.

"I tried to make it very plain that I was not trying to keep law-abiding people from getting a gun if that's what they wanted to do," says the soft-spoken Casey, today the head of security for a Tennessee chemical firm. "I wasn't talking against handguns. I just didn't see anything wrong with a waiting period to check somebody out."

But the NRA did, and it mailed a four-page letter to all NRA members in the state of Tennessee telling them so. The letter asked members to (as the headline read) HELP STOP NASHVILLE POLICE CHIEF'S LIES NOW. Despite the letters and phone calls to Nashville mayor Bill Boner calling for Casey's dismissal, the campaign, as in McNamara's case, had no effect. At least it didn't have the effect the NRA had expected. Once again, the attack on a police chief served to stiffen the resolve of the law enforcement community. The IACP countered the NRA's letter with a "Special Bulletin" of its own. Marked URGENT * URGENT * URGENT, the letter to IACP members ran under the headline IACP PRESIDENT JOE CASEY UNDER ATTACK FROM NRA, LETTER CALLS CASEY A LIAR.

The letter outlined the situation and concluded with the following appeal to police chiefs:

> When Joe Casey is attacked, IACP is attacked and, therefore, *you* are attacked. You must act to protect your citizenry, your department and yourself. . . . Police executives must stand united. Work with your fellow chiefs, and don't let NRA victimize you. If you see a problem developing, contact IACP headquarters and your state association. We don't run away when thugs try to claim turf in our communities, and we shouldn't be intimidated by political extortionists like the National Rifle Association.

Meanwhile, throughout 1987, a bill to ban "plastic guns" continued to ride the legislative roller coaster, and here the NRA was having more success than in its head-on battle with police groups. While most public attention concerning the bill was focused on debates and hearings on Capitol Hill, the real battle was being slugged out at the Justice Department and farther down Pennsylvania Avenue at the White House. While police groups were growing adept at playing the image game—dubbing the armor-piercing bullets "cop-killers" and framing other issues they cared about as either being pro- or anti–law enforcement—they were still no match for the NRA at back room lobbying. The police simply weren't as well connected as the NRA, which now had a decade of experience playing the game of power politics. All of which helps to explain why, just as the Reagan administration was about to unveil legislation banning plastic guns in the fall of 1987, the bill was suddenly, and unceremoniously, killed. While there was little doubt that the NRA had masterminded the legislative slaying, Attorney General Edwin Meese, at the urging of Vice President George Bush, actually pulled the trigger.

Meese had found himself in the extremely uncomfortable position of being caught between two important constituencies: the police and gun owners (represented by the NRA). As the nation's top law enforcement officer, and as a genuine hard-line supporter of "law and order," Meese *wanted* to back the police. He also knew he owed them a favor after the administration's support of the recently passed McClure-Volkmer bill. That support had caused great bitterness on the part of police toward the Reagan administration in general and toward Meese and the Justice Department in particular. Backing the plastic gun legislation was seen as an important opportunity to mend fences with law enforcement.

But the National Rifle Association was not about to stand silently to one side as Meese threw the police a bone. The NRA unleashed a furious back room campaign to do the bill in. On October 6, 1987, NRA lobbyists Wayne LaPierre and James Jay Baker, and newly retained Tom Korologos (the former White House insider whose help had been so effective in the armor-piercing-bullet debate), met with Meese at the Justice Department in an attempt to persuade the attorney general to scuttle the bill. It was the kind of power meeting that the police groups were not yet able to set up. But the NRA didn't depend on this one meeting alone to sway Meese. It mounted several other lobbying assaults simultaneously—on agencies involved with the legislation (such as the Office of Management and Budget) as well as on the White House itself, where the NRA concentrated its efforts on the office of Vice President George Bush.

LaPierre had Senator James McClure contact Bush personally, asking him to put pressure on Meese to kill the legislation. LaPierre also complained about the bill to Bush assistants Lee Atwater and former Justice Department official Phil Brady, who relayed the NRA's concerns to friends at Justice, who in turn passed the message along to Meese. Finally, Meese felt he had no choice but to kill the legislation.

"Ed [Meese] was in a very difficult position," admits Law Enforcement Steering Committee head Neil Behan. "He was very supportive of law enforcement, coming from California as a prosecutor. He understood our problems. But he was working in an environment that has other political views. You're talking about law enforcement on one side and politics on the other and they're not always compatible. He was caught between the two forces. And I think he tried very, very honestly and diligently to be loyal to both."

But no one on the pro-gun-control side was feeling very charitably toward Ed Meese back then, especially after *The Washington Post* ran a front-page article under the headline NRA GETS MEESE TO WITH-DRAW PROPOSAL TO BAN "PLASTIC GUNS." *Post* columnist Mary McGrory wrote that those who wailed about the power of liberal lobbies to defeat the nomination of Judge Robert Bork to the Supreme Court didn't know where the *real* power in Washington was. "Compared with the National Rifle Association," McGrory wrote, "[liberal lobbies] are as the water pistol to the Stinger missile."

Democratic representative Edward Feighan, a supporter of gun control from Ohio, wrote Meese a scathing letter questioning the attorney general's decision to shelve the bill.

"I am especially disturbed by the NRA's apparent veto power over governmental agencies," penned Feighan (in a letter also signed by thirty other representatives). "I have never known the NRA to be an agency of our government. Why then have you granted this gun lobby the right to veto legislation that has been approved by both the Department of Justice and the Department of the Treasury?"

(Feighan had apparently struck a nerve. The Justice Department did not reply to his letter until the following April—five months later—and then the response was addressed to Congressman Pete Stark, a Democrat from California and one of the co-signers of the original letter, rather than to Feighan himself. In addition to a rather curt cover letter, Acting Assistant Attorney General Thomas Boyd sent a copy of a letter he had written to Senator James McClure in March outlining the administration's stand on the plastic gun issue.)

After Meese shelved the plastic gun legislation in October 1987, proponents of the bill decided not to wait for the administration to come up with a new proposal. Instead, they sought to offer their own bill, which was to be introduced in the Senate by Howard Metzenbaum. Once again, the NRA computers spun into action. On December 8, NRA members across the country received an "emergency alert" warning them of the "antigunners'" latest machinations:

SENATOR HOWARD METZENBAUM WILL OFFER A GUN BAN BILL
WITHIN THE NEXT TWO WEEKS. . . . THE BILL BANS ALL PISTOLS AND

REVOLVERS WITH LESS THAN 8½ OUNCES OF STEEL—THOUSANDS OF
QUALITY FIREARMS THAT YOU AND YOUR NEIGHBORS OWN. S.465
ALSO BANS ANY FIREARM THAT THE SECRETARY OF THE TREASURY
DETERMINES IS NOT READILY DETECTABLE—UNDER AN ANTI-GUN
ADMINISTRATION THAT COULD MEAN ALL FIREARMS. . . .

THE ANTI-GUNNERS ARE CLAIMING THAT BANNING YOUR FIRE-
ARMS WILL STOP TERRORISM. THEY'RE CALLING ALL SMALL PISTOLS
AND REVOLVERS PLASTIC GUNS AND THEY'RE CLAIMING AIRPORT SE-
CURITY DEVICES CAN'T DETECT THEM. WE ALL KNOW THE ONLY
PLASTIC GUNS ARE IN TOY STORES, BUT THESE ANTI-GUNNERS DON'T
CARE ABOUT THE TRUTH.

METZENBAUM AND THE NATIONAL COALITION TO BAN HANDGUNS
HAVE CONVINCED THE MEDIA ELITE THAT THEY CAN WIN ON THIS
ISSUE. THEY'VE CONVINCED MANY PEOPLE THAT BANNING FIREARMS
IN AMERICA IS THE WAY TO FIGHT TERRORISTS. THEY MAY CONVINCE
YOUR SENATOR, TOO.

A few days later, this alert was followed by a four-page letter calling
the Metzenbaum bill "the first federal gun ban bill in America" and
painting the battle in near-apocalyptic terms: "You and I are in the
middle of the most urgent and critical federal gun battle we have faced
in 12 years. Without your help we could lose."

But a vote on Metzenbaum's bill was put off until the next year.
The dire rhetoric of the NRA's "emergency alerts" aside, the momentum now clearly favored the gun lobby. Or at least it did until a
cold night in February 1988, when George Bush, stumping for the
Republican presidential nomination, showed up at a candidates' debate
in New Hampshire armed and—at least as far as the NRA was concerned—dangerous.

The surprising development occurred at a Concord motel conference center during a forum sponsored by the Gun Owners of New
Hampshire, an anti-gun-control group affiliated with the NRA. When
the talk turned to the issue of gun control, Vice President Bush pulled
a tiny translucent revolver from his breast pocket. Plastic guns were
a threat to the American public, said Bush.

"Conflicts sometimes arise between gun owners and law enforcement officials and you've got to work this out," he told the crowd,
holding the tiny .22 revolver aloft. "It's not always easy striking a
balance. The answer should be detectability. I'm making a pitch here
for reason."

That fact that Bush, who had so recently been the object of such intense lobbying by the gun group on this very issue, should speak out in favor of a ban on plastic guns was a surprise and a disappointment to the NRA. But even more discouraging, from the NRA's perspective, was the reaction of the audience to Bush's remarks: They applauded. And then, one after another, the other candidates stood and declared support for Mr. Bush's remarks—and also received a round of applause.

"The vice president has put his finger on a very critical and important issue," said retired general Alexander Haig. "The good of all Americans on special occasions requires compromise."

The dreaded "C" word—and the gun fanciers applauded him, too. It was a somber night at the NRA headquarters.

But disappointment for the NRA didn't translate into immediate political gains for the police. Despite the heartening news from New Hampshire, backers of the ban on plastic weapons heard nothing positive coming from the Justice Department. Representatives from the Law Enforcement Steering Committee met with Meese in early March to express their displeasure over Justice's decision to support a bill by Senator James McClure that the police considered too weak. While the bill, which was supported by the NRA, called for a ban on "undetectable" guns made from plastic or ceramic, it set no minimum amount of metal required for detectability, meaning that the government would have to prove that a weapon was undetectable. The police wanted a standard of 8.5 ounces of steel, the amount specified in Metzenbaum's bill. The issue once again appeared to be deadlocked.

Then, in mid-April, law enforcement officials were summoned to the Justice Department for another meeting. Although reports would later say that a "compromise had been hammered out" at the hour-long meeting, that gives a false impression of the gathering, one that implies negotiations. There was no bargaining done at the meeting; the police were simply told that Justice had decided upon a bill that would include a detectability standard of 3.7 ounces of stainless steel. That amount was under half of what the police had wanted, but at least the bill did contain a specific standard, something the NRA had fought.

"The bill was presented in a way that would lead us to believe that we had some influence on it," recalls former IACP director Jerald Vaughn, who attended the meeting. "But when you cut through all the BS, the bottom line to it was they told us what they were going to give us."

The police were in a take-it-or-leave-it situation, much like the one they had faced with armor-piercing bullets in 1984. And once again the police opted to take what Justice offered.

"We assessed what we had before and what was being offered *and* what we were likely to get if we didn't accept the compromise," says Vaughn. "We saw ourselves in a losing position."

Still, many of the police officials left the meeting feeling jubilant. "When you're dealing with a lobby as powerful as the NRA and you can in any way influence the outcome of things to be other than exactly the way the NRA wanted it, you have to feel pretty good about it," explains Vaughn.

The bill easily passed both houses of Congress, and on November 11, 1988, President Ronald Reagan signed the undetectable-weapons bill into law.

Today, even some who fought the NRA on the issues of armor-piercing bullets and plastic guns admit that the dangers posed by these weapons were overstated. The Glock 17, the "plastic gun" that started the uproar, quickly became the standard handgun of scores of police departments across the nation, earning a reputation for reliability, accuracy, firepower, and ease of use.

"There are no plastic guns. There never were," says Eric Sterling, the onetime counsel to the House Crime Subcommittee. "The Glock was made a fall guy in this thing. This airport security stuff—there was a lot of bullshit floating around here: Did Muammar Qaddafi have a bunch of these guns that he ordered? Was there a KGB plastic gun?" Today, Sterling just laughs at these stories.

But others, like former IACP executive director Jerald Vaughn, maintain that the legislation was not misguided. "As a proactive measure [the plastic gun bill] was important," insists Vaughn. "As a real problem—in all honesty, it was not a real problem at that time. But the advent of the technology certainly led us to believe that there was a serious *potential* problem out there. Rather than react after the fact, we felt it was important to be proactive on the issue."

But while the merits of various bills designed to counter plastic guns and armor-piercing bullets can be debated, there is no doubt that the battles over those bills had far-reaching consequences for the NRA.

"There's no question about it," admits Wayne LaPierre. "We took a terrible bath in public relations."

To LaPierre, this had been the cause of the NRA's difficulties: inadequate PR and nothing more.

"The problem is not so much what [the] NRA has done on those issues legislative-wise, it's that we didn't tell our story to America," he argues. "Cop-killer bullets—or armor-piercing bullets, as we call it, the media call it cop-killer bullets—what we said in Congress was that the bill is too broad and it needs to be narrowed, and we oppose it in its present form. The press reported 'NRA OPPOSES COP-KILLER BULLET LEGISLATION' and never told the rest of the story.

"Senator Moynihan said, 'What's wrong with the NRA? What's wrong with *those people*? Are deer wearing armor vests these days? Is that why we have to have these rounds?' And everybody laughed about it."

LaPierre shrugs. "It was a witty comment."

But the NRA's problems were caused by more than just a lack of public relations savvy or a biased press. It is certainly true that the threat posed by both plastic guns and armor-piercing bullets was exaggerated by supporters of gun control. And it is also true that the NRA's opponents were aided in their attacks on these weapons by some in the media who were gullible at best and prejudiced against the NRA and gun owners at worst.

But the gun lobby was its own worst enemy in these confrontations. From the outset, its position was not to find a way to write reasonable legislation but "to kill the issue outright," as Warren Cassidy himself admitted. Even many NRA members—staunch supporters of law enforcement—had their doubts about this course of action and urged the leadership to come to some sort of accommodation that would protect the police while at the same time preserving the ability of hunters and target shooters to buy the firearms and ammunition necessary for their sports. In the end, that's exactly what happened, but only after the NRA was forced to compromise.

Even more damaging to the gun lobby, however, was its heavy-handed, personalized attacks on the leaders of law enforcement groups and on individual police chiefs who differed with the NRA on gun-control issues. The ad hominem assaults led to a schism between the NRA and the police that would never heal. It would, in fact, grow, coming back to haunt the gun group as Americans, alarmed by rapidly escalating gun violence on city streets, turned desperately to law enforcement—and to Congress—for help.

# 5

# A WAR
# IN THE STREETS

*THE BIG MAN in the jaunty white suit hesitates in the doorway, the key
still dangling in his hand. There is a sound on the landing behind him.
He turns and spots the younger, smaller man standing in the shadows.
The older man betrays just the slightest hint of fear, an almost imper-
ceptible tightening of the muscles around the mouth and eyes, before
a smile of recognition flutters across his face.*

*"What have you got there?" he asks, gesturing with a friendly
tilt of his chin at the towel that is wound around the younger
man's arm.*

*As if in reply, the young man steps smartly forward into the harsh
light. He moves like a flamenco dancer, smacking the heel of his right
boot down hard on the wooden floor so that a crack like a gunshot
echoes down the narrow hallway. At the same moment he extends his
towel-wrapped arm directly at the older man's chest. There is a second
sharp noise, this time much louder, as the cheap revolver hidden
beneath the towel goes off.*

*The older man looks down quizzically at his chest, where a small
neat hole now mars his shirt. He pulls at his suit with thick, suddenly
clumsy fingers as if to get a better look. His assailant fires again, this
time hitting the large man two inches below the right eye.*

115

"Ouch," says a lanky man dressed in green surgical scrubs and sprawled over the couch. "I bet that hurt."

*The young man walks over to the inert body that has come to rest against the wall. He places the gun into the dead or unconscious man's mouth and pulls the trigger.*

"Ohhh-kay," says a woman on the couch, also wearing green scrubs, as she leans forward to take the last slice of pizza from a grease-stained cardboard box on the coffee table. "That's it for him."

It is still early on a warm Saturday night, and most members of the Washington Hospital Center's MedSTAR team are taking it easy in the lounge watching a video of *The Godfather, Part II*. As they watch, they offer prognoses for the victims of the movie's mayhem. Vito Corleone (played by Robert De Niro) exacts revenge on the man who had had his family wiped out decades earlier, slipping a knife into the old man's ample belly and drawing it up effortlessly to a point just beneath the wattle of his neck. The feat draws low whistles of admiration from around the room:

"Sharp knife."

"Smooth incision."

"That'd take a good eight hours in the OR to fix up," says the woman who took the last piece of pizza.

She ought to know. She and the others in this room treat more serious wounds in a single week—gunshots, stabbings, and assorted traumatic injuries—than many doctors do in the course of several years. They operate on the front lines of a war fought in America's streets. The MedSTAR (Medical Shock Trauma Acute Resuscitation) concept, in fact, is based on medical techniques developed on the battlefield. The team, a civilian version of the military MASH unit, handles only the most critical of the many serious cases coming out of metropolitan Washington, D.C.

Like all great capital cities of the world, Washington, D.C., is not one but several capitals. Best known as the seat of government, the District of Columbia is also a capital for historic archives, national monuments, and museums of all kinds. In recent years, Washington has achieved another distinction: It has become the murder capital of America. In 1990, 483 residents of the District were murdered, a rate of 76 homicides per 100,000 people—seven and a half times the national average. Washington's homicide rate is the highest in the nation, and has shown an almost tenfold increase over the last two decades. In 1987, MedSTAR personnel treated 351 cases of serious gunshot and knife wounds. In 1990, that number had almost doubled to 685 cases. These wounds have become so common that military surgeons now train at Washington Hospital Center to gain experience in battlefield medicine.

The center is part of a sprawling medical complex of modern glass-and-chrome buildings tastefully set on rolling lawns dotted with beds of purple and pink petunias—all conveniently located in the middle of the D.C. war zone. A tall fence topped with triple-strand barbed wire surrounds the area. On the other side of this fence lies a very different world, a land of crumbling brick apartment buildings and crack houses, where small knots of men hang out on street corners day and night, getting drunk or high or both in a world marked by unemployment, poverty, and escalating violence. The sound of gunfire is so common in the streets surrounding the Washington Hospital Center that when a car backfires, people for a block around dive for cover.

"If somebody cuts you off in traffic on your way over here," a hospital employee warns a reporter who will be spending the night on the Trauma Unit, "don't honk at them. If someone is double-parked and you can't get around, don't yell at them. Those are good ways to get killed around here."

These two Americas, separated by the fence surrounding Washington Hospital Center, overlap in the Trauma Unit.

Terry Powers has worked as a flight nurse on one of MedSTAR's two helicopter crews for the last four years. For the past two and a half years, the thirty-seven-year-old nurse, who bears a more than passing resemblance to actor Michael J. Fox (only with more nervous energy), has staffed the particularly violent weekend shift.

"We've always seen a lot of gunshot victims," Powers says as he leans back against a gurney and folds his arms across his chest. "But now . . . man, we have some nights when that's *all* we have. That's new."

Powers explains that the MedSTAR Trauma Unit serves as a kind of emergency room for other Washington-area emergency rooms.

Originally, ERs were designed to handle the most critically injured patients and those needing immediate attention. When a growing demand for ER services outstripped their ability to treat patients, trauma units were introduced to handle the very worst off among ER patients.

Potential Trauma Unit patients have to meet a strict set of guidelines before they're brought here. Their blood pressure must be dangerously low. Their breathing is either very slow or extremely fast. They have to have a penetrating injury—usually gunshot or knife wounds—to the head, neck, chest, abdomen, or groin. Or at least two broken bones. Or burns on more than 10 percent of their body, or on critical areas. Or they have to be paralyzed or have at least one limb amputated.

In short, these are the patients who will likely die unless they can be stabilized immediately. Even with all these rigorous requirements, more than 3,000 people qualify for treatment at the MedSTAR unit each year. Almost miraculously, most of them survive.

To all outward appearances, the unit is indistinguishable from a traditional hospital emergency room. There are six bays, each about twelve feet by twenty feet, with a portable table in the middle, floors of gray Formica tile, and blue curtains that can be stretched across the front of each area. The bays contain basic emergency medical equipment, familiar to us from countless medical television shows and movies: defibrillators, IV racks, trays full of surgical implements, packs of gauze. Several of the bays are also stocked with specialized equipment to handle one particular injury, such as shock, various medical emergencies, and burns, for example.

"We're equipped and staffed to handle anything," says Powers proudly. "And 'staffed' is the key word."

You must look past the gleaming medical equipment to understand that the key to the many life-and-death dramas played out here every day is not hardware but *people*. From the moment a patient is wheeled into the unit, he or she is surrounded by a platoon of nurses, doctors, and various technicians. A single MedSTAR team consists of two attending physicians, a fourth-year resident, one or two first- or second-year residents, a couple of medical students, a MedSTAR nurse, a MedSTAR paramedic, an intensive care nurse, a respiratory therapist, a cardiovascular technician, and technicians from the blood bank and

X ray. The workers swarm around the patient, working in concert, but each also paying particular attention to his or her own special area of responsibility. To an outsider, the unit can appear to be in a state of total chaos when only a single bay is filled.

"You should see it when four bays are being used," says Powers with a boyish grin. "Now *that's* crazy!"

It takes a certain kind of person to work on the Trauma Unit. Even among other health-care workers the MedSTAR teams have a reputation for a sort of brash competence and derring-do. What strikes you first about the MedSTAR personnel is their age: Almost without exception, they are quite young. As they sit around the television in their lounge joking and eating pizza, they seem like any group of amiable and bright young professionals—stockbrokers, up-and-coming ad-agency executives—getting together for a quiet good time. The talk is about baseball scores, whose baby did what in the past week, and where a certain kind of "bitchin' " new shoe can be procured.

Then a call comes in: A helicopter is needed to bring in a shooting victim from a site five miles away.

The young woman with waist-length blond hair who only a minute ago was sitting cross-legged on the couch sipping a Diet Pepsi and complaining about a funny noise in her new car is now zipped into a green flight suit straight out of *Top Gun* and is dashing out the door in a desperate race to reach the victim before he bleeds to death. The tall guy in wire-frame glasses who had been sitting next to her anguishing about the inability of the Yankees to recruit good outfielders is scrubbing his hands and arms with disinfectant, preparing himself for what will happen when the barely breathing shooting victim comes rolling into a bay in a few minutes and he will be called upon to repair the damage done by four copper-clad hollow-point bullets hurled at a speed of over 680 miles an hour into the collection of soft tissues, muscles, blood vessels, and assorted organs that make up the human body.

They may seem like other people their age when not actually working, but the daily procession of exploded bodies and mutilated limbs that passes before them does leave its stamp on the MedSTAR workers. Just as Washington Hospital Center is separated from the violent world surrounding it by a tall fence, the doctors and nurses who staff the MedSTAR Trauma Unit erect their own internal walls to distance themselves emotionally from the carnage they see every day and night. That wall is often made of sick jokes—humor with barbs as sharp as those atop the hospital fence.

"I hope our banter doesn't bother you," flight nurse Barbara Ozmar warns a visitor at the beginning of a shift. "You have to understand: We deal with a lot and see a lot. Sick humor is a way of handling it."

That humor is apparent in the most serious conversations—*especially* in the most serious conversations. Sitting on a couch in the lounge while *The Godfather, Part II* continues on the television, a nurse is discussing the epidemic of drug-related executions in Washington. With growing frequency, she says, MedSTAR helicopters are called in to collect victims whose hands are tied behind their back and who have a single bullet wound to the back of the head. To have a person killed in Washington costs around $25—about the price of a good meal, without wine.

"At least they're getting better at it," the nurse says, deadpan. "We used to get the same guy back in here two, three times before they'd finish him off. We'd patch him up and they'd have another try at it. Sometimes I've wanted to tell the so-called assassins, 'Look, if you're going to kill somebody, *kill* him.' " She sits back on the couch, running a hand through her short blond hair.

"That's the trouble with this country," she says, and sighs. "Nobody takes pride in their work anymore."

Washington's MedSTAR teams are not alone in dealing with this escalation of violence. While the District may lead the nation in homicides, the problem is growing in cities across America, from Houston to New York, from Los Angeles to Miami. Just days after the firing stopped in the Persian Gulf War, President Bush reminded a group of law enforcement officials (as if they needed to be) that during the opening days of the allied ground offensive "more Americans were killed in some American cities than at the entire Kuwaiti front."

"Think of it," said the president, "one of our brave national guardsmen may have actually been safer in the midst of the largest armored offensive in history than he would have been on the streets of his own hometown."

A MedSTAR nurse who had served in a military hospital during the Gulf War was asked to describe her experience there. She hesitated a moment, and then smiled as she replied, "It was like a vacation."

The list of casualties from this country's gun violence does, indeed, read like the body count of a major war. In the United States today, one person dies by gunshot every eighteen minutes, twenty-four hours a day. In a year, that adds up to nearly 30,000 deaths. In two years, more Americans are killed by guns here at home than died in the entire Vietnam War. Of that annual total, about 15,000 commit suicide, 11,000 are murdered, and some 1,500 die in accidents involving guns. Handguns account for 45 percent of all murders, or about 8,275 deaths a year. In addition, guns are used in 181,000 robberies each year, 164,651 aggravated assaults, and 2,759 assaults on law enforcement officers. In the 1980s, a total of 330,000 Americans were killed by guns, or about three times the number of AIDS fatalities during the same period. Since 1933, more Americans have died from gun injuries here at home than in all the wars our country has been involved in since—and including—the American Revolution.

The statistics on gun deaths, particularly handgun deaths, are even more appalling when compared to the rates in other countries. In 1990, there were 10,567 handgun murders in the United States. In the same year, a total of 291 people were murdered with handguns in Japan, Great Britain, Switzerland, Canada, Sweden, and Australia. (The total population of this group of countries is slightly less than that of the United States. However, after adjusting for this population difference, the number of handgun murders in these countries rises only to 305.)

No group or locality is immune from this violence. Some Americans are, however, at more risk than others. African-Americans, particularly young black males, are disproportionately affected. Gunshot wounds are the leading cause of death among young black males, with one of every two deaths among black male teenagers due to firearms. Only about two in ten white male teenagers die in this manner. Black girls are also being killed by guns in record numbers. The percentage of African-American girls aged ten to fourteen who died of gunshot wounds doubled between 1987 and 1988.

Louis Sullivan, Secretary of Health and Human Services in the Bush administration, was hardly exaggerating when he called the rise in gun deaths among blacks an "American epidemic." It is a sobering measure of this plague's terrible cost to the African-American community to realize that if young black males had been dying from gunshot wounds at the same rate as their white counterparts between 1984 and 1988, there would be 14,000 more young African-American boys and men alive today.

As in all epidemics, the rise in gun violence has created a financial as well as a health-care crisis at hospitals across the country. The taking of a life may be dirt cheap in Washington, but the cost of *saving* that same life can be astronomical. Treating gunshot wounds is an extremely expensive procedure—to save the life of a single victim of a serious gunshot wound can cost $150,000 to $200,000—or more. And generally it is the hospital or the taxpayer who ends up footing the bill. "Gunshot wounds have overwhelmed emergency rooms across the country," says MedSTAR nurse Barbara Ozmar. "They're draining this country's health-care system."

Washington Hospital Center is itself a good example of the problem. In 1990, the hospital—which is a private institution—had to cover some $26 million in indigent care for Trauma Unit patients, mostly to pay for victims of gun violence. A recent study published in the *Journal of the American Medical Association* estimated the annual cost of treating gunshot wounds in America at $1 billion. The taxpayer funds about 85 percent of this amount, or $850 million each year.

The rise in gun violence has been accompanied by a dramatic increase in the number of privately owned guns in this country. Counting firearms has always been a difficult and controversial task in America, where no central list of gun owners exists. The National Rifle Association has successfully blocked the creation of such a list for decades, contending that it would be the first step down the path to gun confiscation.

Every decade or so, however, some government agency guesstimates the size of America's private arsenal. In 1950, experts said there were somewhere in the neighborhood of 54 million guns owned by individual Americans. In 1969, the National Commission on the Causes and Prevention of Violence upped that figure to 90 million firearms (35 million rifles, 31 million shotguns, and 24 million handguns). By 1980, the Bureau of Alcohol, Tobacco and Firearms estimated that there were 59 million rifles, 54 million shotguns, and 52 million handguns, for a total of 165 million firearms.

During the early 1980s, domestic gun manufacturing and imports of foreign-made weapons declined. That trend was reversed after passage of the McClure-Volkmer bill in 1986, when weapons from both sources began to flood the American market. Today, the United States, a country with a population of approximately 247 million people, has a gun "population" of over 200 million. For the first time, the number of handguns has surpassed the supply of shotguns, probably reflecting an increased desire for self-protection on the part of crime-weary Americans. According to a recent ATF study, we are the proud owners of almost 73 million rifles, 66 million handguns, and 62 million shotguns, making us by far the most heavily armed nation on earth.

While many gun owners have more than one gun, the total supply of firearms is surprisingly widespread: An estimated half of the nation's households contain at least one gun, and almost one third own a handgun. (By comparison, less than 14 million households have personal computers.) We have become, as Senator Ted Kennedy warned back in 1982, a nation "armed to the teeth against itself."

While a large percentage of these new guns were bought for sporting purposes (hunting and target shooting were two of the fastest growing sports in the '80s) and for self-protection, many are used for illegal purposes—even a large number of those originally bought for legitimate reasons. Every year, between 200,000 and 225,000 guns are reported stolen, a figure that undoubtedly represents only a fraction of those actually taken.

Not only are more guns being bought each year, but the firepower of the American arsenal is also escalating. As the Cold War winds down we find ourselves in the midst of a domestic arms race. Just ten years ago, the six-shot revolver, the same basic gun that "won the West" a hundred years ago, accounted for seven out of every ten handgun sales. No more. Today's handgun of choice is the 9-mm semiautomatic pistol, a weapon that fires a more powerful ammunition, more quickly, and holds more of it than the revolver. These pistols can hold between twelve and twenty bullets, with the ammunition carried in a removable clip to allow for quick reloading. A standard revolver fires a bullet at a muzzle velocity of 925 feet per second; a round from a 9-mm handgun travels at 1,250 feet per second.

Criminals today disdain the small, inexpensive, low-powered, and inaccurate handguns called Saturday Night Specials. These guns were once so popular with street criminals (or thought to be) that many gun-control advocates made banning them their highest priority. But a new kind of criminal has turned to a new class of high-powered firearms. Drugs, and the money that comes from the illegal drug trade, have changed the nature of the domestic arms race. For narcocriminals, high-powered military-style weapons are simply "tools of the trade."

According to James Wright, a sociologist at Tulane University and one of the nation's top researchers on criminals and their guns, firearms and drugs are intertwined.

"These days, most of the people doing crime are also doing drugs," says Wright. "People who are in the market to buy drugs also buy, sell, and trade guns. They are obviously into an entire package of illicit uncondoned activities. There also seems to be some sort of technological escalation going on, due to drugs. We're seeing a move to bigger and better equipment. . . . [Drug criminals] are about as well armed as you can be short of hand-held nuclear weapons."

Today's up-to-date narcocriminals use semiautomatic and fully automatic weapons (semiautomatic guns fire one round every time the trigger is pulled; fully automatic guns continue to spray bullets as long as the trigger is depressed). These guns come equipped with silencers, flash suppressors (for night use), and laser sights. Their arsenals include grenades (some of which can be shot from launchers fixed to guns), plastic explosives, small rockets, lightweight Kevlar body armor, and night vision devices.

"It seems that the bad guys and the good guys alike are interested in these guns for the same reason that we wanted to make sure we had bigger and more bombs than the Soviets," says Wright. "Anybody who anticipates a firefight wants to be at least as well armed as the adversary. That means that the cops want to carry better guns than the bad guys. The bad guys want to carry better guns than the cops. And private citizens want to carry the best kind of weapons they can afford."

The arms race for the "biggest and baddest" weapons has trickled down to the level of the small-time operator, who now carries at least a 9-mm semiautomatic pistol. On the streets of America today, the once-dreaded Saturday Night Specials are carried only by sissies.

ALTHOUGH HE IS only thirty-six years old, D.C. police sergeant William Nesbitt jokes that he already has plans for his retirement. "I'm going to sell police tape," he tells flight nurse Terry Powers when he drops in for one of his regular visits to the MedSTAR Trauma Unit. "You know, the kind that says 'POLICE LINE—DO NOT CROSS.' Yeah, I could make a lot of money selling that these days."

"I hear that," Powers says, nodding emphatically.

Nesbitt is a seventeen-year police veteran. ("I got out of high school on Friday and joined the force the next Monday.") Over the years, he has watched as the witches' brew of poverty, drugs, and firearms turned his hometown into America's murder capital. He speaks slowly and sadly of these changes, with a slight drawl, leaning his six-foot-three-inch frame wearily against the empty table in bay number two. The night air is humid even inside the unit, and Nesbitt removes his police hat after every few sentences to wipe the perspiration off his brow.

"Everybody's got to have a nice gun these days," he says. "They went from twenty-twos to thirty-twos to forty-fours and forty-fives, to nine-millimeters and Uzis [Israeli-made submachine guns]. You used to see one or two wounds on a person. Now, it's fourteen or fifteen wounds. Slight injuries have become serious injuries and serious injuries have become fatalities. And they're much more willing to use their guns. It doesn't mean anything to them, shooting someone. Everybody here is desensitized to the killings. I mean, there used to be a sense of shock about it. Now, I'll be checking the scene out, a body's lying there with blood all around, and the little kids will crowd around me and say, 'Oooo, look; the cop's got a Glock [a type of pistol]!'"

Are drugs usually involved in the shootings?

Powers fields the question immediately. "With young black males," he says, "drugs are *always* involved."

The policeman nods in agreement.

"A lot of times," Powers continues, "you'll be cutting the clothes off of a victim and—uh-oh." He opens his eyes wide and drops his jaw with mock surprise. "A plastic bag full of vials of crack! Sometimes, the first thing a relative will say when they come here is, 'Did he have a little bag with him?' or 'Can I have his beeper?' It's sad, man, really sad. These people have nothing to live for."

Another nurse walks by and puts her two cents in.

"This is almost a rite of passage now, getting shot and coming here," she says. "There was one man who recently died here of a gunshot wound. A relative told us, 'You know, his brother died here the same way. And his father, too.' " She shakes her head. "It's madness," she says, and walks away.

Nesbitt and Powers both watch her as she leaves. Nesbitt removes his hat to mop his brow.

"Yeah, it's mostly drug related now," he says. "I can't remember the last I saw a domestic shooting. A few suicides. Drugs have changed everything. You see Help Wanted [signs] in McDonald's now. You never saw that before. How do you tell a kid who's making fifteen hundred dollars a night selling drugs that he should be working down at McDonald's? Forget it. And what most of these guys know of the world is less than what Christopher Columbus knew. I've asked some of them before, 'You ever been out of the District?' Some of them had crossed the Potomac. And then came right back. That's it. This"—he jerks a thumb over at the glass doors to the unit, indicating the streets just a quarter mile away—"is their world."

"Man, people think my job is rough," says Powers, shaking his head with admiration. "Uh-uh, man. You got the rough job."

"Well, you see the end product; we see the beginning," Sergeant Nesbitt answers.

"I hear that," replies Powers. There is a brief lull in the conversation during which both men are alone with their thoughts. Then Powers, the unit's resident optimist, suddenly brightens.

"You know, it gives you a better sense of life," he says.

Nesbitt just stares at him.

Powers struggles to find the right words. "It's like . . . when I leave here sometimes . . . after an especially bad night, I'm walking down the steps and it hits me: 'Hey, man: I am *walking down the steps. I'm alive.*' It makes you happy."

Although he is a year younger than Powers, Nesbitt looks much older than the flight nurse. Where Powers has the lithe body of a natural athlete, the policeman has developed a good-sized spare tire over the years. But the difference goes beyond the physical—there is a hangdog sense of world-weariness that suffuses Nesbitt's character. He greets Powers's comments about life-in-the-midst-of-death with the same lack of enthusiasm you imagine he'd show if Powers had suggested that they go jogging sometime.

"Yeah," Nesbitt replies, and then stretches his large frame and yawns. He shakes his head as if trying to clear it, pauses, and says quietly but firmly, "The way I see it, there are two hundred people alive at this moment in this city who'll be dead by Christmas."

What about gun control?

The policeman says he is in favor of strict gun laws, but adds that he doesn't think politicians are willing to put their careers on the line for it.

"I don't know what it'll take for this country to wake up and say 'No more guns,' " he adds. "Maybe it'll take someone with an automatic takin' out half of Congress. It'll have to be like Pearl Harbor to wake people up."

And as to the National Rifle Association's claim that gun ownership is a constitutional right, Nesbitt is unimpressed.

"Yeah, well, maybe," he says without conviction, and then stares silently out the glass doors of the unit.

It is very quiet now. A nurse had said earlier that it is always good luck to have a journalist visiting. "We don't get any calls then," she had joked. Tonight, that luck is holding. The only sound comes from the dispatch room at the end of the unit, where a young woman with lipstick the color of ripe plums and bright red nail polish thumbs idly through the latest issue of *Cosmopolitan*. A tape of Jimi Hendrix's "Foxy Lady" plays on a boom-box behind her.

The silence is finally broken by Sergeant Nesbitt, who still has his eyes focused on some indeterminate point beyond the glass doors, out toward the lights of Washington.

"Maybe it's a constitutional right, but maybe it's time to suspend the rules for a while," he says, mopping his forehead with his shirt-sleeve without taking his eyes off whatever it is that has caught his attention outside. "The NRA hasn't changed, but the world has."

# 6

# HOLDING ACTIONS

THE NATIONAL RIFLE Association—as with any Washington pressure group—is like a three-ring circus. To gauge its success or failure over the long haul it's necessary to look at how the organization performs in three distinct, but connected, "rings."

The center ring is devoted to legislative affairs—that is, after all, the reason these organizations are located in the nation's capital. Assessments of the organization's achievements here are based on its ability to push its legislative wish list through Congress (and, to a lesser extent, through state and local governments). Equally important—and in the NRA's case, even more important—is the group's ability to block bills that run counter to members' interests.

The second ring beneath the Washington big top overlaps the first one slightly. In this ring the group's *electoral* abilities are revealed. How successful is the organization in getting its supporters elected to office? How successful is it in preventing its opponents from being elected or in ousting them from office?

No matter how well an organization performs in the first two rings, it is doomed to failure if it neglects the third, that of institutional operations. Is there enough money to run the group? Does the organization communicate well with its members? Does it retain its membership base? Is the morale of its workers high or low? In short, the third ring is home to all the boring yet essential minutia that have been making or breaking bureaucracies for centuries.

Admittedly, this is the least interesting of the three rings—at least to outsiders. Stories about its activities rarely show up in the morning headlines or on the evening news unless some scandal is involved (preferably concerning sex and/or large sums of money). It is as if the first two rings of a circus contained clowns and trapeze artists, dancing elephants and trained horses, and in the third were the accountants, cleanup crews, and ticket takers. They may be vital to the success of the circus, but who wants to watch them in action?

The National Rifle Association's record in the first ring is legendary. Opinion polls have consistently shown that although Americans overwhelmingly support gun-control measures, the NRA has managed to beat back all major pieces of such legislation for decades. Even the rhetoric they've used in opposing such legislation has remained remarkably consistent over the years. For example, when NRA official General M. A. Reckord testified before a Senate committee in 1930 against a bill that would have required citizens to apply for a permit to purchase handguns, his words could as easily have been uttered by a representative of the gun lobby today:

"We seriously object to the requirement under which an honest, reputable citizen would have to ask anyone if he could purchase a pistol or revolver," said the general. "We believe that this bill, if enacted into law, will make it so hard for the honest citizen to have a pistol that he will not have one and so it will virtually arm the crook rather than disarm the crook."

While this statement lacks the lilting cadence of the more modern NRA mantra—"When guns are outlawed, only outlaws will have guns"—the sentiment behind the two is identical.

And more recently, as in 1930, the lightning rod for gun-control advocates has often been the handgun—especially the cheap, short-barreled, poorly made, and often inaccurate revolver dubbed the Saturday Night Special. To its critics, the Saturday Night Special is both a symbol of growing American street violence and the major cause of the terror stalking more and more urban citizens. Legislative efforts to control gun violence have often centered on attempts to regulate or ban these guns.

But to NRA members, as to gun owners in general, there is nothing special about Saturday Night Specials. As one NRA member alert put it: "The only difference between a short gun and a long gun is a hacksaw. *All* our guns are at stake." The NRA views assaults on Saturday Night Specials as the first step toward confiscation of all firearms, and so it pours its resources into defeating legislative initiatives aimed at them, even though its members are not likely to own such inexpensive, inaccurate weapons.

After years of trying to pass legislative restrictions or prohibitions on Saturday Night Specials, gun-control advocates in Massachusetts in 1976 set their sights on *all* handguns—just as the NRA had been warning. It was the first major legislative test of the NRA's fledgling lobbying wing, the Institute for Legislative Action, which had been founded just a year earlier. The proposed law had the support of then-governor Michael Dukakis and many other officials, but still the measure was soundly defeated in a statewide referendum, thanks in large part to the campaign waged by the ILA. The NRA's reputation for legislative invincibility received a tremendous boost from the victory.

But even as the NRA's star was rising, there appeared on the horizon a small trouble spot, a harbinger of major problems to come for the gun group.

On a warm spring day in April 1981, Geoffrey LaGioia walked into the village hall in Morton Grove, Illinois—a prosperous if somewhat sleepy Chicago suburb—and applied for a business permit to open a police supply store. The twenty-five-year-old LaGioia planned on offering a variety of security equipment at his store—flashlights, holsters, guns—but the heart of the business was going to be a bullet-reloading operation that would, LaGioia hoped, supply discount ammunition for police training courses throughout Illinois. After buying expensive computer-operated reloaders, an alarm system, a walk-in safe, and signing a lease on a small shop in a local strip mall, LaGioia's plan ran into trouble. The local authorities refused to grant him a business permit. LaGioia was furious.

"I had researched everything at the library," he says. "There were no laws against opening a gun store, and I had followed all the rules. I didn't understand it."

As part of the permit-application process, LaGioia had met with Morton Grove's chief of police, who, LaGioia maintains, told him that he just didn't want to see "a gun store in his town." In fact, LaGioia says, there were already two other stores in Morton Grove selling guns—one a general sporting goods shop, the other devoted exclusively to guns.

"In my opinion," says LaGioia, "the real motive was that the chief's good friend owned a competing store in the next town. And the guy who owns the other gun store here is an ex–police officer. I think there was a little something going on there."

But according to Neal Cashman, a Morton Grove village trustee (the equivalent of a city council member), LaGioia's charges were baseless. Cashman and many others in town just didn't want someone else selling handguns in Morton Grove—particularly because LaGioia's location was just down the road from the village's junior high school.

"We didn't want the kids looking in the window, dreaming of guns," Cashman said.

Cashman phoned the village attorney and asked if there was any legal means of refusing LaGioia a permit. After looking into the matter, the attorney got back to Cashman and explained that the village could pass a resolution banning the sale of handguns within the village limits. Cashman thanked the attorney for his idea and the two were about to hang up when the attorney mentioned that if the trustees wanted to they could probably ban the *possession* of handguns, too. The idea instantly appealed to Cashman.

In the meantime, LaGioia contacted the NRA.

"I told them that I wanted to open this gun store, that it's perfectly legal, and they're not going to let me," says LaGioia.

He says that the NRA told him that while it sympathized with his plight, there was nothing it could do to help him. "They told me: 'Well, the Constitution says you have the right to *bear* arms, not *sell* them.' "

At the next regular Monday meeting of the trustees, Cashman proposed a ban on the sale of handguns and the measure easily passed. The body was preparing to turn to other business when Cashman suddenly offered a ban on the private possession of handguns. The trustees weren't prepared for this development, and voted to take no action on the measure. Instead they scheduled a public hearing on the issue, after which they'd approve or reject it.

The proposal caused an instant sensation. Media from across the country, and soon from around the world, flocked to the small village. Because of the added prohibition on the ownership of handguns, the NRA now made the Morton Grove ordinance a priority fight. If passed, the bill would be the first comprehensive ban on the private ownership of handguns. Washington, D.C., had passed a handgun ban some years earlier, but that ordinance contained a grandfather clause allowing owners to keep their firearms. The Morton Grove ordinance would require owners to surrender their handguns; violators would face a $500 fine. Many crime-weary Americans considered a ban on handguns reasonable, but the NRA warned that such a move threatened all gun owners and must be stopped. One NRA board member declared that "the membership did not want to be 'reasonable' anymore; they wanted to stake out a clear legislative position and stick to it at the federal, state, and local level."

Which is what the NRA did. The lobby bussed scores of gun supporters from rural areas into Morton Grove to make their presence felt at the June 8 hearing. Trustee Greg Youstra, a gun enthusiast who was expected to vote against the ordinance, remembers the night of the hearing with distaste.

"[T]hey [gun supporters] surrounded the village hall where it was fifty deep," he was quoted in *In Our Defense* by Ellen Alderman and Caroline Kennedy. Youstra, who holds a black belt in karate, added, "This guy doesn't scare very easily, but I was scared that night. I was afraid I was going to get shot."

Youstra had good cause to worry. After four and a half hours of raucous debate, the six trustees began voting on the ordinance at 1:00 A.M. With only Youstra left to vote, the tally stood at three in favor of the ban and two against. If Youstra voted against the ban, as expected, the trustees would be deadlocked and the measure would die. But Youstra had no intention of voting against the measure. Despite the fact that he himself used guns for sport, Youstra considered the ban on handguns sensible.

As Youstra told the authors of *In Our Defense*: "When I said, 'I vote for the ordinance,' [there were] boos and 'You sold us out, you dirty commie.' It was unbelievable."

Even Geoffrey LaGioia was turned off by the actions of the NRA representatives. "To be honest," he says, "if I had been just a member of the general public, after seeing the people the NRA sent out here, I would have probably been for the ban, too. They sent some kind of fanatical-looking and fanatical-acting people out here. It really blew a lot of my confidence in the NRA the way they handled the situation."

The passage of the Morton Grove handgun ban gave the still mostly inchoate gun-control movement encouragement—and set off warning lights at the NRA headquarters. If Morton Grove could pass such a sweeping bill, both sides realized, so could other towns. Just days after the Morton Grove vote, in fact, local officials in several nearby communities announced their intentions to pass similar legislation. The NRA mailed members a typically frantic legislative alert warning. This time, however, the call to arms rang true:

> The village of Morton Grove, Illinois, has passed the unthinkable— a ban on the private possession of all handguns for all law-abiding citizens—with enforcement permitting the police to *search* any home, to *seize* and *confiscate* strictly on a suspicion that there may be a gun in the home.
>
> The village of Wilmette will vote June 16 on a similar proposal. . . . What was once the unthinkable has now become reality. . . . We must stop a possible domino effect . . . these fanatics must be stopped—NOW!

The picture painted by the NRA of police making unannounced random raids looking for guns was pure fabrication—the ordinance permitted no such intrusions—but the concern about a possible domino effect seemed justified. Rather than try to fight every battle at a local level, the NRA's strategy was to challenge the Morton Grove ordinance in court, hoping to quash such bans once and for all.

The National Coalition to Ban Handguns (NCBH)—the Washington, D.C.–based organization composed mostly of church groups— also saw Morton Grove as the beginning of a trend that could sweep across the country—if it survived the NRA's court challenge. The group's executive director, Michael Beard, mailed coalition members his own "legislative alert":

> By now, you've probably heard about the Miracle of Morton Grove. "Miracle" may be too strong a word for what is, in reality, a triumph of common sense and humanity. But these days, such triumphs are

not common. . . . [W]e're gearing up for the fight of our life—the
most critical battle NCBH has yet been called upon to engage. We've
got to help this small island of sanity. . . .

A little farther down the page followed a rather predictable request
for donations:

We need your help, and the need is most urgent. We must build an
emergency legal fund immediately. I can't emphasize strongly enough
just how important this battle can be to America as a whole. I hope
we can count on you again. Please—please—stretch your generosity
to the limits.

Not to be outdone, the NRA mailed out its own fund-raising appeal
in October, calling Morton Grove "the watchword for the most dangerous attack ever staged against the right to keep and bear arms!" To
highlight the importance of the battle, on the final page of the NRA
letter was a copy of the NCBH's fund-raising letter, over which was
scrawled, "Without your help, there could be a Morton Grove in your
future!"

The NRA's court challenge hinged on the argument that the handgun ban violated the Second Amendment to the U.S. Constitution—
a provision so important to the gun group that its words are bolted to
the side of their headquarters in Washington, D.C., in large metal
letters: THE RIGHT OF THE PEOPLE TO KEEP AND BEAR ARMS SHALL
NOT BE INFRINGED.

It's impossible to overstate the hold these words have on the gun
group. NRA members consider the Second Amendment the most
important of the ten original amendments. It is, they contend, the
queen of the Bill of Rights, the linchpin of democracy, the one loose
thread in the protective cloak of the Constitution: Pull it out and the
rest of the Bill of Rights unravels. That's because—to the NRA's way
of thinking—only an armed citizenry can prevent a tyrannical government from abolishing the rest of our freedoms.

Like a cross to a devout Christian, these hallowed words are apt
to show up anywhere and everywhere in an NRA home. When members sip their first cup of coffee in the morning, many do so from mugs
bearing the legend THE RIGHT OF THE PEOPLE TO KEEP AND BEAR

ARMS SHALL NOT BE INFRINGED. If they light up a cigarette with their coffee, chances are good they'll use a lighter adorned with those same words. And when they go out into the world, their pants may be held up with a belt whose buckle boldly proclaims: THE RIGHT OF THE PEOPLE TO KEEP AND BEAR ARMS SHALL NOT BE INFRINGED.

At first glance, these words appear to be a clear, seemingly unambiguous declaration protecting citizens from gun control. But the words on the side of the NRA headquarters (and on mugs, lighters, belt buckles, and so forth) are a conveniently edited version of the Second Amendment. The full text reads: *"A well-regulated militia, being necessary to the security of a free State,* the right of the people to keep and bear arms shall not be infringed" [emphasis added]. It is this first clause, the one the NRA goes to such great lengths to obscure, that is the source of much controversy.

When confronted with the missing clause the NRA doesn't miss a beat. "The militia clause doesn't change a thing," it maintains, because the "militia" the founding fathers had in mind included all white adult males. Today this category includes all adults, regardless of gender or race. By this reasoning, the Second Amendment protects the right of all adults to own the firearms of their choice. End of argument.

Gun-control advocates disagree with this interpretation, of course. They say that the word *militia* in the Second Amendment refers to what is now known as the National Guard—state military forces capable of protecting the states from an overpowerful central government. In legal terms, the Second Amendment, then, protects only a "collective right" to firearms, not an *individual* one.

Most legal scholars—liberal and conservative alike—find the "collective right" position more convincing than the NRA's interpretation. Erwin Griswold, a former dean of the Harvard Law School who served as solicitor general in the Nixon Administration, has called the right to bear arms the "Phantom Right." Former Supreme Court justice Lewis Powell also failed to find much to recommend the NRA's position, saying, "With respect to handguns . . . it is not easy to understand why the Second Amendment, or the notion of liberty, should be viewed as creating a right to own and carry a weapon that contributes so directly to the shocking number of murders in the United States." And the American Bar Association's official stand on the matter is even more cut-and-dried: "Neither the United States Constitution nor any of its amendments grants anyone the right to keep and bear arms."

The most outspoken opponent of the way the NRA has interpreted the Second Amendment is, surprisingly, the conservative former Supreme Court chief justice Warren Burger. Burger, a lifelong hunter and gun owner, has called the gun lobby's interpretation "one of the greatest pieces of fraud, I repeat the word *fraud*, on the American public by special interest groups that I have ever seen in my lifetime. . . . [The NRA has] misled the American people and they, I regret to say, they have had far too much influence on the Congress of the United States than as a citizen I would like to see."

U.S. courts have almost never ruled in the NRA's favor in Second Amendment cases, a pattern that held for the Morton Grove litigation. In December 1981, the Federal District Court for the Northern District of Illinois ruled that the Morton Grove ordinance did not violate either the United States or the Illinois constitutions. That verdict was upheld by the Seventh U.S. Circuit Court of Appeals in 1982, and was eventually affirmed by the highest court in the land when the Supreme Court declined to rule on the case in October 1983.

But despite these legal victories, the "domino effect" fretted about by the NRA and hoped for by gun-control advocates never happened. A few cities clustered around Morton Grove passed ordinances similar to the town's, but there was nothing like the wave of legislation both sides had predicted. Among major cities, San Francisco was the largest to pass a handgun ban. That ordinance, however, was later rejected by the California Court of Appeal.

The Morton Grove initiative also prompted a backlash among gun owners. In 1982, the town of Kennesaw, Georgia, passed its own gun bill—this one *requiring* all households to keep a gun and ammunition at the ready. When San Francisco passed a handgun ban, Kennesaw mayor Darvin Purdy wrote the mayor of San Francisco, asking her to send any confiscated weapons "so that we may issue them to our indigent citizens."

Even Congress got into the act, when Idaho senator Steven Symms introduced a Firearms Ownership Rights Act, which would have prohibited granting federal law enforcement assistance funds to local governments that ban handgun possession. The bill went nowhere.

Another effect of the handgun ban was that it spurred the NRA to give higher priority to an initiative it had started even before Morton Grove—a campaign to persuade state legislatures to pass laws pre-empting local gun ordinances.

At about the time the Morton Grove fight was taking place, an even larger legislative battle was brewing on the West Coast. Again, the fight concerned handguns, but this time the proposed restriction on these firearms was to cover the entire state of California. Proposition 15 would have banned the sale of new handguns, limiting the number of pistols and revolvers in the state to those owned on April 30, 1983. The measure would have allowed handguns to be exchanged, and, as an additional sop to gun owners, forbidden the state legislature from passing legislation to confiscate existing handguns or to restrict the sale of rifles or shotguns.

A citizens' group headed by public interest lawyer John Phillips and bankrolled largely by Max Palevsky, a liberal philanthropist, had planned an ambitious and savvy media campaign to win over the middle third of California voters, who pollsters reported were on the fence concerning the proposition at the outset. The NRA saw the California campaign as a must-win situation—far more important than the Morton Grove battle, due to the far greater number of people affected by a gun-control victory in California. To spearhead their efforts, the NRA hired veteran political consultant George Young, who had once worked for NRA supporter and U.S. senator James Mc-Clure.

Although the pro–Proposition 15 group, California Citizens Against Street Crime, had widespread support among large seg-ments of the state's population, California voters rejected the gun ban by the overwhelming margin of 63 to 37 percent in November 1982. An NRA spokesperson proclaimed the referendum "a great, great shot in the arm for us. . . . What this means is that when the public has a chance to vote on a poll about gun control, the vast majority will be on our side."

The opposition, of course, had a different interpretation of the California vote. They maintained the loss was due to money—or, to be more precise, to their own lack of dollars and the NRA's abundance of them. The gun lobby had outspent the opposition by at least two to one, using its money to buy all-important television advertisements during the closing days of the campaign, when the gun-control group was broke.

Over the next several years, no serious challenges to the NRA's growing power were mounted. Even the Morton Grove conflict had amounted to little more than a symbolic victory for gun-control advocates. And with the passage of the McClure-Volkmer Act in 1986, the gun group solidified its reputation as a near-invincible legislative powerhouse.

But by the later years of the decade, shifts in the ever-changing American political landscape began to spell trouble for the gun lobby. The cracks that had been slowly forming in the NRA's empire now showed themselves in what had been the NRA's most dependable turf: the legislative arena. Public outrage over rising gun violence and the erosion of support for the NRA among law enforcement officials led, in 1988, to the gun lobby's first major legislative defeat since its rise to power. Ironically, the NRA's reversal of fortune took place in Maryland, a state revered by many in the gun lobby as the site of its earliest political victory—the 1970 defeat of gun-control advocate Senator Joseph Tydings. While this was an oversimplification (there were several reasons for Tydings's loss), following that election, Maryland became for many NRA members what Plymouth Rock is to many Americans. But in 1988 the sacred ground of Maryland became the site of the NRA's Waterloo.

Once again, the target was the Saturday Night Special. In April 1988, a group of key Maryland state legislators, organized by state attorney general Joe Curran, pushed through a bill banning the manufacture and sale of these guns. The bill had appeared stalled in the Maryland Senate Judiciary Committee with no hope of getting out when, four days before the legislature's scheduled adjournment, and with several important bills still pending on the floor, Senate president Mike Miller blocked consideration of *all legislation* until the Saturday Night Special ban was voted out of committee. The tactic worked. The ban was voted out of the committee that afternoon and passed the Senate on the following day.

When Maryland's governor signed the bill into law a few weeks later, some 200 uniformed police officers stood at attention around him. There could have been no clearer indication of the magnitude of the NRA's mistake in alienating the police over the last few years than this blue line of support for the nation's first statewide ban on Saturday Night Specials. The day of the signing an NRA official was asked his organization's opinion of the new law. He had no comment.

Though stunned by the loss, the NRA quickly regained its composure. Opponents of the new ban began collecting the 34,000 signatures needed to put the law to a statewide referendum that fall. Petitions were posted in nearly all the state's gun shops and in a matter of weeks the requisite number of names had been gathered. Both sides began gearing up for what they knew would be a fierce and important battle. The NRA brought in its biggest hired gun; George Young, the hero of the lobby's 1982 California fight, was hired to direct the Maryland campaign. The NRA knew that more than just the fate of Maryland's law was at stake.

"If the people of Maryland reject the law," George Young told a reporter, "their vote will have national impact."

And on this one point, at least, the two sides agreed.

"Our triumph in Maryland will give us the momentum we need to enact stronger handgun laws in states across the country," declared an article in a pro-gun-control newsletter. "Already, other states are looking to Maryland as a model for legislation and as a textbook case on how to beat the NRA."

The fight was made even more portentous because the battlefield was in Congress's backyard. Senators and U.S. representatives followed the fight in Maryland closely, considering it a proving ground for national legislation.

With so much riding on the results of the referendum, it's not surprising that the fight turned unusually ugly in its waning days. The NRA-backed opposition sent canvassers into poor, mostly black neighborhoods of Baltimore, telling residents that the Saturday Night Special ban was a racist law that would disarm them while leaving higher-priced weapons in the hands of wealthy whites.

Gun-control advocates couldn't claim the moral high ground in the fight, however; their rhetoric was equally inflammatory. The director of the Baltimore Archdiocese's Justice and Peace Commission sent a letter to area priests urging them to speak out at mass for the law, referring to opponents of the bill as "apostles of violence." Catholic gun owners responded by dropping used ammunition cartridges into collection plates.

The NRA was kept busy passing its own hat to finance the increasingly expensive Maryland campaign. In one fund-raising letter, members were warned that if they didn't send in their dollars immediately, "the cancer" (the gun ban) "will spread" to their state next. The opposition, the letter continued, "have run hateful ads lying about the NRA on issue after issue . . . spreading their message attempting to weave American firearm owners into their nasty anti-gun web."

By the day of the referendum the NRA had spent a whopping $6.8 million on its bid to defeat the ban—nearly $1.50 for each man, woman, and child in the state of Maryland. The bill's proponents spent just $400,000 for their fight. But for once the NRA's monetary advantage didn't win the day. After the votes were tallied in the early morning hours of November 9, 1988, the nation's first statewide ban on Saturday Night Specials remained on the books; the law had been upheld by a margin of 58 percent to 42 percent.

Immediately, the "spin doctors" went to work.

"They just got blown out of the water," observed one gun-control activist gleefully. "And it happened on the front door of Congress."

The NRA's Richard Gardiner tried to back away from the lobby's earlier claims that the vote in Maryland had national significance. "Members of Congress are responsive to their own constituents," he explained, "not the constituents in Maryland."

But the defeat could not be minimized by fancy footwork. Maryland represented an unprecedented blow, and not only for the 49,000 NRA members who lived in that state. Whether the gun lobby was willing to recognize it or not, the loss was a clear indication that the time had passed when it could take easy legislative victories for granted.

Some experts, however, argue that the NRA's strength has always been "soft" by Washington standards. "Their power was never this omnipotent 'We-can-throw-around-as-many-bucks-as-anyone-in-creation' kind of power that someone like the American Medical Association *does* have," says an experienced House aide. She points out that the public rarely hears about the political battles of the most powerful Washington lobbies. "They find a way to make sure their issue stays noncontroversial. *That's* real power. But the NRA's fights are always public. That means they've already failed at some level."

And yet, it is also true that the NRA has usually come out on top—regardless of where these battles have been fought. Ultimately, that's what counts.

For many years, the NRA had also enjoyed a reputation of omnipotence in the electoral—as well as the legislative—ring.

Whenever a seasoned legislator would take a freshman colleague under his wing, one of the first bits of sage advice offered was, "Whatever you do, don't cross the NRA." It seems that everyone in Washington has a story of how this senator or that representative (always an incumbent who had otherwise voted with the gun lobby for years) had opposed the NRA just once—on a quite modest piece of legislation—and was then targeted for defeat by it. And these cautionary tales always have a similar ending—the errant legislator was inevitably clobbered at the next election. The NRA had become known as the Terminator of American politics. As journalist Bill Keller once put it, "The National Rifle Association wears the adjective 'powerful' like a bayonet, fixed to its name."

It was to avoid being skewered by that bayonet in the electoral ring that many politicians voted with the gun group in the legislative ring. On the same November night in 1988 that gun lovers were mourning their anomalous defeat in Maryland, they had much to celebrate in the electoral arena. There, the NRA had contributed to an impressive rout: the defeat of Michael Dukakis for the office of the presidency of the United States.

While few Americans had heard of Dukakis before the primary campaign, he was already well known in gun circles. As governor of Massachusetts, Dukakis had earned the undying enmity of the gun lobby because of his outspoken support for a variety of gun-control measures, starting with the proposed state ban on handguns in 1976. Standing on the steps of the Immaculate Conception Church in Malden, Massachusetts, in October of that year, Dukakis had launched the campaign for the ban with words that would be used against him in the presidential campaign more than a dozen years later.

"We must disarm society," the governor had told the small crowd gathered on the sidewalk in front of the church. "We must realize that violence only begets violence. Only when we ban handguns will we reduce violence. I hope we have a strong domestic effort to do so."

Dukakis added financial injury to insult when he added that although he *hoped* federal funds would be available to compensate gun owners for their confiscated weapons if the measure passed, he couldn't promise the money would be there for such a program. In that case, the governor explained, the weapons would be confiscated with no compensation.

Gun owners were outraged. Many felt they were being treated like second-class citizens simply because they owned firearms. A hint of the animosity—and real venom—provoked in the gun lobby by these actions was revealed when Michael Yacino, head of the Massachusetts Gun Owners Action League, and an NRA board member, referred to Dukakis as "that stinking Greek." The NRA was convinced that a Dukakis presidency would be its worst nightmare come true and it pulled out all the stops in its effort to defeat him.

Following the strategy developed for the Nixon campaign two decades earlier, the gun lobby focused its efforts on swaying southern Democrats. In the case of the 1988 election, the hot issues the NRA would exploit were gun control and crime, not race per se. The NRA leadership believed that if it could just make Dukakis's pro-gun-control record known to the mostly anti-gun-control southern electorate, voters would cross party lines and support George Bush. In an open letter to NRA members published in the *American Rifleman*, Bush tried to paint himself as a kindred spirit to the mostly Democratic NRA supporters (41 percent are Democrats, 21 percent are Republicans, and 38 percent are Independents).

"As a military veteran, hunter and a Life Member of the National Rifle Association," Bush wrote, "I've owned, used and respected firearms for most of my life. . . . You can support my opponent and give up the rights you cherish, or you can support me and maintain your right to keep and bear arms."

The NRA activated all of its considerable resources to get this message out, spending over $7 million on the bid to defeat Dukakis. It sent campaign materials (flyers, letters, bumper stickers) to the nation's 14,000 hunting clubs. It shelled out $2 million for radio spots in some thirty states. It mailed over twenty million pieces of literature in an attempt to reach a significant portion of the nation's seventy million gun owners. In Michigan, there were more NRA DEFEAT DUKAKIS bumper stickers than official Bush campaign bumper stickers.

The 1988 election was a campaign by sound bite, and the NRA offensive was no exception. While Dukakis had a long record of support for gun control, the NRA wanted a single short, pithy, and provocative statement by the governor on the issue that could be put before the electorate—a statement that NRA strategists hoped would make Democratic and Republican gun owners alike lunge for the Bush/ Quayle lever when they entered the polling booth on November 8.

The Dukakis quote they found was perfect. Wayne LaPierre (the head of the ILA in 1988) knew from the moment he heard it that his crew had struck pay dirt. It was concise and showed beyond any question how Dukakis viewed guns. The quote was potentially so damning that it became the source of intense conflict, raising threats of lawsuits on both sides in the frantic final days of Campaign '88.

According to the NRA, Dukakis uttered the words that would cause him so much trouble at an impromptu three-minute meeting with black activist Roy Innis, head of the Congress of Racial Equality (CORE), in the governor's office at about 10:00 A.M. on June 16, 1986. Innis, who is also a board member of the NRA, had addressed a rally held outside of the state capitol building that day in support of legislation to weaken existing gun-control laws. Because of his leadership position with the African-American community, Innis carried more weight with Dukakis than did other leaders of the "gun owners' rights" movement, and he was invited into the governor's office. Accompanying Innis was Michael Yacino, executive director of the Gun Owners Action League and also a board member of the NRA. Yacino took notes on the back of a manila envelope during the conversation.

"We hadn't been in there for very long when Dukakis just blurted it out," says Yacino. "He said, 'I don't believe in people owning guns, only police and military. And I'm going to do everything I can to disarm this state.' "

Yacino claims that the governor's aide, who was watching the gun activist taking notes, immediately leaned over and whispered something in the governor's ear.

"I assume it was 'Shut your mouth; you're talking too fast,' " says Yacino. The meeting ended a minute or so later.

"It was strange for [Dukakis] to blurt it out," says Yacino. "I was a full-time lobbyist. It wasn't like he didn't know who I was. He's an arrogant son of a gun. He *knew* I'd use it against him."

Which Yacino did almost immediately. A story containing the Dukakis quote appeared in the July 4, 1986, issue of *The New Gun Week* magazine, but caused no stir at the time. The same quote received a lot of attention, however, when it appeared over two years later in stark white letters nearly an inch high, printed against a jet-black background on the cover of *American Rifleman*. The NRA also gave the quote prominent play in advertisements in newspapers across the country, in national magazines, and in a score of radio spots.

"I'm going to do everything I can to disarm this state," Dukakis was quoted endlessly, followed by a dire warning: "Now he wants to disarm America."

Realizing the harm this campaign could do to their candidate, Dukakis's staff tried to take the offensive, denying that the governor had ever uttered the offending words and threatening to sue both the NRA and any radio stations that aired the charges. Daniel Taylor, the Dukakis campaign's general counsel, fired off a letter to Wayne LaPierre calling the ads "false and misleading" and adding that "the NRA and any newspapers, radio, or TV stations which republish this material must bear the legal consequences for publication of those statements."

The Dukakis campaign had played right into the NRA's hands. The threat of such a lawsuit generated even more publicity for the NRA's charges and at the same time made the Dukakis organization look like a bully.

"[The letter shows that Dukakis] has as much respect for the First Amendment right of free speech as he does for the Second Amendment's right to bear arms," intoned a pious Wayne LaPierre.

The NRA responded to the Dukakis campaign in the lingua franca of late twentieth-century America: It threatened to sue. "We believe that your effort to coerce radio stations to discontinue airing the Association's political speech constitutes a wrongful, unlawful, and tortious interference," wrote Washington lawyer Charles Cooper on behalf of the NRA. "We shall not hesitate to take legal action to prevent and/or redress such conduct should it continue."

And on October 26, two weeks before the presidential election, the NRA made good on its threat by filing suit against the Dukakis campaign in federal district court in Washington, D.C.

But the NRA was not particularly interested in a court victory. The real battle, as everyone knew, was fought in polling booths across the country on November 8, and in that all-important arena the NRA emerged victorious. While Dukakis was defeated for a variety of reasons, the gun issue was one of a handful of crucial issues that worked against him. He lost in Pennsylvania, for example, by a margin of less than 2 percent—in a state in which more than 2 percent of the electorate lives in households belonging to the NRA. Dukakis also lost in progun Texas, where, as NRA activist David Kopel pointed out, "No Democrat has ever won a presidential election in this century without carrying Texas. No presidential candidate who is antigun can carry Texas."

NRA leaders were jubilant about the Dukakis defeat. Even the loss in the Maryland handgun referendum—painful as it was—couldn't diminish that victory. Following the election, the gun lobby's reputation as the Terminator of opponents' campaigns was as solid as ever. Few now questioned the wisdom behind statements like the one made by Richard Davis of Virginia, who lost a bitterly contested Senate race after the NRA unleashed an eleventh-hour letter-writing campaign against him. "Don't take on the National Rifle Association," a woeful Davis warned other candidates. "It's bad news and you cannot win."

But Davis's advice was overstated. The truth is that the NRA's power in the electoral ring has always been exaggerated—its record is spotty, as a few knowledgeable opponents have been pointing out since 1982, when the National Coalition to Ban Handguns (NCBH) conducted a study of the NRA's record of financial contributions to candidates running for the U.S. House of Representatives. That analysis found that the NRA usually contributed to incumbents who were running in "safe" districts—those in which they won by at least a 10 percent margin. Of the 157 winning candidates backed by the gun lobby in 1982, 123 were from these easily won districts. In open races (where no incumbent ran), the NRA candidates lost in over half the cases.

Nor did the NRA electoral record improve over the decade—even though its reputation did. When Handgun Control, Inc., analyzed the NRA's record of support for Senate elections, it found a pattern very similar to the one in the NCBH study. Between 1983 and 1988, some eleven NRA-supported incumbents *lost* their Senate seats. At the same time, the gun lobby was unable to throw out of office a single pro-gun-control incumbent. And in open Senate races, NRA-supported candidates won less than half the time. All totaled, the NRA lost twenty-one Senate seats between 1983 and 1988, while picking up only five. In the 1990 elections, only one incumbent senator was defeated: Rudy Boschwitz of Minnesota. And, much to the NRA's embarrassment, Boschwitz had run with the gun lobby's backing. It is true that—in the words of an NRA spokesperson—"We punish our enemies and support our friends." But that punishment is evidently not so terrible, nor the support quite as valuable as many have long believed.

What, then, accounts for the persistence of the myth of the NRA's invincibility at the polls?

First, it should be remembered that the myth originated in Washington, D.C., a city made of equal parts marble and fantasy, where perception is reality's stand-in. It is also a city uniquely devoted to the veneration of Conventional Wisdom. Once an idea becomes entrenched inside the Beltway, it is not easily dislodged. The NRA's reputation persists, in large part, simply because Conventional Wisdom *says* the NRA is invincible.

As the NCBH's Michael Beard points out, through most of the 1980s the press had helped to perpetuate the myth by endlessly repeating, instead of critically examining, reports of the NRA's electoral strength.

"Have you ever seen a reference to them in any newspaper or magazine that doesn't say 'the all-powerful NRA'?" he asks. "The adjectives 'powerful' or 'rich' are always used with the NRA in any news story. That sticks in people's minds and is never questioned. We try to raise this issue, but nobody wants to deal with it. It's much more fun to talk about the powerful NRA, the mighty NRA."

It wasn't until the NRA's electoral weakness started showing up in the legislative arena in 1988 that the press—and congressional offices—began to scrutinize the gun lobby's record in supporting candidates. Almost overnight, the "all-powerful" NRA became known as the "washed-up" gun lobby, an analysis that was as flawed as the earlier assessment.

All this is not to say that there wasn't truth to the stories of NRA strength, but the lobby's real power at the polls has always been very site-specific, determined largely by the region in question. Both the South and the West, where gun ownership enjoys a strong tradition, are NRA strongholds. The organization's power gradually diminishes heading north and east through the Midwest, drops precipitously in the Mid-Atlantic states, and then becomes stronger in New England. But even within these regions the strength of the NRA varies widely, remaining roughly proportional to the size of the rural population. Candidates running in congressional districts with a preponderance of rural voters may very well be voted out of office if they support the most modest gun-control initiatives.

One congressional staffer says that he knows several representatives who would "love to vote against the NRA," but can't because the states they represent are too rural.

"It's like [former Arkansas senator] William Fulbright," he explains. "Back in the days of civil rights, he acknowledged he had to vote contrary to his conscience, or he would have been voted out of office. Some of these guys held their nose in 1986 and voted for McClure-Volkmer because they felt they *had* to."

A lobby doesn't need to be very sophisticated or resourceful when it has the kinds of numbers the NRA has traditionally enjoyed throughout much of rural America, points out Rachael Gorlin, legislative assistant to Oregon Democratic representative Les AuCoin. "The NRA has sixty-two thousand members in Oregon," she says. "You'd have to be a complete screw-up not to figure out how to turn that into something at the polls."

But where NRA membership dips—generally in large urban and suburban districts—so does its power. There is, therefore, more than a touch of hypocrisy to the lofty appeals made by urban legislators who urge their rural colleagues to, like them, "have some guts" and vote against the "all-powerful" NRA. Those representing mostly urban constituencies and who vote for gun control are just as guilty of doing the easy thing politically as are rural legislators who vote *against* such measures.

Since 1985, however, even rural politicians have been able to defy the gun lobby on occasion, thanks in part to increasing concern about crime and to the support shown for pro-gun-control measures by the police. For years, the NRA was able to paint gun issues in simple conservative-versus-liberal terms. Conservatives were against gun control and for tough law-and-order measures. Liberals were for gun control and were soft on crime. But the schism that developed between the NRA and police in the mid-1980s allowed politicians to come out for gun-control measures *and* appear tough on crime.

"This is the first time people have cover because they can stand up with law enforcement," explains Dennis Burke, an aide to Arizona senator Dennis DeConcini. "These guys *love* it. What's better than to be able to stand up next to your local sheriff—the man in blue? They just love to do a commercial with Dewey Stokes [president of the Fraternal Order of Police]. They didn't have that cover four or five years ago."

Longtime Ted Kennedy staffer Jerry Tinker agrees, adding that the advocates of gun control were quick to exploit this division. "They saw the schism as a way to break out of this mold that they were in," he explains. "Before, it was the 'wine-and-Brie' set on one side, and 'law-and-order' over on the other. Suddenly there was a confluence of interest with law enforcement. There's no doubt that it was a critical moment."

Changing American demographics also played a part in diminishing the NRA's influence in elections during the 1980s. A deteriorating farm economy and a more generalized rural decline prompted millions to leave the American countryside in hopes of finding work in the nation's cities. In 1985–86 alone, some 632,000 people left rural areas —the largest one-year population decline in half a century. This erosion of the NRA's rural constituency will lead to a further loss of political power for the gun group as congressional redistricting eliminates several rural seats in the coming years.

WHATEVER POWER THE NRA has enjoyed in either the legislative or the electoral arenas has always come from the neglected third ring containing the group's organizational abilities. Legislators think twice about opposing the gun lobby because they fear the NRA's proficiency at mobilizing its vaunted three million members, inciting them to call or write their representatives, or even drop in for a visit, and generally make life miserable for any elected official who falls off the progun wagon. It is for this reason that the National Rifle Association is considered the granddaddy of grass roots lobbying.

At the heart of the complex communication system that the NRA has developed over the years is the "legislative alert," usually a four-page letter mailed to members when gun-control bills appear on the horizon. The mailings, though expensive (a full national alert costs the group $500,000), almost always include a fund-raising appeal that results in donations that more than offset the cost of the letter. In the first half of 1990 alone, the NRA sent out 51.3 million pieces of mail, including:

| | |
|---|---|
| • 344 ILA legislative alerts | 3,547,649 pieces mailed |
| • 67 ILA fund-raisers | 14,292,561 pieces mailed |
| • 14 membership promotions | 19,537,294 pieces mailed |
| • 3 insurance promotions | 9,195,914 pieces mailed |
| • 15 miscellaneous mailings | 4,726,986 pieces mailed |

Just processing the address labels for all these mailings kept the NRA's computers humming for one solid week.

The NRA's Richard Gardiner estimates that in 1991 the lobby spent close to $10 million on these mailings. "That's our biggest expense," he says. "We spend it because our primary obligation is to keep our members notified as to what's going on. In real emergencies we can use telegrams. We can turn short messages around overnight. If we have a little more time we have forty-eight-hour mail, sent by computer to local post offices and then sent first-class and bulk mail."

Despite the name signed at the bottom of these alerts (usually the current head of the ILA), these letters are written chiefly by independent contractors who have developed a standard formula for their client. One leitmotif found in almost every NRA mailing could be called the "Armageddon Appeal." As NRA chief Ray Arnett told journalist Dan Moldea in a candid moment, "You keep any special interest group alive by nurturing the crisis atmosphere: 'Keep sending those cards and letters in. Keep sending money.' "

The NRA has managed to keep its members dedicated to the cause by proclaiming each and every battle (real, planned, and imagined) "the most important fight yet!" Here is how the Armageddon Appeal has looked in legislative alerts over a span of several years:

The bill . . . should sound as a call to arms for every American sportsman.

Unless you call, write, help organize and deliver the vote of your Congressman, I guarantee you that strict, total gun control will be imposed on all of America.

Our backs are against the wall. The anti-gunners are running wild in Washington, D.C. The atmosphere is the worst for American gun owners in over 20 years.

[This bill] is the worst gun legislation ever to be seriously considered on Capitol Hill. . . .

It's now or never for our gun rights.

[I]f you have already called, call again—or write. If you have written, write again—or call. But KEEP UP THE PRESSURE! You may not get another chance.

Now the stage is set for advancing their [gun-control advocates'] entire national anti-gun agenda. *Every gun owner in America better wake up to this harsh reality.*

If ever there was a time to stand together and stave off *every* attempt to deny us our constitutional rights, THIS IS IT!

You'd better make your calls now. There won't be time later.

*In the entire history of the NRA Institute, American gun owners have never before been under such constant, vicious attacks from the gun banners to which the truth means nothing* [emphasis in the original].

When asked about the purple prose contained in these warnings, an NRA spokesperson just shrugs. "We're pretty much subject to the constraints of the direct-mail industry," he says a bit sheepishly. "There are certain formulas that are always applied."

It's true that much advertising—political and commercial—depends on hyperbole to achieve its desired effect, but in its legislative alerts/fund-raisers, the NRA consistently sails right up to the boundary that separates mere exaggeration from pure fiction. In one case, in fact, the gun group appeared to leave the realm of fact entirely, entering the forbidden territory known as mail fraud.

The incident involved a fund-raising letter sent by the ILA to members and some nonmembers in New York State following the trial of Bernhard Goetz, a commuter convicted of a weapons charge for shooting four teenagers (with an unlicensed weapon) after the four had tried to rob Goetz in a New York City subway just before Christmas 1984. The Goetz case made headlines for weeks because tied up with it were so many of the pressing issues of the day: crime, race (Goetz was white, the teenagers black), the right of self-defense, and, most important to the NRA, gun control.

The NRA letter itself was a rather standard solicitation for funds, which could be mailed to the gun group with the donor signing the following statement:

DEAR WAYNE [LaPierre]:
I AGREE THAT EVERYDAY BERNIE GOETZ SPENDS IN JAIL IS A TRAVESTY TO THE BILL OF RIGHTS AND COMMON LAW PRINCIPLES OF SELF-DEFENSE THAT HAVE BEEN AC-CEPTED FOR CENTURIES.
I WANT TO HELP FREE BERNIE GOETZ AND MAKE THE WORD JUSTICE MEAN SOMETHING AGAIN!
ENCLOSED PLEASE FIND MY MOST GENEROUS CON-TRIBUTION TO HELP FUND OUR CAMPAIGN TO PARDON BERNIE GOETZ AND PROTECT YOUR GUN RIGHTS NATION-ALLY. ENCLOSED IS:
( ) $15    ( ) $25    ( ) $35    ( ) $50    ( ) $300    ( ) OTHER

There was nothing illegal about the appeal itself. The problem arose because of a short message appearing on the outside of the envelope. There, next to the address, the NRA had printed a single sentence, which it hoped would prompt the recipient to open the letter and send a contribution. The sentence read: "If you fail to respond to this letter you could face a jail term."

After examining the letter, the New York State Attorney General's office made a preliminary determination that "the NRA had engaged in misleading and possibly fraudulent solicitation practices while collecting funds from the public." For months, the NRA stonewalled the New York authorities in their investigation. When subpoenaed to turn over other mail solicitations for inspection, the NRA's lawyers refused, arguing that as an "undeniably patriotic" organization, the gun group was exempt under an obscure New York law from complying with the subpoena. Actually, the law cited by the NRA's counsel only allowed patriotic groups to forgo normal registration requirements for soliciting funds; it did not exempt them from following the law in other regards.

Assistant New York Attorney General Moira Morrissey notified the NRA's counsel of this fact in a letter, adding archly: "In light of your client's professed allegiance to the republic, we hope that they will reconsider their seeming disregard for a lawful inquiry by the government of one of its several states." After nearly two years of legal foot-dragging, the NRA finally complied with the order.

The case was settled when the NRA agreed in the future not to state that failure to open its letters could result in a jail term.

In addition to the Armageddon Appeal, another highly successful NRA mailing leitmotif is the Patriotic Imperative. Members are presented with a single, simple formula, repeated so many times that it is not even questioned: Support for the NRA equals support for America. Here, the NRA exposes its military origins. The organization was founded, after all, with the specific goal of improving the marksmanship of American militiamen. For decades, these close historic links with the military gave the gun group's claim to be "undeniably patriotic" some legitimacy. But with the transformation of the group, first to a hunting organization in the late 1940s and 1950s, and then to a gun lobby in the late 1970s, the Patriotic Imperative began to ring hollow. Still, the NRA is able to maintain this artifice by continually retelling American myths about guns, particularly about the supposed importance of firearms to the American national identity.

The author of an NRA-produced book used this technique as he waxed nostalgic for the good old days: "In every household, rich or poor, country or town, a gun of some kind stood in a convenient corner or hung on pegs over the fireplace." It was thanks to the "intimate familiarity with firearms" afforded by their omnipresence that America obtained its freedom from England, wrote this same author.

> During the War of Independence (the American Revolution) 2000 citizen-soldiers at Bunker Hill had shown to the world that they could stand up to a trained force of 2500 redcoats which included five of the crack foot regiments of the British Army, among them the famed

Welsh Fusiliers, the King's own regiment. A few days earlier the members of that stalwart American force had been farmers, mechanics, shipwrights, lawyers, students and teachers, shopkeepers and blacksmiths. The example shown by these citizen-soldiers hardened the resolution throughout the colonies and converted what might have been an abortive rebellion into a full-scale war for independence.

However, George Washington himself complained about the unreliability of these citizen-soldiers in battle, griping once that they were not "fit for the real business of fighting. I have found them useful," he said, "as light Parties to skirmish in the woods, but incapable of making or sustaining a serious attack."

According to historian Richard Hofstadter, the reputation of the citizen-soldier for being a great marksman was wholly undeserved, although widespread even at that time. It was technology, not talent, that made the colonists appear to be better shots than they actually were. Many citizen-soldiers used a firearm known as the Pennsylvania rifle. With its bored barrel giving bullets a straighter trajectory, the Pennsylvania rifle was far superior to the British Brown Bess, a musket accurate for only a few yards. It was this difference in technologies that more than anything led to success and, writes Hofstadter, "helped to instill in the American mind a conviction of the complete superiority of the armed yeoman to the military professionals of Europe."

The crafty General George Washington exploited this myth by having his regular troops dress as woodsmen. Washington knew that the British soldiers believed the stories about "crack-shot" frontiersmen and hoped to frighten the enemy soldiers by making them think they were facing an army of such citizen-soldiers.

While the NRA uses this myth to its advantage, one of its founders gave tacit recognition to the fact that Americans were not good marksmen when he explained his reasons for starting the gun group.

"I believed," wrote General George Wingate, "that if I could help to dispel the prevalent ignorance about rifle shooting I might bring our American Rifleman nearer in actuality to his legendary stature."

NRA members today are told that they are the modern incarnation of the citizen-soldier who fought to make the country free—a fight, members are reminded ceaselessly in the mailings, that continues to this day. Usually these historical allusions are made implicitly rather than stated outright, but sometimes the NRA makes the link quite baldly, as when it cautioned members in a mailing: "We cannot afford to let the anti-gun-for-any-reason crowd return to the tactics of King George's army, tactics that they used 200 years ago."

Another alert began: "Every freedom we have as Americans was won with the blood of sacrifice of our forefathers. . . . Before the Revolutionary War, the British tried to take away our firearms. We fought to keep those guns as well as win our freedom from British rule. . . . Since others fought to and died to guarantee our rights, it's our obligation to defend them."

In a pattern familiar to psychiatrists as well as advertising executives, the further the NRA has gotten from its military roots, the more it ballyhoos love of country. Today, when the group has virtually no links to the military, patriotic references and nationalistic icons festoon NRA literature like red-white-and-blue bunting at a Fourth of July picnic. (Many of the mailings, in fact, are printed in red and blue ink on white paper and so resemble bunting.) U.S. flags, five-pointed stars, drawings of colonial minutemen, and bald eagles clutching rifles are all commonly found on NRA mailings, informational pamphlets, and promotional literature. The organization's use of these symbols is so extensive that in the agreement with New York State in the mail fraud case, the attorney general's office felt it was necessary to include the following additional provision:

> The NRA shall not affix to any direct mail appeals or solicitations any seals, insignias or emblems that can be construed to belong to a government entity or might lead the recipient to believe that the solicitation was from a government entity.

Patriotic paraphernalia is everywhere in the NRA universe. When the organization created a major donor program, it called it "Madison's Eagles." A service in which members are telephoned within forty-eight hours when the NRA learns that a gun-control vote has been scheduled was dubbed the "Minuteman Alert Team." And all of this occurs in peacetime. Times of actual warfare afford the NRA a unique opportunity to exploit increased American patriotism, as the recent war with Iraq showed. As the fighting was just beginning in January

1991, the NRA mailed a fund-raising letter tying America's fight in the Persian Gulf to the NRA's battle against gun control in Congress:

> Your contribution at this time is an investment in freedom. It will serve as a shining symbol for our troops abroad that though there are those who would destroy freedom, the NRA and its membership support *all* the freedoms for which they fight. . . . What's more, our failure to act would be a terrible signal to send our soldiers in the Middle East. If we are willing to send them to defend freedom abroad, are we not willing to stand up and defend our own Constitutional rights here at home?

The letter closed with a P.S. informing recipients that for every $25 sustaining membership received from the appeal, one dollar would be used to mail a copy of one of the NRA's magazines (*American Hunter* or *American Rifleman*) to a soldier or sailor in the Gulf.

Another fund-raising letter, mailed soon after the first, hammered home the same Patriotic Imperative: "If hundreds of thousands of our brave young men and women can travel halfway across the world to fight for our freedoms," reasoned the text, "certainly we can back them up by supporting one of the greatest battles for freedom this Congress will ever see."

Included with this appeal was a small window decal that proclaimed: "OPERATION DESERT STORM—SUPPORT OUR TROOPS AND THEIR FAMILIES. PAID FOR BY THE NATIONAL RIFLE ASSOCIATION/ILA."

Of course, the NRA wasn't alone in commercializing the Gulf War. Companies large and small cynically reduced the heartfelt call "Support Our Troops" to a slogan for peddling beer, cars, and assorted widgets. But that is precisely the point. The NRA attempts to portray itself as a uniquely patriotic organization dedicated only to the common good of all Americans—instead of the typical consumer/manufacturing special interest group it actually is.

A logical corollary to the Patriotic Imperative formula is that those who *don't* support the NRA also don't support the USA, and the NRA has never been squeamish about questioning the loyalty of those who advocate gun-control measures. From reading its literature one might get the idea that disagreeing with the NRA is a treasonous offense.

"I'm not sure how you define these gun-banners," muses the NRA in one member letter. "Certainly, they cannot be called patriots."

In its most malignant form, this tactic takes the form of red-baiting the opposition. The NRA reminds members time and time again that "the first thing Communists do when they take over is register all guns."

"Imagine a knock on your door," begins one NRA letter. "It's government agents come to confiscate your guns.

"Are you in Gorbachev's Lithuania?

"Think again. It can happen right here."

And from another letter: "Government snooping and background checks on law-abiding citizens—This is America, not Leningrad!"

In the 1988 campaign, then–NRA president Joe Foss wasn't coy about red-baiting Michael Dukakis. "A nation under Michael Dukakis," wrote Foss, "promises to be one based on creeping socialism and unfettered federal power. . . . Dukakis themes contain a contempt for individualism reminiscent of the aristocracy our forefathers fled and that we all still fear today. . . . Michael Dukakis wants to sap the strength of this nation through his so-called social reforms."

The NRA created a small controversy in the advertising world in June 1989, when it created a full-page magazine and newspaper ad attempting to use, for promotional purposes, the Chinese Communist government's recent bloody crackdown on prodemocracy forces.

"The students of Beijing did not have a Second Amendment right to defend themselves when the soldiers came," reminded the NRA in the advertisement. "The right to own a firearm is a statement about freedom." Accompanying the text was a chilling photograph of a frightened Chinese student surrounded by soldiers. Some magazines and newspapers refused to publish the advertisement.

The NRA's policy of red-baiting those who oppose it at first appears ironic, given the gun lobby's own warnings about anti-red hysteria during the Cold War–McCarthy era. When fear of the red menace prompted calls for the registration of all weapons in 1951, the president of the NRA, Major General Merritt Edson, called for calmer thinking, declaring that registration "will contribute nothing to the defense of your community."

Even then, the organization was really worried about the narrow issue of gun control and not about the more general erosion of civil rights that occasioned the Cold War. Registration was bad, the NRA president warned, because the plan would "boomerang" as communists here at home obtained copies of the registration lists.

"The accepted fifth column technique calls for raids on the homes of citizens who possess firearms," Edson explained. "Such raids may be in the form of burglaries, in order more adequately to arm the fifth column group while at the same time reducing the ability of the citizens of the community to defend themselves."

By welding the Patriotic Imperative to the Armageddon Appeal, the NRA created a powerful rhetorical device for recruiting new members and activating present ones; over the years, membership in the gun group swelled to almost three million. But using such techniques also created problems for the lobby. It produced a climate of pseudo-patriotic paranoia that easily gets out of hand, leading to the kinds of vicious attacks on opponents that hurt the lobby's credibility and result in a backlash. In addition, such rhetoric may have been well suited to the Cold War era and to the neo–Cold War period that occasioned the early years of the Reagan presidency—not coincidentally, the time of the NRA's greatest growth—but an organization that still red-baits its opposition after the collapse of communism appears foolish and not a little delusional.

By the end of the 1980s the NRA was faltering in all three rings. Legislatively, while the organization was still strong, the defeat in Maryland had proved that it was not invincible and gave hope to pro-gun-control forces. In the electoral ring, a few people had begun to notice what had long been true—that, here too, the NRA was not the colossus it claimed to be.

And in the final ring, the membership—the power base on which all other NRA functions were dependent—began to dwindle. The trend started as a slowing of the phenomenal growth that characterized the early 1980s, and after a period of stagnation, the group started shrinking. The trickle quickly turned into a hemorrhage: The organization that boasted close to 3 million members in early 1989 had only 2.3 million in 1991.

Clearly, the NRA was now foundering on hard times. The gun group had lost the support of law enforcement, and its blustering "you're-either-with-us-or-agin-us" attitude had also alienated many politicians, even some longtime friends. Alarmed by violent crime,

Americans were now demanding some modest form of gun control. Gun-control advocates were themselves becoming better organized. And now large numbers of members were jumping ship.

Another organization, finding itself in a similarly besieged position, might have made modifications in policies or, at the very least, in tactics, compromising sometimes where necessary. But the NRA could not follow this path even if its leaders had wanted to. The group had built its reputation on a refusal to compromise and that inflexibility had become institutionalized. A kinder and gentler NRA was out of the question. Besides, NRA leaders didn't feel that they, or the policies or tactics they had developed, were responsible for the group's problems. No, they knew very well who was to blame for the difficulties: their implacable enemies outside the group, and the traitors within.

# 7

# ENEMIES WITHIN
# AND WITHOUT

*Yes I'm proud to say*
*I'm the NRA*
*Born in America*
*And this is where I plan to stay.*

The song boomed over the massive public-address system at the San Antonio Convention Center's North Banquet Hall as the members filed slowly in, many of them bleary-eyed, some cringing visibly at the loud music, still feeling the aftereffects of a night spent renewing old friendships with gun lovers from around the country, swapping hunting tales over glasses of Jim Beam, or—in deference to local tradition—pitchers of sangria.

*Yes I'm the NRA*
*Ask me why, and I'll say*
*It's a God-given freedom,*
    *a God-given right*
*A God-given duty . . .*
    *AND WORTH THE FIGHT.*

*I'm the NRA.*
*I'm the NRA.*

Some 20,000 NRA members and spouses had made the trip to San Antonio in April 1991 for the organization's annual convention, but no more than a few thousand showed up for this business meeting on a dazzlingly bright Saturday morning.

> *And I'll be there to defend your right*
> *To protect your family and home,*
> *And I'll be there to train your kids*
> *About safety and the sportsman's code. . . .*
> *But I'll throw the book at all the crooks*
> *Who abuse these precious rights,*
> *And I'll stand and cheer—and shed a tear—*
> *When they hoist those Stars and Stripes.*

The music was switched off when the hall was nearly filled. Dick Riley, a former gun shop owner and the current NRA president, a man who bore more than a passing resemblance to North Carolina senator Jesse Helms—both physically and politically—took his place at the microphone at the front of the hall and, with a brisk and business-like manner (a by-product of his having served two terms in the New Hampshire state senate) attempted to call the meeting to order.

*Bam. Bam. Bam.*

Riley struck the table with a wooden gavel and waited impatiently for the room to quiet down.

*Bam-bam-bam.*

"This meeting *will* come to order," Riley called out, his flat Yankee accent sounding strange and a little grating to members whose ears had already begun to grow accustomed to the more melodious drawl native to the region.

Officials of the NRA had known exactly what they were doing when they selected San Antonio as the conference site. They had chosen this south Texas boomtown not simply because it offered first-class hotel accommodations and an exhibition hall capable of housing one of the largest gun shows in the nation—although those factors surely worked in San Antonio's favor. Nor was the deciding factor the charming jumble of outdoor restaurants and stylish shops clustered along the banks of the slow-moving San Antonio River as it wound through the city center, a popular area known as the River Walk.

The real reason for choosing San Antonio had more to do with myth than practicality, for the journey to San Antonio was intended to be a sort of pilgrimage for NRA members. Right in the heart of the city center, shouting distance from the convention site, was a grove of ancient oak trees, a world apart from the surrounding urban hubbub. The dusty plot of ground encompassing no more than an acre or two was the touchstone of all those American values the gun group liked to claim as its own: an uncompromising attitude, unabashed love for this country, and a readiness to fight her enemies—no matter what the odds.

For here was the Alamo, the American shrine where 155 years earlier Jim Bowie, Davy Crockett, and some 140 others had fought to the death rather than surrender to Santa Anna's much larger Mexican army. Only days before the enemy's final assault, William Travis, the young lieutenant in charge at the Alamo, managed to get a letter out, addressed to "the People of Texas and All Americans in the World." Travis asked for reinforcements, although he knew none were likely to come.

"I shall never surrender or retreat," he promised. "If this call is neglected, I am determined to sustain myself as long as possible & die like a soldier who never forgets what is due his honor & that of his country. VICTORY or DEATH."

Thirteen days later the Alamo fell, and just as Travis had pledged, the defenders—to a man—died fighting.

The NRA felt this was the perfect place to rally the troops. Like the men trapped inside the Alamo a century and a half earlier, the NRA felt besieged by hostile forces. Its leaders had hoped that some of the courage of those earlier patriots would rub off on members who would head home on Monday, their resolves stiffened and spirits renewed by cries of "Remember the Alamo!"

The timing of the convention was as good as the location. Most Americans were still exuberant about the recent military victory over Iraq in Operation Desert Storm. With that success came renewed support for the military—support the NRA hoped to steer its way, linking the fight in the desert to the battle at home over gun control.

Indeed, on the night before the Saturday meeting, the NRA hosted a gala "Celebration of the Bicentennial of the Bill of Rights," which, from the endless stream of references to the recent war, could have been more accurately named the "Victory in the Gulf Party."

At a little before 6:00 P.M., when the event was set to start, a phalanx of grave-faced Cub Scouts took up positions along an area near the front of the convention hall. When a middle-aged woman whose name tag identified her as a member from Michigan tried to enter this zone, a sandy-haired scout politely but firmly informed her: "Ah'm sorry, ma'am, but this section is reserved fer NRA board members an' thay'er families."

Suspended from the ceiling at the front of the hall was a giant American flag (at least as large as those found above many car dealerships), flanked by immense clusters of red-white-and-blue balloons. In front of the giant flag, and only slightly smaller than it, stood a replica of the Statue of Liberty. Toward the edges of the cavernous hall hung enormous movie screens that provided the crowd toward the back with a better view of the festivities.

While there were some young people in the room (in addition to the Cub Scouts) most celebrants were in their sixties and seventies. These were die-hard NRA members, the ones who were given to saying things like, "If you want to take my guns, you'll have to pry them from my cold, dead fingers." Several of them, in fact, had apparently come to the celebration armed. Some of the men wore hip pouches on their belts, bags that might have contained a pipe and tobacco; but given their resemblance to holsters advertised in the current issues of *Guns and Ammo* and *Shooting Times*, the safe money said these men were packing heat.

The celebration opened with a video montage in which slow-motion scenes of U.S. troops returning home triumphant from the Gulf were intercut with images of ordinary Americans holding guns. Black men with shotguns. White women with revolvers. Asian and Caucasian men with target pistols. Children of all races cradling BB guns or small 22s.

This film was followed by a marching performance by the University of Texas Army ROTC color guard; the Pledge of Allegiance, led by a local 4-H teenager; and "The Star-Spangled Banner," accompanied on the movie screens by flashing patriotic images. The audience applauded wildly when (on the line "the bombs bursting in air") there appeared film of Patriot missiles ramming incoming Scuds over Riyadh, showering the night sky with incandescent debris that looked like fireworks on the Fourth of July.

After the movie ended, and with the audience properly warmed up, Wayne LaPierre, head of the ILA, was introduced to cheers.

"What a night . . ." LaPierre declared in a voice amplified by the PA system so that it echoed around the hall like a roll of thunder, pausing dramatically before completing the thought: ". . . for patriots!" The crowd roared back in delight.

"You know, while I was watching that magnificent film, I thought of an old saying." Pointing to the giant flag behind him, LaPierre cried out: "These colors don't run!" Once again, the crowd hollered its agreement.

Then LaPierre continued, as if the thought had just struck him, as though he were speaking now off the top of his head and not off the TelePrompTers that flanked him: "And the NRA does not run!"

More cheers.

But LaPierre was not the main act. A special guest was waiting backstage, LaPierre told the crowd, an old friend of the NRA, a true patriot and a great American. And suddenly, there he was, standing alone in the spotlight, waving energetically like a prizefighter entering the ring: Charlton Heston.

The crowd was instantly on its feet, cheering the movie star long associated with the National Rifle Association and conservative causes.

"I'm proud to be among friends," Heston told the crowd in his distinctive clipped voice, the voice of Moses and Ben Hur. Speaking over a lush musical background, Heston delivered a patriotic recitation, interweaving personal recollections about growing up in the "dark, deep woods" of Michigan ("Oh, the thrill I felt when a Civil War veteran let me heft his old campaign rifle") with broad historical themes ("The American settlers planted freedom and liberty was the harvest"). Heston concluded his short address by saying that after serving proudly in World War II, he had returned home with his service revolver.

Almost shouting to be heard over the music that had been slowly swelling throughout his speech, Heston declared, "If I give up that gun, I break my bond with every American who rode into the west wind."

With a quick wave to the adoring crowd, the movie star left the stage to another standing ovation. Then, as a choir of children walked out onto the darkened stage, each one carrying a lighted candle, the army of Cub Scouts dashed around the room handing out small American flags affixed to tiny dowels. Gathered on the stage for the last performance of the night, the children, who were of all ages and races, lip-synched to a recording of "America the Beautiful."

After the event, hundreds of happy NRA members burst from the hall and poured down a flight of stairs—the small American flags waving above their heads all the while like a swarm of red-white-and-blue butterflies—to where white-gloved attendants were waiting to serve them hot dogs and beer at a party hosted by the Philip Morris tobacco company.

The mood was quite different at the members' meeting the next morning, a disparity apparent in Dick Riley's opening remarks.

These were troubling times for gun owners, admitted Riley. Like the defenders of the Alamo, decent, law-abiding shooters were under siege from hostile forces. The NRA faced many opponents, said Riley. "Without a doubt," he declared, "the most formidable adversary" was the American news media.

Riley's charge was just the first of many unleashed against the media throughout the meeting. Robert Corbin, second vice president, and a former state attorney general from Arizona, likened the media to Santa Anna's army outside the Alamo 155 years before. "They paint us as hoodlums, hoods, the KKK!" cried Corbin in a fire-and-brimstone speech that was interrupted several times by applause and calls of "That's right!"

"Where is the truth, where is the fairness in the media?" Corbin asked rhetorically.

"Because of the media attacks, even some of our *own members* are starting to believe in a negative version of the NRA," complained Gary Anderson, NRA vice president for general operations. "Have the media talked about police training, hunting, safety, legislative victories? No, they play up the negatives."

It was a complaint heard throughout the convention: The media is the enemy; the press is to blame for our problems. The theme was not new for the NRA; press bias had long been attacked by NRA officials. When he testified before Congress in 1975, Harlon Carter argued that "people in the media . . . seem to blame crime on everything in our society except the criminal and want to punish anyone and anything except the criminals."

In one sense, the NRA's antipathy for the press was rooted in the group's earliest days. When he helped found the National Rifle Association, William Conant Church was editor of a national military newspaper begun during the Civil War to counter the effects of the "disloyal" press. But as long as the NRA dealt primarily with hunters' education and training, the modern gun group enjoyed good relations with the press. As calls for gun control grew and the NRA entered the political arena in force, however, these relations grew strained.

In the drive for gun control that followed the wave of political assassinations of the 1960s, the NRA lashed out against the press, both for running hard-hitting pro-gun-control advertisements as well as for its alleged negative portrayals of gun owners. Specifically, the gun group objected to a series of six advertisements created and offered to the press at no charge by a Chicago agency, North Advertising Inc. The ads were indeed emotionally charged, not surprising given that they were created only months after the assassinations of Martin Luther King, Jr., and Robert Kennedy and just five years after the killing of President John Kennedy.

"Write your Senator [supporting gun control]," implored one of the advertisements, "while you still have a Senator."

The NRA called the advertisements part of "an enormous, concerted and deliberate campaign . . . to downgrade and demoralize" the gun group. Striking back in the pages of American Rifleman, the NRA published a picture of the North Advertising employees who had created the ads, as well as a list of several of the agency's largest clients.

Also in the NRA's magazine, there appeared at the same time a study conducted by an NRA member who alleged that over a two-year period, 60 percent of the references to the NRA and to guns appearing in The New York Times were negative. The member charged that the press "contributes much more to the current violence, crime and lawlessness than any lack of firearms registration laws."

Even the popular "I'm the NRA" advertising campaign used so effectively from 1982 to 1989 became a source of animosity between the NRA and the press. While the ads ran in some forty-five magazines during those years, a few publications refused to print them. *Modern Maturity, Better Homes and Gardens, Audubon, Ebony,* and *McCall's* rejected the ads outright. *Reader's Digest* and *Southern Living* accepted the ads only when the pictures showed individuals holding long guns.

The NRA also listed some forty-four television stations across the country that refused to run its commercials.

"They rejected them over the phone," says an obviously peeved spokesperson for Ackerman McQueen, the NRA's affiliated advertising agency. "We always ask for a letter explaining their reasons, but they never send one. We think the whole thing is very unfair."

By the late 1980s, the NRA considered the media to be public enemy number one. Media bashing had, over the years, become a staple theme in NRA legislative alerts and fund-raising letters:

> The national press bosses and the anti-gun politicians know they can't beat us in a fair fight.
>
> I am sick and tired of the national press beating up on responsible American gun owners.
>
> . . . the elitist media tycoons who live behind private security systems and have armed guards. . . . These yellow journalists would like to turn the United States and its citizens into meek victims, passive and unarmed, where only criminals and the government own guns!
>
> The national media sitting in their ivory towers in the heart of New York City simply do not care about gun and hunting rights and just how important they are to you, and me, and tens of millions of law-abiding citizens throughout America.
>
> The NRA is the only force standing between the anti-gun media, their political allies, and your gun rights.

In his January 1990 *American Rifleman* column, Warren Cassidy blasted "the major media's single-minded hatred of the NRA and gun owners."

Biased editors and programmers sought to destroy the NRA by repeating ad nauseam that we had lost our way, reached our zenith and
were doomed to failure as a political force. . . . The national news
media in general seems determined to defeat us. Destroying Second
Amendment freedom appears second only to covering demands for
increased freedom abroad. What bitter irony!

This antipress sentiment is always close to the surface in interac-
tions between the media and NRA officials. Even as he was sitting
down for an interview, NRA leader Richard Gardiner warily eyed the
journalist before him. "Look," Gardiner said in a testy voice, "all we
ask, though we never get it, is that you just tell the truth. We're
looking for one honest reporter. So far there aren't any. But I suppose
there must be one somewhere."

Michael Isikoff doesn't look like anyone's idea of an "elite media
tycoon." Seated at a desk in the sprawling fifth-floor newsroom of *The
Washington Post*, Isikoff looks like a typically stressed-out reporter at
the weary end of the day. His longish black hair is disheveled; the tail
of his rumpled blue-striped shirt hangs out. Isikoff sips coffee from a
paper cup as he talks, his eyes bloodshot behind large, dark-framed
glasses. Hired by the *Post* in 1981, Isikoff has covered the criminal
justice beat since 1988. It is a large territory that emphasizes drugs,
guns, violence—and the National Rifle Association. Isikoff doesn't take
the NRA's attacks on the media personally, or even very seriously.

"The media bashing is for the membership's sake," he says. "Certainly the editorial positions are against them—ours and *The New York
Times'*. The NRA is so used to being maligned there that they expect
articles that aren't sympathetic to their point of view. I think the
editors around here do strive to make the articles balanced. They
sometimes bend over backwards to present the NRA's side."

To say that the *Post's* editorial positions are against the NRA is like
saying that Ronald Reagan disliked Communists. On few if any other
issues does the *Post* so regularly and vehemently editorialize as on the
issue of gun control. In early 1965, the newspaper ran pro-gun-control
editorials on seventy-seven consecutive days. Today, the target of
these editorials is, more often than not, the National Rifle Association
itself.

But, as Isikoff explains, there is almost always a wide divergence between a paper's editorial stance on issues and how it reports on those same issues in its news pages. The NRA counters that the *Post's* bias against guns extends to the news sections of the paper.

Isikoff also has another explanation for the NRA's hostility toward the press. "You've got to remember one thing. Public opinion is overwhelmingly against the NRA's views," he explains. "The NRA would like issues framed in a way that's favorable to *their* position, but the media generally represents the mainstream. Groups outside the mainstream will always complain that their side isn't 'represented' adequately. We [the *Post*] are not left-wing revolutionaries or right-wing kooks."

Certainly the existence of an "antigun media elite" plotting the demise of the NRA is a creation of the NRA public relations department, a fiction used to create the kind of crisis atmosphere that helps fund-raising and membership drives. But there is an important element of truth underlying some of the gun group's charges.

Most reporters, editors, and TV producers are notoriously ill informed about firearms. It is common, for example, for news reports to use the terms *automatic* and *semiautomatic* interchangeably when discussing weapons—although the distinction between the two is crucial to the debate over gun control. The field of firearms is, perhaps, the only area in which a reporter's ignorance is not only not a cause for shame but, on the contrary, often appears to be a source of genuine pride.

This ignorance, however, is not limited to the press. As American society has become more urban, fewer professionals—including journalists—are raised and live in areas where people hunt. These city dwellers are neither familiar with firearms nor, all too often, respectful of those who are. To many journalists, just as to most other urban professionals, all gun enthusiasts are kooks unless proven otherwise. Still, the important schism here is not so much between the media and gun owners as it is between urban and rural experience and values. To the average city resident, a gun is an instrument of crime and mayhem. To the average rural citizen, a gun is both the basis of a pleasurable sport and, for farmers and ranchers, a necessary tool of the trade. To them, a gun is no different, in principle, than a hammer or a posthole digger.

The leaders of the NRA, however, pretend that their differences are primarily with the media. What group, after all, admits that it is out of step with mainstream America? Then the NRA magnifies the contradictions ("These yellow journalists would like to turn the United States and its citizens into meek victims"), creating a convenient and traitorous scapegoat for its problems.

Some NRA leaders also criticize the entertainment media for glamorizing gun violence. Shoot-'em-up TV police shows and Rambo movies with their orgies of firepower all give responsible gun users a bad image, complains the NRA.

"It's not that Hollywood has made a conscious effort to be antigun," explains Richard Gardiner, the ILA director of state and local affairs. "Most of it is that they want to be entertaining and violence sells movies."

Gardiner singles out the TV show "Miami Vice" for special criticism. "That one show has done us more harm than anything else," he says. "It has nothing whatsoever to do with reality. People believe that if you go to Miami, there is a good likelihood that you'll be machine-gunned. It's not true, but it's great entertainment. I mean, I even watch the show."

Yet, it is hard to take NRA complaints about Hollywood very seriously. They have never threatened action against sponsors of ultraviolent shows, as they have repeatedly done in cases of programs and documentaries that call for gun control. And while Gardiner says "Miami Vice" is the worst offender in presenting a poor image of guns and gun enthusiasts, that hasn't stopped the gun lobby from using Michael Talbott, one of the show's co-stars, as a spokesperson for NRA events.

But if the NRA has created a bogeyman in the form of an "antigun media elite," there *is* a real outside threat to the gun lobby's interests, one that had been growing, almost imperceptibly, for several years.

After a September 1981 speech before the New York State Conservation Council, Harlon Carter was asked about the "gun-control movement." The NRA chief just smiled.

"There is no gun-control movement worthy of mention," he said. "There are a few isolated situations, but no large movement of people."

Practically speaking, Carter was right. The National Coalition to Ban Handguns (NCBH) was just a pesky gadfly, buzzing irritatingly around the behemoth National Rifle Association, but by and large posing little threat to the gun lobby's interests. There was one other small group, Handgun Control, Inc., which was less sweeping in its advocacy of gun control. Rather than calling for a ban on all handguns, HCI advocated a variety of measures, such as instituting a federal waiting period for handgun purchases, and a ban on Saturday Night Specials. HCI was different from NCBH and many other ad hoc gun-control committees in that it was, from the start, an organization of conservative Republicans. The group was formed in the early 1970s (under the name National Council to Control Handguns) and headed by Ed Welles, a retired CIA agent. In 1976 Pete Shields became the group's executive director. Shields had been a successful executive with E I. du Pont de Nemours and Company—and a conservative Republican—when he received a phone call in the middle of the night on April 16, 1974, telling him that his twenty-three-year-old son, Nick, had been shot to death, the latest victim in a string of San Francisco murders dubbed the "Zebra killings."

The senseless killing changed Pete Shields's life. He began reading everything he could about the issue of gun control, and in early 1975 he learned of HCI's existence; in May he took a year-and-a-half's leave of absence to work for the organization, and when that time was up, he took early retirement to work for gun control full-time.

Despite the group's modest approach to gun control, it remained small and not very influential, especially when compared to the mammoth NRA. Numbers and/or dollars equal power in Washington, and HCI had few of either. Harlon Carter had every reason to be confident when he dismissed the idea of a powerful gun-control movement.

But on March 30, 1981, a mentally disturbed young man named John Hinckley, Jr., changed the equation. On that rainy Monday afternoon, Hinckley stood as part of a crowd gathered outside the Washington Hilton Hill Hotel, waiting for President Ronald Reagan to appear after delivering a lunchtime address to a convention of the Building and Construction Tradesmen. At twenty-five, Hinckley already had a long history of mental illness. He had arrived in Washington by bus the day before, carrying a Saturday Night Special, a .22-caliber RG 14 Rohm revolver he had purchased at a Dallas, Texas, pawnshop for $29.

For years, Hinckley had nursed an obsession with the actress Jodie

Foster, writing her desperate letters, calling her on the phone at night, even leaving poems and notes on her doorstep in New Haven, Connecticut (where she was a student at Yale). But Foster wanted nothing to do with Hinckley. At some point, Hinckley figured out a surefire way to impress her, if not completely win her over: He would assassinate the president of the United States.

Hinckley first stalked President Jimmy Carter, but didn't have the nerve to put his plan into operation when he had the opportunity. Several months later, after Ronald Reagan had replaced Carter as president, Hinckley arrived in Washington, hoping to catch a bus to New Haven and once more attempt to woo Foster. But while reading the March 30 edition of the *Washington Star* in his hotel room, an item on page 3 caught his eye: President Reagan would be addressing a convention not far from Hinckley's hotel. It was the perfect opportunity.

Hinckley loaded his gun with six Devastator bullets, rounds designed to explode on impact. Then he wrote a letter to Foster, asking her to "please look into your heart and at least give me the chance with this historical deed to gain your respect and love." He placed the gun in the right-hand pocket of his brown tweed sport coat and caught a cab to the Hilton.

At 2:27, the luncheon address delivered, the president's entourage exited the hotel's VIP door and headed for the waiting limousine. Reagan was just feet from the small group of press and passersby in which Hinckley was standing when the deranged man acted. Hinckley pulled out his gun and dropped into a low combat position—bent at the knees, the revolver in his right hand, his left hand cradling the right—and began firing. He was wrestled to the ground in less than two seconds, but that was all the time he had needed. In 1.8 seconds Hinckley had managed to empty the revolver.

Only one of the shots hit President Reagan, and that one by chance, ricocheting off the back of the car and striking him in the chest. The bullet lodged inches from the president's heart. Luckily, the Devastator had failed to explode. Two of the other bullets had hit no one. One bullet had struck Washington, D.C., policeman Thomas Delahanty in the back. Secret Service agent Timothy McCarthy had been hit in the chest, the bullet puncturing his liver and one lung.

The most seriously wounded was James Brady, the president's

forty-year-old press secretary. The bullet that struck him was the only one of the Devastators to work as intended. It hit him in the forehead, just above the left eyebrow, and exploded into twenty to thirty whirling metal fragments that spun into the flesh around his nose and eye. A few of the fragments went deep into his brain. In nine out of ten cases, a head wound like Brady's is fatal. In fact, when the press secretary was first wheeled into the emergency room, doctors there did not expect him to survive. But Jim Brady was lucky; he survived because he was rushed to the George Washington University Medical Center, where he was being treated less than ten minutes after the shooting. Brady's life, however, would never be the same.

Besides the physical trauma to brain tissue caused by the bullet fragments, the Devastator had severed two important arteries that deliver oxygen-rich blood to the brain. The effects of these brain injuries were far-reaching, although their very severity at first kept Brady from realizing how permanent the damage was. The brain's ability to reflect on itself, to take an inventory of its own skills, is often impaired in head injury cases. Two weeks after the shooting, Brady was on the phone to the White House, telling officials there that he would soon be returning to work. It took several months for him to realize just how gravely injured he was.

Brady would never return to his position at the White House, although he retained the title to the job and eventually would go in to his office for a few hours each week. He would need to use a wheelchair. He would spend hours every day in excruciatingly painful physical therapy sessions trying to restore his limbs to partial use. He had to relearn simple tasks, such as eating and shaving. For months he battled life-threatening health crises precipitated by the shooting. His memory was erratic, communication difficult. The brain injury also resulted in a condition called perseveration, which caused Brady to repeat things, verbally and physically. When asked a question, Brady might answer, "Yes. Yes. Yes. Yes . . ." until someone stopped him. Or it might cause him to continue scratching at an itch for hours.

The injury also diminished Brady's ability to distinguish between appropriate and inappropriate behavior, although it is uncertain to what degree, since even before the shooting Jim Brady was notorious for this "condition." This was, in part, what endeared him to the Washington press corps, despite the fact that Brady had only been on the job for a few months when he was shot. One infamous example of Jim Brady's inclination to play the enfant terrible occurred in 1979 when he was still press secretary to presidential candidate Ronald Reagan. At the time, many reporters were still snickering over Governor Reagan's recent statement that most air pollution was caused by trees, and not human activity.

A few days later, the campaign plane, "Leadership '80," was flying over a forest fire while heading to a rally. Suddenly, Brady ran into the press area and pointed out the windows. "See, killer trees! Killer trees!" he cried.

After the story appeared in print, some of the senior men surrounding the future president were not amused and Brady was reprimanded. But Brady was irrepressible. A few months later, he closed the press conference announcing his appointment as the president's press secretary with a credible imitation of Richard Nixon: head down, arms held aloft, hands arranged in the V sign, and insisting "I am *not* a crook! I am *not* a crook!"

To all outward appearances, Jim's wife, the former Sarah Kemp, is her husband's exact opposite. Both of the Bradys are tall, but Jim is big-boned, with a cherubic face and a nose only slightly smaller than W. C. Fields's. Everything about Sarah Brady is angular: Her face is long and narrow, dominated by an equally long and thin nose and a fetchingly toothy smile. But the two are quite similar in other ways. The media had painted Sarah Brady as being prim and proper, a bit of a prig even, perhaps because that makes for an interesting contrast to her outlandish husband. But while Sarah does have her conservative side, she is no Victorian. She is a straight-talker, passionate yet often humorous, possessing a large, bass laugh and a vocabulary that might not be as earthy as her husband's but that would still make a debutante blush. And at the end of a hard day, there is nothing she enjoys more than a cold beer and a cigarette. The two are, in fact, a very well matched couple. They met in 1970 in Washington, D.C., at a Republican party function that Sarah had helped organize, and were married two years later.

Jim's shooting was not the first time Sarah's life had been bruised by gun violence. In 1971, a good friend and colleague named Janet Dent was shot and killed by her boyfriend. "They were evidently having an argument," recalls Sarah. "Janet said, 'George, if you feel that way, why don't you shoot me?' He picked up the handgun he had given her for self-protection and shot her."

She sighs at the painful memory. "The second he shot her, he realized what he had done and called the police. It was a tragedy, a moment of anger."

In the months and years immediately following Jim's shooting, Sarah Brady was kept busy just caring for her husband and their two-year-old son, Scott. At that time, the issue of gun control was, she says, the furthest thing from her mind.

Then, in the fall of 1982, one of the organizers of Proposition 15 (the California ban on the sale of new handguns) contacted Sarah, asking her to speak out in favor of the measure. She considered the proposal, which she favored, but decided that as the wife of President Reagan's press secretary it would be inappropriate for her to publicly support the measure. Reagan was, after all, against Proposition 15.

"Going into his home state in an election year? It just wasn't my place," she says. "And I thought I'd just sound like an aggrieved victim's wife. I *certainly* didn't want that."

She told the organizers, "Sorry," and didn't think about gun control again until 1985. That summer, the family was visiting Jim's relatives in southern Illinois when a friend dropped by to take Sarah and Scott swimming. Scott, then six, climbed into the friend's pickup truck first, picked up a pistol that was lying on the seat, and playfully aimed it at Sarah.

"Scott," she admonished him, "be careful. Don't even point a toy at someone." She took the gun away from him. Then she looked more closely at the revolver. It was heavy; made of metal, not plastic.

"I realized it wasn't a toy, but a *fully loaded* twenty-two," she recalls, the anger still evident in her voice, even years after the incident. "I was really upset that anyone would be that dumb."

That episode was still fresh in Sarah's mind when, back in Washington, she read that the Senate was about to vote on the McClure-Volkmer bill, the NRA-backed effort to roll back federal gun control. She was stunned that anyone would propose such a measure. "That's when I called HCI back up and said, 'Hey, I'm ready to get involved now.' "

Her first act in support of gun control was to write a personal letter to each senator explaining why she felt they should vote against

McClure-Volkmer. A week later, the Senate overwhelmingly passed the bill.

"The McClure-Volkmer act was really an *extreme* stand," she says. "I was just irate when I heard that it passed. I was home cooking dinner at the time, and I was so mad I didn't know who to complain to."

Sarah was aware, however, that the NRA had been lobbying for the bill, so she called and asked to speak to someone in the organization's legislative affairs department. When a man's voice came on the line Sarah told him, "I'm Sarah Brady and I just heard that you all have been lobbying for this bill and I think it's absolutely horrible. I want you to know that I'm going to make it my lifetime mission to see that you are destroyed."

Sarah laughs at the memory of her impulsive call. "And remember, this was at six-thirty or seven o'clock at night. It was probably some poor security guard I was telling off. I think his response was something like 'Thank you for your views.' "

In October 1985, Sarah Brady joined the board of HCI. She began speaking out in public against the NRA measure, writing newspaper op-ed pieces, appearing on television talk shows. Although the legislation eventually passed the House, some of the provisions that Sarah considered most onerous were stripped from the bill—particularly the section that would have made it easier to sell handguns. "I'm delighted we beat the NRA on the big one," she told reporters.

In just a short time, Sarah Brady had become the most visible— and persuasive—gun-control advocate in America.

There were several reasons for her popularity. The first was clearly political. Sarah Brady was the quintessence of mainstream America. As she explained in a speech to the San Francisco Commonwealth Club in 1985, "I am a Republican and a conservative. A good many people whose political views are similar to mine say they are against 'gun control.' As they define it, so am I. That definition would include more controls on hunting weapons, gun bans, or gun confiscation. I am against these things too."

A favorite tactic of the NRA was to smear all "gun grabbers" with a red brush. Sarah's middle-of-the-road perspective and conservative bona fides made that tactic impossible. Sarah Brady's husband had been part of the most conservative administration in decades. And as the wife of a well-known victim of gun violence, Sarah Brady put a recognizable face on an issue that was beginning to alarm more and more Americans. Sarah Brady did for gun victims what basketball player Magic Johnson would later do for victims of the AIDS epidemic. But Sarah did not wear the role of victim comfortably. "I don't want your pity," she once told a congressional committee, "I want your *action*."

But clearly it was sympathy for the tragedy that had befallen the Bradys that caused many people to look at gun control in a new light. Almost from the day Sarah joined the board, HCI's ranks had begun to grow, much to the consternation of the NRA. In 1985, HCI had 120,000 members and a budget of $3 million; by 1991, both the group's membership and budget had more than doubled. Harlon Carter's statement that there was "no gun-control movement worthy of mention" in America was no longer true.

"The NRA *seemed* invincible for a long time," says Rex Davis, the former director of the Bureau of Alcohol, Tobacco and Firearms. "But that's only been true because they've had no meaningful opposition until recently. Handgun Control and the Coalition to Ban Handguns were fairly naive and had limited resources. That's changing. Especially Handgun Control has gained expertise and resources."

Realizing the threat, the NRA hit back hard, alleging that Sarah Brady was a "tool" manipulated by liberal gun grabbers. The NRA used HCI's support of the proposed Maryland ban on Saturday Night Specials as proof that Mrs. Brady's gun group wasn't as moderate as she claimed.

"Sarah Brady and HCI demonstrated that they will ban firearms across America if you and I don't get more active in fighting back," warned an NRA legislative alert. To further cast HCI as a gun-grabbing, rather than gun-controlling, organization, the NRA started referring to Handgun Control as the Gun Ban Lobby.

"Let me tell you right now," warned an NRA fund-raising letter, "nothing makes Sarah Brady and the Gun Ban Lobby more furious than your consistent support of the NRA-ILA."

And when HCI stepped up its attacks against the NRA, taking out full-page newspaper ads suggesting that "the NRA has gone off the deep end" for fighting "cop-killer bullets" and "plastic guns," the NRA responded in kind.

"The only political groups doing well in America right now are those preaching hate," claimed the NRA in a member mailing. "And the No. 1 group on the list that is selling hate to raise funds is Handgun Control, Inc."

The fight between the two organizations escalated in 1987 when Wayne LaPierre wrote NRA members that he had discovered an HCI plan to "spread misinformation and to paint me and your leaders of the NRA as crazy extremists." This "disgusting effort," wrote LaPierre, was called "Operation Alienate."

"I have in my hand as I write this letter this outrageous plan of 'Operation Alienate,' " he continued. "It is budgeted at well over $1 million, and it is laid out on two pages with budget figures included."

But LaPierre was himself spreading misinformation. The $1 million plan he was writing about was actually called "Campaign '88," and consisted of a ten-point "blueprint for action." Operation Alienate was HCI's name for the sixth element, which was allocated just $78,000. According to the two-page HCI document referred to by LaPierre, the purpose of Operation Alienate was "to undermine the NRA's extremist leadership in Washington."

The document goes on to explain:

> Many reasonable NRA members become outraged when they discover how they are being misrepresented by the organization that is supposed to be looking out for their interests. "Operation Alienate" will spread the word through a targeted mail and print ad campaign on what the NRA leadership is up to today so that members can see how their dues are really being spent. Few sportsmen want to be associated with the defense of machine guns, plastic handguns, cop-killer bullets and other extremist stands being taken by today's NRA leadership. And many of them are now supporting Handgun Control, Inc. "Operation Alienate" will win thousands of additional disaffected NRA members over to our side.

Sarah Brady wasn't the only conservative breaking ranks from the gun lobby during this period. A rift had developed between the NRA and leaders of several powerful conservative organizations during the second half of the 1980s. The erosion of support among one of the gun lobby's primary constituencies was caused by the NRA's refusal to compromise on several firearms issues supported by law enforcement, particularly on plastic guns and armor-piercing bullets. Right-wing leaders were also angered by the NRA's refusal to support conservative candidates running in key elections. The rupture broke into the open in 1989 when conservative leader Patrick McGuigan blasted the NRA in *Policy Review*.

"During the past few years, the [NRA] has refused to play coalition politics," complained McGuigan.

> A go-it-alone approach and a refusal to compromise on less than critical issues is jeopardizing the NRA's effectiveness in winning political support on those issues that it considers most important. . . . The NRA also refused to cooperate with conservatives during one of the most important fights of the last decade: the Bork nomination. . . . We badly needed the NRA's help and didn't get it.

The NRA had decided not to support Bork because, after a perusal of Mr. Bork's writings, it was decided that he was unlikely to suppress the exclusionary rule, which disallows evidence gained in illegal searches. The NRA leaders favored the exclusionary rule because it protected gun owners and dealers whose weapons had been wrongly seized by agents of their old nemesis, the Bureau of Alcohol, Tobacco and Firearms. Paul Weyrich, of the conservative Coalitions for America, asked Senator James McClure to persuade the NRA to back Bork.

"McClure communicated with every member of the NRA board of directors," wrote McGuigan. "A major confrontation ensued, in which those who wanted the organization to stay out of the battle prevailed."

The gun lobby's failure to come to the aid of conservatives in what the right wing considered its hour of greatest need poisoned the already ailing relationship between the NRA and conservatives. Richard Gardiner says that although he regrets the ill feelings, when it gets right down to it, there is nothing that the NRA could or should have done differently.

"Look, we're not a *conservative* organization," he stresses. "We're a *progun* organization. Most of the time that results in supporting candidates that people would consider conservative. But we do not get involved in anything but the gun issue."

BY THE TIME of the San Antonio convention, these outside forces, taken together, were clearly taking their toll, resulting in the siege mentality that marked much of the proceedings. But there was another element to the gun lobby's problems, one that was not discussed openly in San Antonio. Rather, it emerged in oblique references and vague formulations, grasped only by insiders.

Take, for example, President Dick Riley's first words after calling the members' meeting to order. When silence finally reigned in the grand hall that Saturday morning, Riley introduced himself with these enigmatic words: "I'm the president of the NRA. The *whole* thing. Not one division or group—but the *whole* thing."

Such proclamations of unity are standard fare at NRA gatherings; they are repeated throughout the organization's magazines, in member mailings, and in NRA press releases. And the propaganda campaign is, on the whole, successful. The average NRA member believes in the unity of the organization—so does most of the American public. But insiders know that high-level intrigues and intense power struggles rage through the massive NRA headquarters building in Washington with a frequency and ferocity normally associated with the Kremlin. A never-ending internal war poses one of the greatest threats to the gun lobby's future.

"The NRA has been its own worst enemy for the last fifteen years," says Dr. Edward Ezell, curator of the Smithsonian Institution's National Firearms Collection and a world-renowned expert on small arms. He is also a former member of the National Rifle Association. "In fact, I join it every now and then just so I can quit when they do something stupid," he jokes.

"They have a seventy-five-member board," Ezell explains. "My God, it's a zoo. What you've got essentially is seventy-five rambunctious individuals, each one with his or her own agenda about where this organization is going to go. A lot of people look at the NRA as this monolithic behemoth. They don't realize how factionalized the whole place is."

Neal Knox, the man who floor-managed the Cincinnati Revolt for Harlon Carter in 1977, echoes Ezell's observation.

"If you want to understand the NRA board," Knox told a reporter in 1990, "you study the Politburo."

If that sounds a bit strident, welcome to the world of the NRA leadership, where the harshest rhetoric is reserved for those insiders thought to be apostates or heretics or—perhaps worst of all—overly ambitious. The board is riven by an ever-changing constellation of factions, each one centered around a single powerful individual, or around a small clique of players. One result is that board meetings often resemble a junior high school classroom in which the teacher has stepped out for a minute.

This divisiveness isn't limited to the board. There are bitter and near-constant battles over resources and prestige between the NRA's lobbying branch (the ILA) and its other divisions. The heads of the education and sport-shooting divisions have become demoralized over the last decade as more and more money has been funneled away from their activities and into the ILA. A general operations staffer once complained that non-ILA workers had become "second-class citizens." The lobbying division has itself often been the scene of the bloodiest battles (not surprising, since that's where the money and power have accrued).

At the heart of most of the power struggles that regularly convulse the gun lobby stands Neal Knox. If the NRA board is the Politburo, as Knox alleges, then he is Rasputin. Despite numerous attempts to do him in—politically speaking—the charismatic former Texas journalist (he edited *Gun Week* and, later, *Handloader Rifle* magazines) keeps returning to torment his enemies inside the gun lobby.

Knox took over as the director of the Institute for Legislative Action in the aftermath of the Cincinnati Revolt led by Harlon Carter, and Knox remained Harlon Carter's right-hand man during his tenure there. He was also Carter's *right-wing* man, a rather extreme position that was destined to get Knox into trouble.

Few, after all, would characterize Harlon Carter as a moderate; until his death in November 1991, he was as uncompromising when it came to issues of guns and crime as anyone in America. In one widely circulated editorial written by Carter in 1989 (when he was in retirement), the former NRA chief showed just how tough he remained when he proposed his "modest solution" to the nation's drug problem. After invoking presidential emergency powers and suspending the "privilege of the writ of habeas corpus," wrote Carter, "those people apprehended in violation of the mandate that this government must win the war with drug dealers, distributors, transporters, possessors and users of drugs unlawfully obtained, would be arrested without warrant and . . . deliver[ed] to a place prepared for internment for the duration of the war on drugs."

The internment camp, suggested Carter, would be located in the southwestern desert, surrounded by double rows of concertina wire, and secured by trained Dobermans and armed guards in lookout towers with searchlights.

"No access [to the camp] would be permitted attorneys, congressmen or sob-sisters, supersaturated with sympathy for somebody—anybody—except at such time in the future as the victorious end of the war would permit hearings," added Carter. Of course, no press would be allowed in and any overflying aircraft would be shot down.

But despite Carter's extremist views, he *did* understand the importance of not making enemies needlessly—especially enemies in Congress—and he understood that political realities sometimes dictated tactical accommodations. Neal Knox was as hawkish as Carter when it came to the issues of guns and crime, but lacked the political instincts of his mentor. Knox seemed to relish making enemies—and then twisting their tails at every opportunity.

In his conservative suits, styled salt-and-pepper hair, and metal-framed glasses, the middle-aged Knox looks more like an industrialist from Omaha or Des Moines than a high-powered Washington lobbyist. But behind the soft-spoken drawl there is an edge that is gun-barrel hard. Less than two years after Knox took over at the ILA, three of the division's top lobbyists quit, citing Knox's belligerent style as reason for their departure.

"Knox wanted to do or pursue things on the Hill that professionally-wise would damage our credibility," complained Wilhelm Pickens, director of the ILA's government affairs division at that time. "There's a difference between taking a hard line and being an idiot. You need to know when to retreat."

"Neal's attitude is that we can put a congressman or a senator to the wall and stick it to him at any time," said another of the former lobbyists. "[Knox doesn't] feel you have to compromise on anything."

John Aquilino, who served as a high-ranking NRA executive for nearly a decade, says that Knox's behavior became more extreme—even bizarre—over the years. "For the first two years it was great to work with Neal. For the last two, it was as if the people across the road [at the Soviet embassy] were zapping him with microwaves and making him crazy."

Dissatisfaction over Knox's behavior finally reached a breaking point in April 1982. One week after the group's annual convention, the board of directors, acting under guidance from Executive Vice President Harlon Carter, asked Knox and his chief assistant to hand in their resignations. In explaining his reasons for ousting his former protégé, Carter later framed the conflict with Knox as a power struggle, pure and simple. "Knox always wanted to be executive vice president," said Carter. "He came to the ILA as a fighter. It wasn't long before he had everybody in the ILA fighting—against each other."

Carter had been suspicious of Knox's ambitions for some time. To protect his own position, Carter told the board in 1981 that if they didn't extend his annual contract to five years he would resign immediately. The board gave in, much to Knox's frustration.

Knox, of course, characterized his firing differently. Carter and others within the NRA had become too willing to compromise on gun issues, he alleged, and declared himself—not Carter—the true embodiment of the spirit of the Cincinnati Revolt. Forced out in disgrace in 1982, Knox remained popular with many members, and managed to get himself elected to the NRA board of directors the following year. From his position there, he could easily harass Carter and his other enemies within the NRA. His detractors looked for a way to get rid of him. In 1984, Knox made the misstep his enemies had been waiting for: He testified at a congressional committee hearing, speaking strongly against certain amendments to the McClure-Volkmer Act, when the official NRA position endorsed those same amendments. The board of directors voted forty-five to twenty-four to remove Knox from the board, the first time such an action had been taken in the NRA's history.

When Knox was fired from the ILA in 1982, Harlon Carter decided to replace him with Warren Cassidy, the man who had led the NRA's successful campaign against the Saturday Night Special ban in Massachusetts in 1976. The gregarious Cassidy could be counted on to smooth the many ruffled feathers left in the wake of Neal Knox—both on Capitol Hill and within the ILA. According to John Aquilino, ILA staffers themselves had hoped that Cassidy would usher in a "kinder and gentler" era at the NRA. Expectations at Cassidy's first ILA staff meeting ran high.

"We were like a bunch of kids waiting for Santa Claus," Aquilino recalls. "Then Cassidy came in. He started out by telling us that he knew he couldn't trust us; that he was going to plant misinformation, and then see who was leaking it."

The honeymoon was over before it had even begun. Cassidy, who had been brought in to heal old wounds within the ILA, proved more adept at creating new ones.

Harlon Carter was alarmed. Cassidy's effect on the ILA would be bad enough, but Carter was even more concerned about the harm that Cassidy could do to the organization as a whole. Traditionally the ILA directorship was a stepping-stone to the NRA's top post, that of executive vice president. Once appointed chief of the ILA, Cassidy's commitment to fighting all gun-control legislation seemed, at least to some on the board, to be less than absolute. They, and Carter, were afraid that if Cassidy were made head of the NRA, he would direct resources away from the ILA.

In late 1984, Carter summoned a group of key directors for a secret meeting. He began the rendezvous by reminding the leaders of three important facts. First, his five-year term as executive vice president would expire in a little over a year. Second, a battle to succeed him would likely be fought between Warren Cassidy and Neal Knox. Despite the fact that he had been booted out of the ILA and then off the board, Knox was still a major force in the NRA and had powerful friends on the board and within the general membership. The third fact listed by Carter was that the ascension of either of these two men would be detrimental to the NRA. The purpose of the meeting was to devise a strategy that would prevent either Warren Cassidy or Neal Knox from taking over. The only way to accomplish this feat, the group ultimately agreed, was for Carter to hand the reins over to a hand-picked successor *before* the end of his term. The group found their man in the person of G. Ray Arnett.

Arnett seemed perfectly suited to the job. Not only was he an avid hunter and a former head of the National Wildlife Federation, he also had strong ties to the White House, having served as Governor Reagan's Director of Fish and Game in California in the early 1970s. When the voters sent Reagan to Washington in 1981, Arnett came along as an assistant secretary of the Interior. Carter hoped that Arnett would heal the wounds created by Cassidy, who had been brought in to heal the wounds created by Knox, who had been brought in to heal the wounds created by the Cincinnati Revolt.

From the moment of his investiture, however, Arnett's tenure was tainted by controversy. How Harlon Carter and his supporters fooled themselves into thinking that the situation could have been otherwise is a mystery. Their end run around Cassidy, and Knox, was bound to cause resentment, and it did.

At the January 1985 meeting of the board of directors, Carter announced that, effective immediately, he was resigning his position as executive vice president. According to NRA bylaws, Gary Anderson, the group's director of general operations, would succeed Carter. But Anderson declined the promotion, forcing the board to elect Carter's replacement. Arnett was nominated; so was Cassidy. Voting by secret ballot, the board elected Arnett the new executive vice president. Cassidy and Knox had been successfully blindsided. Both, however, refused to go gently into the good night, as Carter had wished.

Cassidy returned to his seventh-floor corner office at the ILA, one floor directly below Arnett's own suite, a perfect location in which to sharpen the knives he'd use in a coup when the opportunity presented itself. Knox continued his sharklike circling from outside the organization. He formed his own firearms lobbying group and took potshots at the NRA in columns appearing in a variety of gun magazines.

The first test of Arnett's strength came at the members' meeting in 1985 in Seattle. Although elected at the board meeting earlier that year, Arnett had to stand for regular elections if he wanted to hold on to the post he had been handed by Harlon Carter. Arnett outpolled Neal Knox, 2,014 votes to 881. The five-year term was now his, but so were the intrigues that came along with the job. Four days after his election, a disgruntled former employee of Arnett's from the Interior Department, Theodore Gianoutsos, who also happened to be an NRA member, filed a petition to recall the new executive vice president.

Gianoutsos had been fired from his position as management analyst at Interior after revealing that the department had lost several million dollars due to gross mismanagement under Arnett. He charged that before his firing, Arnett had attempted to buy his silence in exchange for a plum promotion, a charge Arnett denied. It is quite probable that nothing would have come of Gianoutsos's drive had Arnett himself not made a number of errors, and had the climate inside the NRA been less contentious.

Arnett's first mistake came while filming a promotional video for the NRA. The burly executive vice president and several colleagues were hunting in Virginia in October 1985, the camera shooting Arnett as Arnett shot wildlife. It was a typical idyllic hunting party staged for the cameras: a beautiful fall day, law-abiding gun enthusiasts, just the image the NRA was trying to portray. Everything was going perfectly until Arnett broke the law by firing at a bird while his motorboat was moving under power. Arnett was charged by state and federal game wardens who were present and later paid the $100 fine. The incident, which was gleefully reported in pro-gun-control newsletters, gave the NRA a black eye at a time when it needed all the good publicity it could get. Soon after the reports of the violation surfaced, the Association of Outdoor Writers canceled plans to have Arnett be the keynote speaker at its annual convention.

The incident wasn't, in fact, Arnett's first serious hunting violation. In 1982, while on a hunting junket to the Cayman Islands in the Caribbean, Arnett supposedly took a shot at an endangered species of parrot. No charges were filed in this incident. The Cayman government quite possibly decided to look the other way rather than humiliate Arnett, a representative of a United States government administration that was then contemplating ending an import ban on Cayman turtle products.

Three months after the Virginia hunting episode, the NRA's thirty-member executive board, meeting behind shut doors, closed ranks around Arnett and ruled that the recall petition was invalid. The move might have temporarily saved Arnett's skin, but to many in the group it simply gave weight to the charges made by Neal Knox that the NRA was abandoning the democratic reforms enacted in Cincinnati. Gianoutsos saw very clearly the propaganda implications of the board's act.

"Do you realize what message you have sent to our friends and enemies?" Gianoutsos and his wife wrote in a letter to the board.

What will they think when they see the shocking spectacle of the entire NRA leadership, the full board and all the officers, so afraid of two NRA members armed only with the truth that they had to retreat with knees knocking and hands trembling behind closed doors to hold an executive session! Is this the mighty NRA in action?

But if Arnett felt secure in his position after the board's January action, it wasn't long before that illusion was shattered. According to division chief John Aquilino, "Arnett fell into puppy love with one of my employees." Arnett and the woman deny they had an affair, but Aquilino says that the "infatuation" created problems, both for him and for others on his staff, as Arnett singled the woman out for special attention.

"[Arnett] came in one day to say that we had to find a way to make her ammunition tax-deductible," says Aquilino. "And as his infatuation grew more open, her work ethic grew more questionable. I'd remind her of her duties and then she'd complain to [Arnett] and I'd get a call asking 'Why are you picking on her?' Finally, he took her out of my department and gave her a position as liaison." The new position came with a large pay increase, a fact that caused more than a few raised eyebrows among the NRA staff.

And there was also the matter of a letter Arnett had written in April 1984 as a character reference for one Duane Wendall Larson, whom Arnett had met in the late 1970s when the NRA chief had been head of the World Beefalo Association. The WBA is a trade organization for ranchers raising beefalos, a cross between bison and cattle, and Larson had been a member of the group. Although the two weren't close, Arnett said that he had socialized with Larson at official WBA functions and could vouch for Larson's "character and honesty without equivocation or mental reservation."

Arnett had written the letter at the request of Larson's lawyer, after Larson had been convicted of running cocaine in the Minneapolis area. The NRA chief might have felt he was simply extending a courtesy to a former business acquaintance, but when Ted Gianoutsos got hold of the letter (it was leaked to him by an anonymous source connected to the Larson investigation), *he* saw something else: The top official of the NRA, an organization that was trying to stem the growing split with law enforcement, had been caught in bed with a drug dealer. Gianoutsos threatened to make the letter public if Arnett didn't resign.

But before Arnett had time to assess the potential damage presented by this latest scandal, the NRA chief created another one. It was to be his last. On the day after the McClure-Volkmer bill was signed into law, just at the moment that Washington and the national media were trumpeting the NRA as the most powerful lobby in the country, Arnett fired the group's entire public education division. On the morning of May 7, all fifteen members of the division (including its head, John Aquilino) were gathered together and informed that they were no longer employed. They were then given two hours to clean out their desks and vacate the building.

Why did Arnett take this drastic action? The reasons vary according to whom you talk to. Arnett himself later told a reporter that the firings were a purely financial matter. "I said to myself, Here's a department that's probably costing me seven hundred to nine hundred thousand dollars a year, and what the hell am I getting for it?" Arnett said to Dan Moldea in an interview published in *Regardie's* magazine in 1987.

Gun-control groups interpreted the firings as a sure indication that the McClure-Volkmer bill was a defeat for the gun lobby, no matter how much the NRA bragged about the victory. "We managed to salvage the most important part of the 1968 gun-control act [the ban on interstate sales of handguns] and in addition stop the sale and manufacture of new machine guns," says Susan Whitmore, HCI's director of communications. "I think it's significant that the day McClure-Volkmer was signed, they fired their PR department. That's what they do when they *win?*"

Others suggest that the mass firing was Arnett's payback for Aquilino's "ill treatment" of the woman the NRA chief favored. Regardless of Arnett's reasons, the result was that NRA board members now agreed the executive vice president had to go.

On May 17, just ten days after the firings, the executive committee of the NRA board met in an emergency session. The night before the meeting, Arnett had been given a list of formal grievances, including:

failure to address falling morale among NRA workers; firing the public education division; failure to get the approval or advice of the board in several instances; using NRA funds for personal hunting trips; promoting the woman with whom he was allegedly having an affair.

Arnett denied all the allegations and called the meeting a "kangaroo court," but there was little he could do or say to save himself. Although it was not mentioned in the board's formal list, many individual directors were most upset by the character reference Arnett had written for the convicted drug dealer. Others were more concerned about Arnett's seeming disrespect for the board, evidenced in his firing of the public education division without consulting them. At any rate, the cumulative weight of the several scandals dogging the executive vice president assured his speedy exit.

The executive board suspended Arnett without pay, effective immediately. When he threatened to sue the organization, the board offered to settle the matter by offering him a $150,000 cash payment, the use of a Lincoln Town Car for one year, and $40,000 for attorney fees. (The board also doled out $39,000 to be split by three Arnett aides also fired at the meeting.) Rather than fight, Arnett took the money and left town.

When it comes to the matter of succession, Neal Knox wasn't far off in comparing the NRA board with the Politburo. Certainly, average NRA members are kept no better informed by their official news organs about internal power struggles than were Soviet citizens of the pre-glasnost era. The May 1986 issue of *American Rifleman* offered no clues that a change in leadership was imminent. G. Ray Arnett's monthly column, ". . . Sincerely, GRA," was devoted to singing the praises of the McClure-Volkmer bill, recently signed into law.

"You have spelled the difference between defeat and victory," Arnett told the members in closing the piece, "and what a sweet, joyous victory it is."

The first indication that anything was amiss at NRA headquarters was found in the masthead of the June issue of the magazine. Beneath the line that contained the magazine's issue date and volume number, where traditionally the reader would find the words "G. Ray Arnett, Executive Vice President," there was, instead, a large empty space. Arnett's name had been deleted.

A few pages later in the same issue, members were provided with as complete an explanation of the shake-up as they were going to get from their leaders for several months: a three-sentence notice that "[b]ecause of a number of matters regarding the Executive Vice President's conduct of his office," G. Ray Arnett had been suspended.

One month later, Arnett was given four column-inches in which to say his good-byes to the membership. He made no mention of the reasons for his sudden departure.

"I sincerely thank you for giving me the opportunity to serve as your executive vice president during this important time," wrote Arnett. "Please accept my best wishes for continued success, good hunting and good shooting."

Beneath Arnett's farewell was an even shorter official message directed to the former chief. "I know the Board joins me in expressing appreciation for the contribution you have made to the NRA," the organization's president, James Reinke, wrote in an open letter to Arnett. "We wish you well in the future."

Nowhere in the NRA hierarchy was the news of Arnett's firing greeted with more enthusiasm than in the office directly below that of the executive vice president. There, at the hub of the ILA, J. Warren Cassidy had been waiting for this day for over a year. Many, in fact, insist that Cassidy had been doing more than just waiting. He was, they said, the fountainhead of the many rumors concerning Arnett's indiscretions and blunders.

"Cassidy carried tales of Arnett's behavior to [Harlon] Carter on a daily basis," charges John Aquilino in *Insider Gun News*, the newsletter he founded after being fired by Arnett.

Regardless of the role played by Cassidy in Arnett's fall, the situation couldn't have worked out better for the ILA chief, whose ascension to the post of executive vice president had been blocked by G. Ray Arnett's appointment. Arnett was now out of the picture; Neal Knox still had significant influence with some board members, but even more of them considered him a pariah. That left Cassidy's route to the office upstairs clear. In the July 1986 issue of *American Rifleman*, in the position on the masthead that had been left suspiciously blank just the month before, there now appeared a new line: "J. Warren Cassidy, Acting Executive Vice President." Soon, the word *Acting* was removed and Cassidy was made head of the National Rifle Association.

For a time, Cassidy and the ILA—now headed by Wayne La-

Pierre—could focus their attention on the slight but growing threats to gun ownership posed by enemies outside the group. By the time of the 1991 convention in San Antonio, however, Warren Cassidy—like G. Ray Arnett, Neal Knox, and the Old Guard before them—would himself fall prey, not to the NRA's foes, but to his many enemies within the NRA.

# PART III

# GUN WARS

# 8

# DRUMS ALONG
# THE POTOMAC

IN THE TWO years after Warren Cassidy took over the helm of the NRA in 1986, there occurred two events that were destined to change the debate over gun control in the United States. Neither favored the NRA.

At the time there were few signs that would have indicated that such a reversal of fortune was imminent. Membership in the association was still growing, and pride over the passage of the McClure-Volkmer Act overshadowed any concern about law enforcement's still mostly inchoate discontent with the NRA. To outsiders especially, the NRA appeared stronger than ever.

The first watershed event was the decision by Sarah Brady and others at Handgun Control, Inc., to center their efforts on one piece of legislation. The bill, which came to be called the Brady bill, mandated a federal seven-day waiting period for the purchase of handguns. The Gun Control Act of 1968 already prohibited the sale of handguns to felons and fugitives, but a convicted criminal could easily circumvent the law simply by lying about his or her criminal past on the federal form when purchasing a handgun. The only way to make the law work, the police told legislators, was to run background checks, and to do so, a waiting period was needed.

The law would also provide a "cooling-off period" during which impulsive buyers with a grudge to settle would have a chance to reconsider their actions. The bill seemed quite modest—too modest, in fact, for some supporters of gun control.

"The Brady bill is a nice, innocuous piece of legislation," says Michael Beard, of the National Coalition to Ban Handguns. "To us it's a *minor* step forward," he adds, stressing the word *minor*.

The principle of a waiting period was so mild that even the NRA had once supported it. "A waiting period could help in reducing crimes of passion and in preventing people with criminal records or dangerous mental illness from acquiring guns," reads an NRA pamphlet from the mid-1970s.

But the NRA's position hardened in the years following the Cincinnati Revolt. By the time the Brady bill was introduced in Congress on February 4, 1987, the organization's position was that *no* new gun-control measures were acceptable—not even a waiting period. "We think this is a major issue," declared the NRA's Wayne LaPierre, and he promised a tough fight on the measure.

The second seminal event came a year later. On March 14, 1988, then–secretary of education William Bennett sent Attorney General Edwin Meese a four-page memo on the subject of drug policy. Under a section titled "Fighting the Pushers at Home," Bennett (who was to become "Drug Czar" under the Bush administration) made the following suggestion:

> The easy access to firearms has put increasing firepower in the hands of drug traffickers. We should consider supporting legislation to better manage the production, importation, and sale of automatic weapons and other firearms, as sought by the major law enforcement organizations.

Since the production, importation, and sale of new automatic weapons had already been outlawed by the last-minute amendment to the McClure-Volkmer bill, Bennett was most likely targeting *semiautomatic* weapons, particularly the class known as assault weapons, semiautomatic versions of popular military firearms. The idea to ban assault weapons did not originate with Bennett, but he was the highest ranking official at the time to suggest such a measure. Bennett's almost offhanded reference was seen by those in Congress who supported a ban on assault weapons as a green light to move on the issue.

For the next several years, these twin measures—the Brady bill and a federal ban on assault weapons—would dominate the national movement for gun control. The fight for the bills would also put the NRA in an unusual defensive position, exacerbating the problems that had been slowly building for the gun group.

When the Brady bill was first introduced in Congress in 1987, most pundits gave it as much chance of being enacted as a bill outlawing apple pie. Despite the fact that polls showed the majority of Americans favored a waiting period, Congress simply wasn't ready to stand up to the NRA. For a brief moment in June 1988, however, proponents of the measure thought their time had come when President Reagan appeared to endorse the Brady bill while answering reporters' questions at an economic summit in Toronto. A waiting period is a good idea, said the president. But before HCI could issue a press release trumpeting the presidential endorsement, the White House press office "clarified" Reagan's support out of existence.

"[The president] thinks a cooling-off period is a good opportunity to check out the background of the applicant," explained White House spokesman Marlin Fitzwater, "but he really felt it should be a *state* law, as opposed to a *federal* law."

Today, Sarah Brady maintains that it was the president's handlers who got it wrong: Ronald Reagan, she says, always supported a federal waiting period. Brady sent President Reagan a short note thanking him for his remarks in Toronto. A few days later, she was cooking dinner at home when the president called to thank her for her note.

"He said we needed background checks," Brady says. "And, yes, on a *federal* basis. I felt a little strange about quoting him because it was a private conversation. I was very dumb, I guess. I should have said, 'Hey, will you come out publicly for the Brady bill?' but I just wasn't quick enough. I could kick myself for not doing it then."

Gun control, like all perennial issues, must be tailored to fit the times. Early gun-control ordinances were aimed at newly freed slaves in the American South. When New York enacted its Sullivan Law in 1911 (requiring citizens to obtain a police permit to possess a handgun) it was presented as a way to control the foreigners then entering this country in large numbers. In the early 1960s, gun control was seen as a way to crack down on the scourge du jour: juvenile delinquency. By the later years of the decade, however, the same legislation had metamorphosed into the antidote to the wave of political assassinations that had claimed some of the country's most beloved public figures.

Almost from the beginning, the Brady bill was custom-fit to the issue of its day: drugs. In October 1982, Ronald Reagan had declared war on drugs, and a waiting period—and later the ban on assault weapons—was cast as a formidable weapon in that fight. For this reason the Brady bill was introduced as an amendment to the House Omnibus Drug Bill; the link was explicit and voiced as often as possible by the bill's backers.

In 1988, HCI executive Pete Shields announced: "Nancy Reagan has been leading the fight against drugs in this country and people are beginning to be aware of the enormous number of drug guns that are being purchased in states without waiting periods." At the same time, the legislative counsel for the International Brotherhood of Police Officers added, "We think this seven-day waiting proposal is very appropriately placed in the drug bill because there is a very close connection between drugs and guns."

After easily passing through the House Judiciary Committee in June 1988, the Brady bill almost fell victim to behind-the-scenes machinations by House Speaker Tom Foley. Foley, an old friend of the NRA's, was from Washington State, a gun enthusiasts' stronghold where, as the Speaker once said, " 'Drop yer guns' is fightin' words." At the NRA's behest, Foley tried to strip the gun-control amendment from the bill *before* letting it on to the House floor. As during the McClure-Volkmer debate two years earlier, process was quickly becoming as important as substance to the bill's chances. If Foley succeeded in his gambit, the Brady bill stood little chance of winning approval on the floor, because it is much more difficult to attach an amendment to a bill during floor debate than it is to let an existing amendment remain on a piece of legislation.

Backers of the bill were lucky, however. Informal House rules also make it politically costly for the leadership to delete amendments already passed by a committee, and Foley was unwilling to pay the price for crossing committee members, where the Brady amendment had passed thirty-five to zero. Undoubtedly, heavy lobbying by police groups also helped Foley make up his mind. Hubert Williams, president of the Police Foundation, let Foley know that "the law enforcement community feels very strongly about this."

As the House prepared to vote on the Brady bill in September 1988, both sides stepped up their lobbying campaigns. The Law Enforcement Steering Committee, an umbrella group (organized with the help of HCI) representing eleven national organizations, with a total of 400,000 police officers, had 120 uniformed officers march through the Capitol building and hand out buttons that read "Cops Know Seven Days Can Save a Life."

Not to be outdone, the NRA staged its own "police action": a press conference *against* the Brady bill with 110 officers and prison guards in attendance—but the effort backfired when it was later revealed that at least two of the police officers attending the press conference hadn't known in advance what the event was about. According to the two, both from Cincinnati, they had been invited to Washington at the NRA's expense to give "support for a new law-enforcement unit [the NRA] was starting." It wasn't until the press conference began that the two realized they were being used to support the NRA's position. One of the officers was actually a strong supporter of the Brady bill.

The gun lobby's practice of painting every battle in the direst of terms—the Armageddon Appeal—combined with its bullying tactics was beginning to cause hard feelings among some House members. F. James Sensenbrenner, Jr., a longtime NRA ally, was particularly incensed by a letter sent to NRA members in his Wisconsin district describing his support of the Brady bill as a vote "to impose total, strict gun control on all America." In a harbinger of things to come, the Republican representative distributed an angry "Dear Colleague" letter (so-called because of its traditional salutation) to other members of the House.

"I certainly have no problems with a lobbying group informing their membership about a certain bill," Sensenbrenner wrote. "In fact, they have an obligation to do so. However, the recent NRA letters are misleading and, in some cases, inflammatory."

At the top of the page, just under the letterhead, ran the words NRA SHOOTS SELF IN FOOT.

Others in both the House and the Senate had previously complained about the NRA's tactics, but Sensenbrenner's letter was one of the most public displays yet of the rising discontent felt by even anti-gun-control legislators. The NRA, however, did not change its strong-arm tactics.

The gun lobby's legislative strategy in this first House vote on the Brady bill was simple. In explaining the plan, Don Morrissey, legislative director for U.S. representative Bill McCollum, quotes a Capitol Hill axiom: "It is easier to defeat something with something," Morrissey says, "than with nothing." In other words: Never allow a simple yes-no vote on a measure you oppose; *always* offer an alternative. Morrissey knows the truth of this assertion firsthand; he helped develop the NRA's alternative to the Brady bill offered by his boss, a moderate Republican from Florida.

The McCollum amendment was presented as a substitute to the Brady bill. It instructed the U.S. Attorney General to design a point-of-sale "instant check" system for handgun buyers. Instead of waiting a week for a police background check to be conducted, under McCollum, gun dealers would have only to dial a special Justice Department number and punch in the name and Social Security number of the prospective buyer. Somewhere, a giant government supercomputer would check the name against a list of all felons and fugitives, and after only a few minutes, the dealer would know if the person on the other side of the counter was prohibited from buying the handgun. The Justice Department would have a year to design the system and report back to Congress. It would then have another thirty days to implement the plan nationwide.

Morrissey, a big and good-looking Texas native with a reputation as a tough political street fighter, bridles at charges that Representative McCollum was simply a conduit for an NRA bill. He insists that the amendment was drawn up in Bill McCollum's offices. "The NRA had nothing to do with putting that bill together," he says. "In fact, we've kept a very hands-off relationship with the NRA. When I came on board in 1986, I asked Bill, 'Have you ever accepted money from the NRA?' We checked. He had taken $250 in 1982, and he's never gotten a single dollar since. I've told the NRA *not* to give us money."

Federal Election Commission records, however, show that McCollum received $250 from the NRA in the 1983–84 election cycle, $5,000 for 1981–82, and another $1,000 in the 1979–80 cycle. Since 1983–84, McCollum has not received any direct contributions from the NRA.

Regardless of who designed the McCollum amendment, the NRA was clearly its strongest supporter, spending an estimated $2 million for advertisements and letters to members backing the plan. Supporters of the Brady bill scoffed at the "instant check" system. Implementing such a system would cost tens of millions of dollars, they said, and perhaps more. Even if funds were found to computerize the states' criminal records, opponents insisted that it would be years before the system were up and running. The McCollum amendment was a pie-in-the-sky concept designed with the sole purpose of killing Brady, they charged.

"I wouldn't quibble with that assessment," says Morrissey. "I think the Brady bill is silly. *It* won't work."

But when the vote was taken in the House on September 15, 1988, the McCollum amendment was presented as a practical alternative to the controversial waiting period, and enough representatives either believed that to be true or at least pretended to believe it rather than incur the wrath of the NRA. On a lopsided vote of 228 to 182, Brady was taken out of the drug bill and McCollum was put in its place. Brady had lost round one.

The vote had broken along traditional lines, with rural and southern districts voting heavily for the McCollum substitute; only 25 of 129 representatives in thirteen southern states voted for Brady. NRA members in those areas had written their legislators angry letters threatening to throw them out of office come election day if they cast their votes for the waiting period. According to Brady bill sponsor Edward Feighan, at least two dozen legislators told him after the vote, "I agree with you personally. It's a sensible, modest amendment, but I can't vote with you because of the forces of the NRA."

Those voting for Brady steeled themselves for the political fallout with gallows humor. Dan Glickman, a Democrat from Kansas who had supported Brady, ran into James Sensenbrenner as the two were leaving the House chamber after the vote. "Well," said Glickman, "do you want to form a law firm with me after we leave Congress?"

The defeat of the Brady bill was quickly followed by the defeat of Michael Dukakis for the presidency. Even the November passage of the Saturday Night Special ban in Maryland didn't stifle the NRA's celebration over George Bush's election. But that celebration was to be short-lived. It ended in the furor over semiautomatic assault weapons that erupted in January 1989, when Patrick Edward Purdy walked onto the playground of the Cleveland Elementary School in Stockton, California, and opened fire with a semiautomatic rifle.

Top officials of the NRA knew they were in trouble the instant news reports of the massacre started coming in. "We knew immediately that there was going to be a hue and cry for gun bans," says the NRA's Richard Gardiner. "We knew that the first thing the news media were going to focus on was gun banning. I knew there would be no discussion of anything other than the gun. And that's exactly what happened."

NRA lobbyist James Jay Baker was sitting in his office at the group's Washington headquarters when the news of the shootings in California broke. He, too, knew that the gun lobby had a public relations catastrophe on its hands.

"I've worked here eleven years so I had a pretty good idea how it would be played," he says. "And sure enough, it didn't take long for the CNN cameras to get there and start focusing on 'that firearm.' "

"That firearm" was a Chinese version of the famous—or infamous, depending on your point of view—Soviet AK-47. With their distinctive "banana clips" (each capable of holding thirty bullets), these guns were familiar to Vietnam veterans—as well as to millions of other Americans who saw them on nightly newscasts. The guns always showed up in film clips of Eastern Bloc soldiers or Communist-supplied rebels throughout the Third World. A total of only 8,000 of the military guns were imported into the United States in 1985 and 1986, but in 1987, the Chinese government needed to channel funds used to produce weaponry into civilian projects. Not wanting to cut back on the industry itself, the government decided to continue producing the guns, but to sell most of them abroad. They dumped some 39,000 into the U.S. market in that year alone and another 40,000 in 1988. Retailing for as low as $300, the semiautomatic weapon was a steal.

When Patrick Purdy fired over a hundred rounds from his AK-47 into a crowded schoolyard, his actions produced two immediate and contradictory results. News of the massacre first led to an increase in sales of the weapons. "I never realized the [AK-47s] were so effective," said one admiring buyer after hearing of Purdy's handiwork. But news of the massacre also prompted others to call for a ban on the assault rifles, just as NRA officials had feared.

Many people were surprised to learn that the guns could be legally sold in the United States. When Barbara Bush was asked if she favored a prohibition on the sale of assault weapons following the Stockton massacre, the surprised First Lady said she thought the guns already were banned. "They should be, absolutely," she told reporters.

Even former president Reagan, the NRA's old friend, refused to defend the firearm. "I don't believe in taking away the right of the citizen to own a gun for sports, hunting, or their own personal defense," Reagan said. "But I do not believe that an AK-47, a machine gun, is a sporting weapon."

Reagan's statement captured the essence of the developing debate. Even many who otherwise supported the right to bear arms saw the AK-47 in a different light. Rifles, shotguns, and handguns were one thing; assault weapons were something else entirely.

But are they? Few of those calling for the abolition of the AK-47s had even a rudimentary understanding of firearms. The media, by and large, was either unwilling or unable to provide even the simplest technical details that would have allowed the public to understand the debate over these guns. The AK-47s imported into this country after 1986 were *not* machine guns. Machine guns, also called "fully automatic" weapons, fire a continuous stream of bullets as long as the trigger is depressed. Those had been outlawed in the controversial last-minute amendment to the McClure-Volkmer bill.

The *original* AK-47 was, indeed, a machine gun. Actually, it was a "select fire" gun, which, with the flip of a switch, could fire *either* as a fully automatic weapon or as a semiautomatic—firing one bullet for every pull of the trigger. The AK-47s sold in America had been modified to work only as semiautomatics. While they can still fire very rapidly, semiautomatics have nowhere near the speed of a fully automatic gun, which can shoot at a rate of 600 rounds per minute. Like the former president, reporters covering the debate on assault weapons seemed to be under the impression that all AK-47s were fully automatic.

Another common myth concerning assault weapons is that they are "high-powered" weapons. They are not. In fact, the ammunition fired by most AK-47s is *less* powerful than the bullets used in a standard deer-hunting rifle. The recoil—or "kick"—delivered to the shoulder when firing a standard military bullet proved too much for automatic firing when the guns were first invented by the Germans during World War II. Each shot sent the end of the gun a few inches into the air. With a single-shot gun, that wasn't a problem. The shooter simply waited for the gun to fall back to its original position before firing again. But even after a short burst with an automatic gun the soldier was left with his gun pointing skyward, the cumulative result of a dozen "kicks." Military engineers quickly redesigned the automatic weapons to fire smaller bullets, backed by a less powerful charge, resulting in a reduced kick. Since most semiautomatic "assault weapons" are based on select fire guns, they, too, use the less powerful ammunition.

In the wake of the Stockton shootings, stories circulated through the press about the horrifying lethality of bullets fired by assault weapons. One trauma center doctor told a reporter that "because of the bullet's high velocity" when fired from an assault weapon "shock waves can shatter bone or explode organs even if not hit directly." The schoolyard killings were used as an example of this phenomenon. San Diego Chief of Police (and gun-control advocate) Joseph McNamara was quoted as saying that "one bullet hitting a child in Stockton took out his entire stomach."

But according to one of the nation's leading experts on bullet wounds, these reports were almost uniformly exaggerated or wholly fabricated. Dr. Martin Fackler, director of combat trauma management at the Letterman Army Institute of Research, analyzed the autopsy reports of the five children killed by Patrick Purdy and concluded that there was no damage done to any organ *not directly struck by a bullet*. All of the children who died in Stockton had been hit in a vital organ. "The magnitude of the tissue disruption reported from fatal wounds inflicted by the AK-47 bullets fired by Purdy," he added, "was, in fact, no greater than that produced by many common handgun bullets."

Fackler warned that these exaggerations not only distorted public policy debate but posed a health risk. Inexperienced doctors, told that the person they were treating had been shot with an assault weapon, might cause additional injuries by probing wounds in search of "exploded organs" and "shattered bones."

While the movement to ban assault weapons didn't start with the Stockton shootings (William Bennett's memo on the subject had been written nearly a year before the killings), the tragedy did thrust the issue into the national spotlight. Bills were introduced in the Senate on February 8, 1989, and in the House on March 1, banning or restricting the importation and sale of several types of semiautomatic assault weapons, including the AK-47.

Opponents of the gun ban looked to George Bush to lead the opposition against these legislative efforts. After all, hadn't Bush written an open letter to NRA members before the November election, telling gun owners, "You can support my opponent and give up the rights you cherish, or you can support me and maintain your right to keep and bear arms"?

Just to make sure that Bush understood how important these issues were to the NRA, ILA director Wayne LaPierre and lobbyist James Jay Baker paid a call on the new deputy White House political director, David Carney, in early February. Was the president considering any new bans or restrictions on semiautomatic weapons? the pair wanted to know. Carney assured them that the administration had no such plans. Bush reiterated this stand in public later that month when asked by a reporter about new restrictions on semiautomatic weapons.

"Look," Bush emphasized, "if you're suggesting that every pistol that can [fire on semiautomatic], or every rifle, should be banned, I would strongly oppose that. I would strongly go after the criminals who use these guns. But I'm not going to suggest that a semiautomated hunting rifle be banned. Absolutely not."

This sounded like a ringing endorsement of the NRA position, but lobbyist James Jay Baker was not so sure. Publicly, Baker told the press that he was encouraged by the president's comments, but in the privacy of his small office at NRA headquarters, Baker felt that something was amiss.

Since coming to the NRA in 1980, Baker had learned to trust his instincts, a course that has rarely let him down. Perhaps it was his training as a lawyer at Catholic University and the two years he served as assistant county prosecutor in Missouri that gave him such unerring gut intuitions about people's motivations and his ability to ferret out the truth behind ambiguous language. Thanks, in part, to these skills, Baker had risen fast at the NRA. As director of federal affairs for the ILA, the thirty-five-year-old native of Washington, D.C., was responsible for handling all congressional gun legislation, as well as serving as a liaison between the gun group and the White House. Although Baker wasn't the head of the NRA, or even of the division in which he worked (Warren Cassidy was executive vice president and

Wayne LaPierre director of the ILA), many on Capitol Hill considered him the real power behind the NRA. Even John Aquilino, the deposed director of the gun lobby's public education division, once referred to Baker as "the gem in the NRA's lobby crown."

Baker stood out for another reason. In a Capitol Hill environment in which the NRA had long since decided it was better to be feared than liked, Jim Baker was universally respected and genuinely admired. Even among the opposition, it's hard to find anyone with a bad opinion of him.

"Jim Baker's really the only one that's allowed to come up here and negotiate," says one congressional legislative assistant who has often found himself on the other side of an issue from the NRA. "The rest of them we won't even talk to."

"Baker's good," admits another legislative aide. "He's knowledgeable. He's a very good strategist. I've got a lot of respect for him."

But former HCI lobbyist Mary Louise Cohen speaks for many on the Hill when she adds that those same qualities that make her like and respect Baker—his reasonableness and amicability—lead her to question his commitment to the NRA's extreme and uncompromising stands. "Jim is a smart and pleasant person. But it's always astounded me the positions he'd take," she says. "I think he's a professional. I never had the sense that Jim believed in what he was doing in his heart of hearts."

Sarah Brady, who has met Baker several times, also doubts that he is a "true believer." "He seems like a pleasant person," Brady says. "I'm shocked he would actually believe these things [NRA positions], but I doubt that he does. He's more like a hired gun. He's paid to do what the board wants him to do and if he wants to keep his job, he's got to perform."

Told of these comments, Jim Baker just laughs—but softly. Although he is unfailingly friendly and, as Cohen says, pleasant, Baker is essentially a serious person who does most of his laughing with his eyes, or with a bemused tug at a corner of his cowboylike mustache. The idea that he is less than earnest in his defense of the Second Amendment just because he's also a nice guy clearly amuses him.

"The people who know me well would tell you that I *am* a true believer," he says. Pressed on the point, though, Baker concedes that there is some truth to the assertion that he is just doing his job. "I represent a client," he explains slowly and carefully, as before a jury. "I think I represent them fairly well. But I think there are differences in my personal beliefs as opposed to some of the beliefs that I espouse for the client."

But then he adds with a quick smile, "But if anything, my beliefs might be *more* radical. Look, this is more than a job to me. For me to tell you that I'm not emotionally involved in this issue, I'd be lying to you."

Jim Baker may be an enigma to people inside the Beltway, but in Missouri there is little doubt in Farrell Hockemeier's mind that the NRA's chief lobbyist is a genuine believer in the right to bear arms. Hockemeier and Baker were roommates at Tulane University for the two years that Baker attended school there before transferring to the University of New Mexico. The two remained friends, and when Hockemeier got a job as county prosecutor in rural western Missouri, he hired Baker as his assistant.

Baker taught Hockemeier to shoot, and the two would often spend their off-hours target shooting. Asked if Baker perhaps got his dedication to the Second Amendment from spending time in rural Missouri, Hockemeier insists it was the other way around.

"There is a big emphasis on letting people go their own way around here, but Jim didn't get that from here," he says. "He brought it with him. If anything, he gave the people here a renewed appreciation for that kind of sentiment. He was born with that sense of freedom and of other people's rights."

Hockemeier wasn't at all surprised when Baker told him in 1981 that he was leaving to work for the NRA in Washington, D.C.

"This is a small county and Jim wasn't cut out for rural Missouri," recalls Hockemeier. "We both knew from the start that he wasn't going to settle down here."

Nor was Hockemeier surprised by Baker's success in Washington. Hockemeier remembers the pride Baker took in thoroughness, an attention to the smallest details that he brought to everything he did, from preparing his cases to doing intricate mechanical work on his BMW 2002.

It was this attention to details that now had Jim Baker questioning the depth of George Bush's commitment to what the NRA saw as the gun owner's nearly absolute right to buy the gun of his or her choice—

including semiautomatic "assault weapons." Baker pored over George Bush's congressional voting record from when the New England transplant had represented Texas in the House. Bush had made the right noises about the sanctity of gun ownership, but his votes on the issue revealed only a lukewarm commitment. There was no mistaking it: George Bush was no true believer. Baker decided the NRA could not depend on the president's support if things heated up.

On March 11, Virginia's lieutenant governor, Douglas Wilder, raised the ante by challenging the president to follow Virginia's example and outlaw assault weapons. "Whatever it takes," Wilder said, "let's show the American people that we are really serious about crime and serious about drugs." As a member of the Democratic Leadership Council, Wilder's message was a clear indication to Bush that the Democrats would use any administration foot-dragging on assault weapons against the Republicans. On the same day that Wilder made his remarks, White House senior staff members and Republican leaders in Congress were holding a powwow in Wilder's backyard, Charlottesville, Virginia. The Republicans were casting about for a hot (but not too complex) issue the new administration could use to prove that it was decisive. *The New York Times*'s political reporter R. W. Apple later theorized that it was at this meeting that the administration seized on assault weapons, an issue that, Apple wrote, "would cost little and it might win widespread support."

The issue was indeed hot. On February 6, the Stockton City Council voted nine to zero to outlaw assault weapons; the city of Los Angeles passed a similar ban the next day. Another six cities rapidly followed suit. Within weeks, at least thirty states and countless local governments around the country had taken up the issue. Maryland weighed whether it should join neighboring Virginia in enacting a ban on semiautomatic assault weapons. California Attorney General John Van de Kamp announced a campaign to outlaw assault weapons statewide. Van de Kamp—who was planning a run against Republican governor George Deukmejian in the next election—caused a commotion when he brandished an AK-47 at a legislative hearing and declared that he could wipe out the entire room in a flash. Not to be outdone, Governor Deukmejian—who had been elected on an anti-gun-control platform—now strongly backed the plan to limit access to assault weapons. The National Conference of Mayors passed a resolution asking Congress to pass legislation banning the guns, as did the leadership of the International Association of Chiefs of Police. On March 13, the California State Assembly voted to outlaw forty models of semiautomatic assault weapons.

On March 14, 1989—one day after the California action—the Bush administration reversed itself and gave in to rapidly escalating pressure for action on semiautomatic weapons. In his first full day on the job as the administration's new "Drug Czar," William Bennett—the man who had first suggested banning assault weapons a year earlier—issued a one-page statement: "Treasury Secretary Nicholas Brady and I have discussed assault weapons and he has decided to suspend, effective immediately, the importation of several makes of assault-type weapons. . . ."

The statement mentioned by name the AK-47, the Israeli-made Uzi carbine, the Austrian Steyr Aug, and two semiautomatics made by Fabrique Nationale of Belgium.

The suspension—the administration went to great lengths to point out that the action was not technically a "ban"—was made under a section of the 1968 Gun Control Act that allowed the secretary of the Treasury to prohibit the importation of guns that were not "generally recognized as particularly suitable for, or readily adaptable to, sporting purposes." The suspension would remain in place for two or three months, until the Bureau of Alcohol, Tobacco and Firearms could complete a review of assault weapons importation. The action blocked the importation of 113,732 weapons already on order—nearly triple the number imported in the previous year. Together, the five guns accounted for 80 percent of U.S. imports of assault weapons.

The suspension was evidence of America's growing concern with violent crime, as well as proof of the gun-control movement's success in bringing the nation's law enforcement community into its fold. Gun control was no longer a "liberal" issue. These facts were apparent in Bennett's explanation for the government's action: "There are a lot of policemen out there who are saying . . . the main purpose of these weapons is carnage and mayhem. It's not going to solve the problem, obviously. But . . . we don't need to add fuel to the fire."

The police also had an inside line to the president in Los Angeles Chief of Police Daryl Gates. The former adviser to the Bush presidential campaign on crime and drugs, Gates had emerged as one of the leading proponents of an all-out ban on the weapons. In impassioned testimony before a Senate committee hearing, Gates had argued that "these [assault] weapons have to go."

> The problem is that we have a proliferation of these weapons; that is the problem. And I cannot see why reasonable people, responsible people, can't understand that. . . . And those who object to gun control had better pay attention because we in law enforcement are facing up to this every single day and I am getting pretty sick and tired of presenting flags to widows and little kids and trying to explain away why it is we have an arms race in the United States.

It was a meeting with undercover Drug Enforcement Administration (DEA) agents on March 9, in New York City, however, that finally convinced Bush to take action. One agent told the president that harsh new sentencing guidelines for drug offenders had resulted in a situation that was putting the agents' lives at increased risk. Facing life sentences without a chance of parole if convicted of drug trafficking, cornered suspects now routinely grabbed their assault rifles and blasted away at police. The agents asked Bush to ban the weapons.

Rather than fight the inevitable, the NRA tried to put the best face on the suspension. ILA chief Wayne LaPierre issued a statement saying that "the NRA trusts that the action will end the rush of ill-conceived and ill-defined legislative proposals that would turn millions of Americans into felons and deprive honest citizens of firearms they have lawfully owned for decades."

Privately, however, the gun lobby was less philosophical about what it considered a double cross by Bennett and Bush. That anger was evident in a caustic letter sent to the drug czar from NRA assistant general counsel James H. Warner. Warner claimed the suspension was unfair to U.S. soldiers serving overseas who wanted to bring assault rifles with them when they returned home.

"While you may not be familiar with the life of a serviceman," wrote Warner—in a jibe at Bennett, who had obtained a student deferment from military service during the Vietnam War—"for many of these men the chance to bring home firearms purchased while posted overseas is small recompense for the . . . risk of overseas duty." Just in case Bennett didn't get the first suggestion that he was a draft dodger, Warner added, "Perhaps you can remember, when you were in graduate school, looking forward with great anticipation to some small pleasure to relieve the tedium of your scholarly pursuits." After advising the drug czar that he should exempt servicemen from the suspension, Warner concluded:

> I know that you are comfortable talking to the press, and that you wish to do the right thing in this matter. Accordingly, I have taken the liberty of informing the Washington representative of the servicemen's newspaper, *Stars and Stripes*, that he might expect a statement from you by 1:00 tomorrow afternoon . . . expressing your regret for any inconvenience to members of our armed forces.

When a reporter later asked Warner if he was calling Bennett a draft dodger, the NRA lawyer answered, "Let people's records speak for themselves. I suppose one has to read into it whatever one sees there. That's as clear as I can make it."

If Wayne LaPierre really believed that the suspension would end the controversy over assault weapons, he was mistaken. The NRA's old nemesis in the Senate, Howard Metzenbaum, pointedly referred to the administration's action as "a major first step," and in the House, California Democrat Pete Stark said that "the next step is how do we keep drug dealers and psychopaths from buying assault weapons cash-and-carry." The suspension might have kept 80 percent of imported assault weapons off the nation's streets, but what Bush and Bennett failed to mention was that at least three quarters of the estimated three million assault weapons already owned in this country were domestically manufactured. The administration had no plans to place new limits or restrictions on any weapons produced within the country.

But two days after Bennett announced the suspension, the manufacturer of one of the best-selling domestically produced semiautomatic assault rifles surprised both the NRA and gun-control proponents when it announced that it was ending production of the gun. That weapon, made by Colt Firearms, was the AR-15, the semiautomatic version of the standard U.S. military infantry automatic weapon since Vietnam: the M16. A Colt spokesperson said that the decision was based on a desire to honor "the spirit of the law."

"Our weapons are for ranchers, hunters, and target sportsmen," explained the representative. "But we sense a great concern on the part of the government toward the possible inappropriate misuse of semiautomatic weapons. We're responding to that concern."

The company's professed patriotism notwithstanding, its decision was probably more a result of the U.S. Army's recent determination to turn over the contract for producing the military version of the gun—which Colt had made for thirteen years—to a Belgian firm. (The company's motives were made even more questionable when, one year later, Colt introduced a "new, modified version" of the AR-15. The gun, which lacked the bayonet mount and the flash suppressor of its predecessor, resembled and functioned like the original in all other ways. Colt emphasized its contention that the new gun fit the ATF's guidelines—"particularly suitable for, or readily adaptable to, sporting purposes"—by naming the firearm "The Sporter.")

Colt's announcement was hailed by gun-control advocates and the Bush administration ("a very courageous action," said DEA chief John Lawn) as another step forward in the battle against crime. The NRA declined to comment—possibly because even as Colt was making its announcement, the gun group was busy behind the scenes twisting the administration's arm in an effort to stop the ATF from adding another twenty-five imported military-style semiautomatic weapons to the five already suspended. After getting wind of the ATF's plan, Wayne LaPierre quickly sought for and got a meeting with White House chief of staff John Sununu. LaPierre reminded Sununu of the NRA's good-faith effort to work with the Bush administration, demonstrated by the fact that the gun lobby went along—albeit begrudgingly—with the first suspension. LaPierre could not promise Sununu that the powerful lobby would be so understanding concerning any further moves to restrict semiautomatic weapons. Only hours after that meeting, the ATF received orders from senior officials at the Treasury Department: No new weapons could be suspended for the time being.

But even the NRA could not forever block the inevitable, and on April 5, 1989, President Bush announced that the earlier suspension on importations of assault weapons—which blocked 80 percent of such imports—was now being expanded to include the remaining 20 percent. Twenty-four models were added to the list after manufacturers of the original five types of weapons complained that other nearly identical firearms should not have a competitive advantage. White

House press secretary Marlin Fitzwater described the move as merely "a midcourse correction." The NRA, of course, saw the matter differently, and officially broke with the administration, charging that Bush had reneged on a campaign pledge to protect the rights of gun owners "in the face of short-term political hysteria."

"Does the Bush administration seriously believe a Prohibition-style approach will stop drug dealers, gang members and other criminals from getting any guns they want?" asked an angry Wayne LaPierre. "We call upon President Bush to stick to his guns."

But by sticking to its (semiautomatic) guns, the NRA was losing support even among its staunchest allies. Former senator Barry Goldwater, a life member of the NRA who had often appeared in advertisements for the gun group, told a reporter for *The Washington Post* that on the issue of assault weapons, he and the NRA no longer saw eye to eye. "I've never used an automatic or semiautomatic for hunting," Goldwater said. "There's no need to. They have no place in anybody's arsenal. If any SOB can't hit a deer with one shot, then he ought to quit shooting."

But the NRA had a far more disturbing "defection" in store.

Soon after Howard Metzenbaum introduced his anti–assault weapons bill in the Senate, a group of leading law enforcement officials called on an old ally: Arizona senator Dennis DeConcini. The police asked DeConcini to support Metzenbaum's bill, which, in addition to banning a large number of imported and domestically produced weapons, would confiscate these guns from *present owners*. The request put the senior senator from Arizona in a difficult position, one that revealed the shifting alliances of the 1980s. DeConcini had been elected to the Senate in 1977 as a "tough-on-crime" conservative Democrat, forging a strong alliance with police groups. The son of an Arizona State Supreme Court judge, and a former county district attorney, DeConcini's primary issue had, from the beginning, been the war on drugs. In fact, President Bush had first offered the position of drug czar to DeConcini—who declined the honor in order to keep his Senate seat.

But DeConcini was also an NRA "100 percenter"—one of a handful of legislators who had never voted against the organization. He had played a leading role on the Senate Judiciary Committee in the passage of the McClure-Volkmer legislation. For his work in defense of gun owners' rights, DeConcini had once been named the NRA "Person of the Month." And in return, when the Arizona Democrat was in a tough reelection campaign in 1988, the NRA mailed out a member letter wholeheartedly endorsing the man it called "one of our best friends" in the Senate.

DeConcini listened to the police leaders explain why they thought he should support the Metzenbaum bill. "Well," DeConcini told them at last, "I'm sorry. But I just can't support something that far-reaching."

It was not just the provisions contained in the bill that bothered DeConcini. The idea of being lumped together with the legislation's sponsor, Howard Metzenbaum—one of the most liberal members of the Senate, and perhaps the NRA's most hated enemy in the body— was enough to give the conservative DeConcini night sweats. Still, the police were asking for help on the semiautomatic issue, and De-Concini felt he couldn't just turn his back on them. He called the NRA and explained the situation to them. "Look, can't we work something out on this?" he implored. Several NRA officials huddled. DeConcini was a loyal friend, and although they wanted to help him, in the end it was decided that their hands were tied. There would be, there *could* be, no compromises. The group had already conceded more than it had wanted on the original suspension order. Some high-ranking NRA officials also felt that their earlier "compromises" on so-called plastic guns and armor-piercing bullets had hurt the group's credibility among hard-line members. On the issue of semiautomatics, the NRA had now drawn a line in the sand.

"Sorry," they told DeConcini. "No compromises."

Now it was DeConcini's turn to choose: the police or the NRA.

On April 11, the mild-mannered fifty-two-year-old senator from Arizona stood at his desk on the floor of the U.S. Senate and took the greatest gamble of his career. "Mr. President," DeConcini said in his usual monotone, "I propose today to introduce the Anti-Drug Assault Weapons Limitation Act of 1989." The bill would ban future sales of several semiautomatic assault weapons, both domestic and imported, but allowed present owners to keep their firearms.

"I am certain that arguments will be made that this legislation does not go far enough," DeConcini told his colleagues. "I am equally convinced that others will contend that the bill goes too far. I view those two arguments as supporting the position that this legislation takes—that there must be a reasonable middle position which will protect the public from physical harm while ensuring protection of constitutional rights under the law."

Far from seeing DeConcini's bill as a "reasonable middle position," the NRA felt betrayed by the senator.

"The NRA went through the roof," says DeConcini's primary aide on gun issues, Dennis Burke. "There was no compromising with them. It was a religious war. You're either with them or against them." And now DeConcini, considered (only the year before) by the NRA to be "one of our best friends in the Senate," was against them—in the NRA's way of thinking.

The gun group unleashed a furious campaign against the apostate senator, mailing letters to the 50,000 NRA members in Arizona telling of DeConcini's "tragic mistake." The bill, according to the letter, "can ban almost all centerfire semi-auto rifles, shotguns and pistols you can buy in Arizona"—charges DeConcini dismissed as "lies and exaggerations." Later, the NRA sent out letters likening DeConcini's bill to Soviet tactics in Lithuania.

"Initially you laugh when you read this because it's so absurd," says Dennis Burke. "But then you think, My God, these guys are *sending this material out to people!*"

And the material was making its mark on Arizona gun owners. Petitions to recall DeConcini began circulating through gun shops. The senator's Phoenix office was inundated with calls and letters blasting him for his bill.

"I believe you have forgotten that you represent Arizona, a Western state that has a very high per capita membership in the National Rifle Association," charged one letter. "Therefore Senator, I believe you are politically dead meat."

"These Elitist Marxists," wrote another constituent, "by what ever name they currently choose to call themselves, are pushing for the destruction, piecemeal if necessary, of the Second Amendment, the Cornerstone of the American Constitution. . . . I realize that I am wasting my time writing to you, but one must make the effort, Comrade."

While the NRA efforts at DeConcini-bashing were taking a toll on the senator, DeConcini himself warned that the gun group was hurting itself more than it was him, describing his own bill as the only thing that could prevent passage of harsher legislation. "The NRA is succeeding only in alienating its friend closest to the fight," he warned.

Bad news continued to pile up for the NRA. Despite continued Bush administration assurances that it was not considering bans on domestically produced weapons ("We'd never get a law passed to ban domestic assault weapons," said Marlin Fitzwater), a letter from Treasury secretary Nicholas Brady listing seventeen domestic assault rifles that *would* be banned if they were made overseas was made public in late June.

Two weeks later, there was even worse news. ATF director Stephen Higgins announced the results of a three-month study of assault weapons: The temporary ban on twenty-nine imported semiautomatic weapons was now made permanent—and expanded to include forty-three models.

The decision satisfied no one. Certainly not NRA members, who began a petition drive to expel Bush from the organization. Although the national body didn't officially sanction the move, Wayne LaPierre let it be known that "the sentiment is pretty wide in terms of the disillusionment, disappointment and anger toward President Bush."

But even those supporting restrictions on the firearms gave the Bush ruling mixed reviews. California representative Pete Stark (who had offered his own bill calling for a more comprehensive ban on assault weapons) praised Bush for "having the guts to stand up to the National Rifle Association," but complained that the prohibition applied only to foreign guns. "This is just a bonus to domestic companies because obviously they can raise their prices now," said Stark. "They won't be faced with cheaper imports, and their demand should go up."

Stark's crystal ball was dead-on. Domestic manufacturers had a hard time keeping up with the increased demand as American gun enthusiasts fell over one another trying to buy semiautomatic rifles. Arms Corporation of America, maker of the semiautomatic M14S, had had to boost production by more than a third in the four months following the announcement of the first import suspension. "Our factory is running around the clock, seven days a week, no holidays and no vacation," reported a company executive.

All over the country, gun stores were finding it impossible to keep semiautomatic assault rifles in stock. Even with prices inflated by 30, 50, or 100 percent, buyers had to put their names on waiting lists for the weapons.

On July 20, 1989, the DeConcini bill faced its first legislative test: a vote by the Senate Judiciary Committee. To insiders, it did not seem to be much of a test, however. In a committee divided equally among Democrats and Republicans, the bill faced an almost certain tie vote— which would have the effect of killing DeConcini's ban without its ever being debated on the Senate floor. The NRA could not have hoped for a better venue, and even DeConcini knew it. In a last-minute effort to make his bill more palatable to the opposition, the Arizona Democrat added a "sunset" provision to his bill: The ban on nine types of assault weapons would expire in three years. During the time in which the ban was in effect, the Justice Department would determine what effect, if any, it had on drug-related violent crime. If the ban proved useful, it could be reintroduced; if not, that was the end of it.

DeConcini's "sweetener" had no effect, however. As the voting began, it was clear that senators were splitting along party lines, as expected. Of course Edward Kennedy, Howard Metzenbaum, and DeConcini voted for the bill. So did the other Democrats. And the Republican conservatives stuck to their anti-gun-control guns. To the few outsiders watching the voting, there was a moment of confusion when the vote stood at seven to six in favor of the bill. It appeared that the bill was heading for passage. Why, then, didn't any of the Republican opponents look worried?

The reason for their calm demeanor was due to their knowledge that Republican committee member Arlen Specter hadn't cast his vote yet. He was sitting in on the impeachment hearings of a federal judge and would arrive at any time to vote with his fellow Republicans. There was nothing unusual about this. Because so much is occurring around Capitol Hill at all times when Congress is in session, legislators are always walking in and out of committee hearings, shepherded by their aides just in time for votes. It is almost unheard of for a committee to meet for a full session with all members present and accounted for the whole time. And everyone was fairly sure of how Specter would vote. As sure as they could be with Specter, that is.

The former district attorney from Philadelphia, a political moderate, was known for being something of a wild card on many issues. This stemmed from Specter's independent voting record, but also from his tendency to refrain from saying how he intended to vote until it was time to actually cast his ballot. Despite a keen—some say "brilliant"—legal mind, Specter's abrasive personality had made him few close friendships in the Senate, and even among his own staff he had a poor reputation, sometimes dressing down staffers in public, sometimes on the record, and prompting an unusually high turnover rate.

But there was little doubt about how he would vote in this case. Pennsylvania had the second highest per capita rate of NRA membership in the nation, and Specter generally went along with this important rural constituency—made even more important by the fact that Specter himself came from the state's largest urban center.

While his fellow Republicans might have been confident about Specter's vote when he got there, with the deadline for voting rapidly approaching, some of them began to grow nervous. Specter had not given his proxy to any of his colleagues, as is usual if an important vote might be missed. Aides were dispatched with instructions to find Specter immediately and bring him in to vote. Concern rapidly escalated to panic as the seconds ticked away.

The Democrats exchanged barely hopeful looks. Was it possible that Specter wouldn't show up, handing them an easy victory? Judiciary chairman Joseph Biden began counting off the final seconds as his Republican colleagues sputtered and fumed.

Just as Biden was about to declare the bill passed by a tally of seven to six, Arlen Specter strolled into the room. The Republicans' sigh of relief was matched by the sound of the Democrats' teeth-gnashing. Neither side, however, was prepared for what Specter did next.

"I'm sorry, Mr. Chairman," Specter told a dumbstruck Biden. "I can't vote on this bill. My staff hasn't briefed me adequately."

Then he turned around and walked out.

Silence held throughout the grand marble room. It took several seconds for the impact of Specter's words to sink in. Then, Chairman

Biden, recovering first, declared the DeConcini bill passed by a vote of seven to six, and swung the large wooden chairman's gavel down on the striker in front of him—*bam!*

The meeting was over. DeConcini's bill was headed for the Senate floor.


THE NRA HAD one last setback waiting for it in 1989. Toward the end of November, Attorney General Richard Thornburgh submitted his study on the feasibility of the point-of-sale "instant" background check for purchasers of handguns mandated by the McCollum bill (passed the year before). To no one's surprise, and although he tried to put the best possible spin on the conclusions, Thornburgh confirmed what critics had charged in 1988: that "a comprehensive, accurate system for identifying felons at the point of sale simply cannot be fully accomplished in the near term. . . ." Thornburgh called the idea a "worthwhile goal," but concluded that it was just not practical right then—it would be too costly and too complex.

"We knew a year ago that a point-of-sale check was impossible to implement immediately and that it would cost an enormous amount of money to put one in place," said an angry Edward Feighan, who had sponsored the Brady bill in the House. He charged that the year-long study had been merely "a delaying tactic."

But with Thornburgh's admission, backers of the Brady bill were now set to push *their* bill again. "This removes any and all excuses for not passing the Brady bill right away, before more criminals buy more handguns over the counter," said an HCI spokesperson.

On the same day that the attorney general sent his report to Congress, the Senate Judiciary Subcommittee was receiving a report of a different sort. The legislators, who were considering the Brady bill, were briefed by Jim Brady himself. Speaking in a slurred monotone, and seated in his wheelchair, Brady made a brief but powerful statement about the consequences of the nation's permissive attitude toward guns.

"I had no choice but to be here today because too many members of Congress have been gutless on this issue," he told the senators. "Are you willing and ready to cast a vote for a commonsense public safety issue endorsed by experts—law enforcement? Or are you going to continue to pander to the special interests that whine about a little inconvenience and other such lamebrain foolishness?"

Brady described the terrible changes wrought in his life by a bullet to the head.

> There was a day when I walked the halls of this Senate and worked closely with many of you and your staffs. There was a wonderful day when I was fortunate enough to serve the president of the United States in a capacity I had dreamed of all my life, and for a time I felt that people looked up at me.
>
> Today, I can tell you how hard it is to have people speaking down to me. . . . [N]othing is harder than losing the independence and control we all so value in our lives. I need help getting out of bed, taking a shower, and help getting dressed. And, damn it, I even need help to go to the bathroom.

The muffled sobs of legislative aides could be heard from around the otherwise silent room as Jim Brady concluded his testimony. "Damn it," he said, half imploring, half commanding, like a modern-day Jeremiah. "Don't let the vocal minority dictate your position!"

A SHOWDOWN WAS now imminent over both the seven-day waiting period and the ban on semiautomatic assault weapons. And for the first time since the NRA had entered the legislative arena in earnest some fifteen years earlier, all bets about the gun lobby's ability to crush its opposition were off.

# 9

# FIRST BLOOD

DENNIS BURKE LAID the single sheet of paper with five short columns of names on his already crowded desk top, beside the metal spindle jammed to the top with pink phone message slips—all of them marked URGENT—and looked out of the floor-to-ceiling window to his left. He had an impressive view of the enormous central atrium of the Hart Senate Office Building. Burke watched the swirl of people that never stopped flowing around the base of a towering sculpture, the last creation of Alexander Calder, three floors below. He saw the harried legislative aides, the bored secretaries, the sharp-eyed lobbyists in $700 suits, the visitors from back home, shy and diffident amid so much marble, energy, and power.

Burke turned his attention back to the piece of paper on his desk and shook his head. His official job title was Majority Counsel to the Subcommittee on Patents, Copyrights and Trademarks of the Senate Judiciary Committee—the body chaired by Dennis DeConcini, his boss. But Burke was really in charge of *all* the senator's Judiciary Committee work—a heady job for a recent graduate of the University of Arizona's law school. At this moment, however, the job seemed a bit overwhelming, for the top item on Burke's agenda was

the upcoming vote on DeConcini's Anti-Drug Assault Weapons Limitation Act, and the sheet of paper he stared at presented a bleak
picture.

Centered across the top of the page were the words:

U.S. SENATE: ASSAULT WEAPON TARGET LIST

And:

UPDATED MAY 14, 1990

Below, in smaller type, were five neat columns showing where the
hundred senators of the 101st Congress stood on the DeConcini bill.
On the far left was the list of those who were solidly for the bill. That
column had the number 1 typed above it. On the right-hand side of
the page were those known to be immovably opposed to the legislation.
Their column was topped by the number 5. In between were the
senators thought to be leaning for the bill (2), those who were undecided (3), and those leaning against the bill (4).

This format is used by every office in Congress and by lobbying
groups throughout Washington, including the NRA. Aides will employ
these enumerations in conversation, a form of verbal shorthand, but
even more, a shibboleth separating Beltway insiders from the general
public. "Kennedy? Oh, he's a One," an aide will say to a colleague,
meaning, "Don't worry about him, don't waste your time—he's on
board." The lists are to congressional aides and lobbyists what the
electronic ticker tape is to the stockbroker: portentous, dynamic, and
all-important.

On the left-hand side of Burke's sheet there were twenty-
five Ones—their votes were secure. But running down the extreme
right side of the page, Burke saw with dismay the longer column:
twenty-nine senators who were sure to vote against the DeConcini
assault weapons bill. There were also fifteen senators leaning for it,
twelve leaning against, and, in the center of the page, nineteen
undecideds.

On most bills, aides could phone the staffers of undecided senators—Threes or even Fours—and ask how to lobby their bosses, what
the right angles to push were, but Burke knew that the time had long
passed for such lobbying on this bill. The legislation had been around
for more than a year.

"I can't recommend anything," one aide had told him recently. "My boss knows this issue. He'll make up his mind for himself."

There was nothing more to do. Burke looked back out his window and frowned.

ACROSS TOWN, JAMES Baker sat in his office, only slightly larger than Burke's, staring at a similar sheet of paper. Although the numbers looked more encouraging to him, Baker was not enthusiastic. It was just too close. He would have liked some more breathing room; fewer Threes, more Fours.

Twice a day, a packet of newspaper clippings containing references to the NRA or to gun issues circulated around ILA offices. On this day, the articles about the assault weapons bill mentioned that the NRA hadn't lost a full Senate vote since it began lobbying in a serious way in 1977. That made Baker feel a little better about his organization's position. Still, like Burke, he knew that despite all the procedural wrangling and the intensive lobbying, despite the fact that he, the consummate detail man, had taken care of every last detail, there was no guaranteeing what would happen once the voting began. Even so, the NRA's record spoke for itself; Baker had no doubt that when the yeas and nays were called out on the Senate floor the gun lobby would prove victorious.

ON THE MORNING of May 22, a balmy Tuesday, Dennis DeConcini sent a letter by courier to the White House. It was a last-ditch attempt, a formality really, to get the president's support for the senator's bill, which would come up for a vote either later that same day or, at the latest, on the next.

In two and a half pages, single spaced, DeConcini listed the reasons Bush should support the measure. But the letter's real message was found at the bottom of the final page, beneath DeConcini's signature, where eight representatives of the law enforcement community signed their names. Included were Robert Scully, president of the National Association of Police Organizations, Dewey Stokes, national president of the Fraternal Order of Police, and Daryl Gates, chief of the LAPD and a former adviser to Bush on crime issues. Their names personalized the plea that ended the letter: "Help us make our streets safe again, and end the carnage of our police officers."

But the president was now moving in the opposite direction. That same day, the White House announced that the Bush administration no longer supported a proposal it had made in 1989, calling for a fifteen-round limit on ammunition clips for semiautomatic guns. Instead, Bush threw his weight behind a bill sponsored by Republican senator Strom Thurmond. That bill, which the NRA had also endorsed, called for harsher penalties for crimes committed with guns, rather than new gun-control measures. The administration's new position surprised no one who had been following the issue during the past year. Ever since the brief flurry of activity in the first half of 1989, Bush had been backing away from his initial stand. This reversal was especially apparent in February 1990, when William Bennett, who had started out as the administration's point man on assault weapons, had had an acrimonious exchange concerning the weapons with Senator Ted Kennedy during a Judiciary Committee hearing.

After praising Bennett's early leadership on the fight against assault rifles, Kennedy asked why the administration had done nothing about new *pistol* versions of the banned guns.

"Have you met with the NRA? Have they asked you to be quiet?" asked Kennedy.

Bennett, obviously irritated by the implication, answered, "No, no, they haven't—well, yes, I guess I did have a meeting with the NRA officials back when, and our relationship has not been particularly amicable."

Kennedy continued to press Bennett, his own displeasure showing. "Why are you silent?" he demanded. "Why are you quiet?"

"Because I have given my advice to the president, Senator," answered Bennett, "and that is where it should lie."

The two continued to spar for some time, interrupting each other, talking over each other, their voices rising until Bennett, when asked if he considered there to be any sporting purpose to semiautomatic assault pistols, shouted back at Kennedy, "I don't know a damn thing about guns!"

A Kennedy aide who was present at the hearing says he was surprised by Bennett's lack of cooperation on an issue he had himself started.

"My clear sense was that Bennett had been reined in at that point," he says. "I never figured out who had gotten to him. Bill Bennett isn't easy to quiet down. I mean, he's a pretty compelling guy. But he got the import ban and then he washed his hands of the whole gun issue in a big way."

By the third week in May there were three separate assault weapons bills in the Senate: DeConcini's, Thurmond's (which didn't mention the weapons by name, but which was understood to be an alternative to DeConcini's bill), and the far harsher measure offered by Howard Metzenbaum. As usual, *how* the amendments were presented would be critical to their chances.

Because his assault weapons ban had been passed out of committee a year earlier, DeConcini's amendment was included in the crime bill. But just days before the vote, Senate Judiciary Chairman Joseph Biden came to DeConcini with some bad news. The Democratic leadership had decided to remove his assault weapons ban from the bill. DeConcini would have to offer his bill as an amendment from the floor.

"Look, you just don't have the votes," explained Biden, who personally supported the measure. "You're just going to screw up the whole bill."

But DeConcini was adamant. The legislation was important to him, and, he argued, it had earned a place in the bill by the committee vote. A high-level meeting took place in the Senate majority leader's office late one night to work out a compromise. Biden, DeConcini, Metzenbaum, and Majority Leader George Mitchell—himself a Three or a Four on the measure—attended the meeting. After much discussion, they decided to keep DeConcini's amendment in the bill. Orrin Hatch, one of the NRA's closest allies, and the leader of the opposition to DeConcini's bill, would have to marshal the votes necessary to take it out. And they agreed that Metzenbaum would first get a vote on his more stringent bill.

That vote took place on May 22. With even DeConcini's milder bill not expected to win, few took Metzenbaum's amendment seriously. Still, the white-haired senator from Ohio spoke out passionately for his position, telling his colleagues: "Don't be afraid of the NRA. The NRA is a paper tiger. Its bark is louder than its bite."

But after two hours of debate, Metzenbaum's legislation was definitively swamped, eighty-two to seventeen. The magnitude of the defeat did nothing to raise Burke's confidence as the body turned to debate Orrin Hatch's motion to strike the DeConcini ban from the crime bill.

Burke had already prepared himself for defeat. No one likes to lose, especially hypercompetitive legislative aides, but he reminded himself that no one had come this close to beating the NRA since 1968, and that was some solace.

So we lose, he told himself. So we get our 40 votes, and then it's over with.

At 10:44 P.M., after the senators had used up all but forty-five minutes of the three hours allotted for debate on Hatch's amendment, it was decided that the Senate should recess until the following day, Wednesday, May 23.

Promptly at 9:30 A.M., Robert Byrd, president pro tempore of the Senate, called the body to order. That job is usually performed by the president of the Senate, Vice President Dan Quayle, but Quayle was on a trip to the Midwest. His absence wasn't surprising. The president of the Senate only votes in case of a tie, and, as Dennis Burke knew, that was not likely today.

The final forty-five minutes of debate began, and soon ended, the only surprise being Majority Leader Mitchell's statement that he intended to vote to keep the DeConcini ban. Then the polling began.

Around the back of the Senate chamber, DeConcini's staff had arranged a number of easels bearing poster-size photographs of the assault weapons to be banned by the amendment. There was the MAC-11, a T-shaped pistol sporting a thirty-two-round magazine and advertised as "the gun that made the eighties roar." Next to it was a blowup of the TEC-9, a 9-mm semiautomatic pistol capable of emptying its thirty-six-round clip in forty-five seconds, a gun federal agents said was popular with drug dealers. Beside the TEC-9 was a photograph of the Striker 12, also known as the Streetsweeper. The Striker 12 was a semiautomatic shotgun capable of firing a dozen twelve-gauge shotgun shells in seconds.

These guns were clearly modeled after military weapons and looked nothing like hunting rifles. And there was no doubt that the guns even *looked* frightening; Burke noticed with satisfaction that senators were standing around the photographs in small groups, shaking their heads. Burke spotted his boss standing before a photograph of the Streetsweeper, asking a colleague, "You're going to go hunting with *this*? You're going to protect yourself with *this*? There's no purpose for this. It's used in South Africa for *riot* control, for God's sake!"

The other senator listened intently to DeConcini, nodding as if in agreement.

Off to one side, Burke noticed Orrin Hatch and Idaho senator James McClure, both fervent NRA supporters. Neither of them was talking. They, too, were watching the other senators examine the photographs of the assault weapons, and both Hatch and McClure, Burke noted instantly, were scowling. A minute later, Alan Dixon of Illinois (a Two, Burke immediately thought) came up and asked if he could have a copy of the gun poster. While Burke was arranging to get Dixon a poster he saw Tom Daschle of South Dakota huddled in conference with DeConcini.

"Don't worry," DeConcini was telling him, "your local police will campaign with you." Daschle looked concerned, but he was nodding. Daschle was a Three, possibly even a Four! Burke had never thought they'd get his vote.

Burke knew that most debate on the floor is designed to explain for the record how a senator intends to vote, rather than to convince colleagues to vote a certain way. Most votes are decided coolly and rationally—that is to say, politically—long before they are actually cast. As Burke looked around him he realized many senators were making their decisions *right on the floor!*

From the conversations he was having with other aides, as well as others he could overhear, Burke understood for the first time just how critical police support had become. He knew firsthand how this worked. After DeConcini had first introduced his bill, he had tried to keep a low profile on the issue for a time, rather than antagonize gun owners, but lobbyists at HCI had prodded DeConcini to speak out forcefully for the ban.

"Do you want me to have Sarah Brady call Dennis?" Gail Hoffman, HCI's chief federal lobbyist, had asked Burke.

"Sarah Brady isn't going to do anything," Burke had told her. "Have Dewey Stokes [president of the police union] call."

Stokes called, several times, as did other police representatives. The result was that the Arizona senator made the assault weapons ban a high-profile issue. And now Burke saw that that same political cover provided by the police was helping many Twos and Threes overcome their fear of the NRA.

Lloyd Bentsen sat in his office following the debate on C-SPAN.

The Texas Democrat, who had received national recognition as the Democratic vice presidential nominee in 1988, had a long anti-gun-control voting record. Although Burke's "Target List" had Bentsen down as a Two, that was a bit optimistic. But when the C-SPAN camera focused on the posters of assault weapons, Bentsen knew what he was going to do. He went down to the Senate floor and sought out DeConcini. "I think you're right," the Texan told DeConcini.

If the bill was to stand a chance, it would need the support of several other southern Democrats, senators used to voting as a bloc *against* gun-control measures. The dean of that group was Georgian Sam Nunn, the arms-control expert (international and nuclear—not domestic and semiautomatic) with presidential aspirations. Before controversial Senate votes, it was standard practice for legislative assistants in the offices of other southern Democrats to phone Nunn's people and ask what their boss was going to do. Nunn had been leaning slightly in favor of DeConcini's bill, but had not declared his intentions. Now, he voted for DeConcini, but would that be enough to sway the other southerners? Burke's tally now showed the opposition still running ahead, but the margin was closing.

The bill took a giant leap forward when Bob Packwood (from Oregon; a Two) and John Warner (a Virginian, and a Three) voted for DeConcini's amendment. They were joined by Oklahoman David Boren and Jay Rockefeller of West Virginia—also Threes. But the biggest surprise was still in store. Tennessee senator Al Gore, a Two, approached the Volunteer State's other senator, James Sasser. Sasser was listed as a Four on Burke's list, but most others considered him a solid Five—dead set against any gun bill. The two were standing at the front of the chamber, in the semicircular area directly in front of the presiding officer's chair, an area known as the "well."

"Jim," Gore said quietly to Sasser, "I really think we should go with Dennis on this. I think we can do all right back home on this." Sasser listened to his colleague carefully. The two talked for a minute or so. Then both men voted in favor of the DeConcini amendment.

The clerk reported the final tally a few minutes later: The Senate had upheld the assault weapons ban by a vote of fifty-one to forty-nine. The progun delegation forced another vote on the measure a few hours later, but the amendment once again carried the day.

Back in his office following the vote and surrounded by cheering staff workers, Dennis DeConcini couldn't stop grinning. It was not only a major legislative victory but a personal triumph for DeConcini, who had endured the wrath of gun owners (egged on by the NRA) for more than a year. Pickets outside his Phoenix office; a vicious recall campaign; harassing phone calls; even death threats. In one of the few actions by a U.S. senator in recent years that would qualify for a "profile in courage," he had gambled his political future on legislation that no one—including Dennis DeConcini—thought would pass.

After thanking his staff, DeConcini told his people to get on the phones and start thanking those senators who had joined his campaign for the ban.

"You have to help Boren and Rockefeller and their staff," DeConcini instructed. "Help them on whatever they need—explaining this bill to constituents, providing cover, whatever they need." Senate staff workers would need a lot of help in the coming weeks. For many of them, the vote came as a complete surprise.

"One moment, their boss was going to the floor to vote no on the bill," says Burke. "A half hour later he comes back having voted yes. A lot of the staff were just blown away. I was on the phone the next two weeks helping them deal with the fallout from this vote."

Meanwhile, the atmosphere at NRA headquarters was funereal; all that was missing was the black crepe. It was the largest setback yet for the gun lobby, and by far the most visible. At tough moments in the past (as in the battle over plastic guns and armor-piercing bullets), the group had switched sides at the last hour, just as defeat seemed certain. Using this tactic, it could at least plausibly claim to have an unblemished record of legislative victories in Congress. This time it was as surprised by the vote as the other side was.

"We never expected to lose," Jim Baker admitted to a reporter. "We knew it would be close, but we didn't expect it to be that close."

In an ILA tabloid newsletter, the NRA later attributed its defeat to the disloyalty of a few senators. Gun owners, the paper reported, "suffered a serious loss . . . due solely to a number of betrayals." The excuse used by many senators to justify their vote for the DeConcini amendment—that they had already voted *against* Howard Metzenbaum's harsher bill—was termed a trick as "transparent as it is underhanded."

"The tactic was as old as mine warfare," said the NRA. "First, you lay the smoke screen, then you plant the mines."

While there is no doubt that Metzenbaum sincerely wanted his own bill to pass, Dennis Burke readily admits that backers of the DeConcini amendment used the earlier vote to give themselves political cover. "Oh yeah," Burke says, "that helped us tremendously. You could go home and say, 'I voted against Metzenbaum. I voted for the DeConcini bill.' We knew that would help us from the beginning."

The article in the NRA paper concluded with a promise to remember both friends and enemies come next election day. "There is a reward for loyalty and a heavy tax on treachery," it declared with typical NRA bombast.


WHETHER THE NRA'S ability to dole out reward and punishment in the electoral arena had ever been anything more than a myth, Tom Andrews was at least certain that it was no longer true, and he was willing to bet his political career on it. The Democratic state senator would do what no one had yet tried: make a run for the U.S. Congress *highlighting* his support for gun control. Making the Brady bill the focal point of his campaign was unusual enough, but Andrews added another wrinkle to the battle. He was running in Maine, the state with the highest per capita membership in the NRA in the nation.

The pundits scoffed. Republicans quietly rooted for Andrews in the primary. Even some of his own advisers thought he was making a catastrophic mistake—but they weren't surprised. Although he was only thirty-seven years old, Andrews had long been a practitioner of what he calls "in-your-face progressivism," taking forceful stands on controversial issues—and never making apologies for it. Andrews had nothing but contempt for timid Democrats who downplayed or denied their liberal ideology. He was a Yankee version of Jim Hightower, the Texan who once blasted "centrist" Democrats by insisting that "the only things that belong in the middle of the road are a yellow line and dead armadillos."

Andrews made sure that his party also supported the Brady bill by introducing the measure as a plank in the party platform at the state Democratic convention in June 1990. The bitter fight that ensued is now hallowed in Maine history as "The Showdown at Presque Isle."

(Presque Isle, the site of the convention, is a small town in the predominantly rural northern section of the state.)

A Maine Democratic convention had never before been held in such an isolated, northern area. Most of the party bigwigs flew into town the night before the convention, socialized with their buddies, gave a speech the next morning, and flew out before noon. Andrews's strategy for passing the plank was simple.

"We waved good-bye to all the politicians as they were driving away from the convention center," he says with a devilish smile, "and *then* we engaged in a debate on the waiting period." There were still enough opponents around to protest the move, however, and vigorously. They denounced the plank, calling it "foolhardy," "a publicity stunt," and "political suicide." "This is going to mean the loss of Democrats all over the state," shouted one man, who was running for a seat in the Maine state senate, "and I hope Tom Andrews is the first."

The absent politicos were stunned when they awoke the next morning and read the headline in the *Maine Sunday Telegram*—DEMOCRATS BACK 7-DAY HANDGUN WAITING PERIOD.

"It was incredible," recalls Andrews. "I was suddenly the skunk at the lawn party at party functions. Even friends from rural areas said, 'You've just shot us in the back.' "

True to character, rather than apologize, Andrews went on the offensive. "I told them, Let's just relax a bit and take a couple of deep breaths. This is not the death of the Democratic party. And besides, it's the right thing to do. It's unbelievable that we can't pass something like this. It just defies logic that a group like the National Rifle Association could make this a litmus test. We should have the guts to stand up to these people."

"And when we do," Andrews promised his colleagues, "we're going to win."

Andrews was a tireless and confrontational campaigner, both for his candidacy and for the Brady bill. Only weeks before the November election, the NRA mailed out a member letter, signed by Jim Baker, charging that Andrews "has taken every opportunity to oppose your right to own firearms. His campaign literature proudly displays the fact that he wants to ban firearms!"

In the past, many other candidates on the receiving end of such a letter kept quiet about it, hoping to minimize the political damage. Andrews took the opposite tack. He distributed copies of the letter to reporters, blasted the NRA for misrepresenting his support for the Brady bill, and called publicly on his opponent to condemn the NRA tactics. "The key is to bring the debate out into the full light of day, for everybody to see," says Andrews. "Then they see that the emperor, the NRA, has no clothes."

As a result of the NRA letters, however, Andrews had to spend much of his time setting the record straight about his stand on gun control. When he'd walk into cafés or mom-and-pop stores while campaigning, Andrews says, the hooting and heckling would start immediately. "You don't have *our* votes," a group would tell him. So Andrews would sit down and talk with them. They were surprised to learn that he didn't want to ban long guns. But even when they believed him, they'd often repeat the NRA line that the Brady bill was just the first step toward government confiscation of all firearms.

"I'd tell them, 'Look, if anyone proposes to take your hunting rifle away or limit your access to buy a hunting rifle, they're going to have to go through me first,' " says Andrews. "And that generally took care of it."

Despite all the fretting of Democratic party regulars, and despite the pundits' predictions that you can't win in Maine supporting gun control, Andrews was elected to the U.S. House of Representatives. For someone to be elected in spite of his stand on gun control would have been a large enough setback for the NRA's reputation. What made the Tom Andrews victory so devastating for the gun lobby was that it came not *in spite* of his support for the Brady bill but largely *because* of it. And it didn't help the NRA that Andrews won in the gun group's greatest stronghold.

On the other hand, you would have a hard time selling Pete Smith on the idea that the NRA was now a paper tiger. Smith, who was elected to the U.S. House of Representatives from Vermont in 1988, has a lot in common with Andrews. Although not as young as Andrews (Smith was forty-eight years old when elected to Congress), he looks much younger than his age, and he, like Andrews, is bright and energetic. Although he is a Republican, Smith is from the party's moderate-to-liberal wing, and takes pride in calling himself a progressive. He also comes from a rural New England background where he grew up hunting. When the NRA sent him a candidates' gun-control questionnaire in 1987, Smith, without even thinking about it, indicated that he opposed gun control.

"If you're raised in the countryside the perceived purpose of guns is hunting," he says. "I never gave the question about gun control a second thought."

Moving to Washington, D.C., caused Smith to think hard about gun control for the first time. The level of gun violence in the nation's capital shocked Smith and his family. "It was like day and night—the difference between back home and Washington," he says. Smith's ten-year-old son refused to watch the evening news—too full of shot-up bodies. Smith gradually came to the conclusion that Congress had to do something, and that something, he decided, was pass the Brady bill and the ban on assault weapons.

When his staff counseled against his decision, Smith scoffed. "It just seemed that in a world in which we license drivers there's no reason not to figure out some handgun bill," he explains, his voice still tinged with incredulity that anyone could find such a mild and reasonable stand offensive.

The NRA was more than offended by Smith's change of heart, however. In an act that Smith now calls "naive in the extreme," he called the gun lobby before going public with his decision. Smith was a former president of the Community College of Vermont (which he helped found in 1970 when he was only twenty-five years old), and he thought that once he rationally explained to the NRA what he saw was the problem (a demographic split in which rural rules—easy access to guns—did not fit urban reality), he could work with the gun lobby to develop a workable compromise on the issue. "I went to them as a lifelong supporter," he explains, smiling now at his own innocence. "I thought I could help them reinvent their policy."

Rather than thanking him for his offer to negotiate a gun bill, Smith says the NRA told him that if he supported the Brady bill or the assault weapons ban, it would see to it that he was crushed at the polls in 1990. The gun lobby's threat offended Smith's sense of fair play and so hardened his position.

"If I backed off they would know, and I would know, that it was because I was afraid of their political power," he says. "At that point it was a matter of personal ethics."

The NRA and local Vermont gun clubs went after Smith as soon as he publicly announced his support for the assault weapons ban. The NRA printed and distributed thousands of bumper stickers urging voters to DUMP PETE SMITH. Then there were the stickers proclaiming SMITH & WESSON (YES)/PETER SMITH (NO). (Smith & Wesson is the name of a popular gun manufacturer.)

Smith says that he knew the NRA would take him on, and he knew the fight would be intense, but what he didn't expect was that the gun lobby would attack him personally on the issue of credibility. "I thought we'd have a debate on gun control," he says, "but we never did."

Instead, the NRA and its local affiliates focused on Smith's switch from anti- to pro-gun-control, telling voters that their representative had been corrupted in Washington. Bumper stickers appeared that read PETER SMITH: THE BIG LIE, and flyers comparing Smith to Hitler showed up in gun shops. His campaign yard signs were blasted with buckshot. Irate gun owners threatened his life. His wife was afraid to stay home alone at night after receiving threatening phone calls. When Congress recessed for the summer, the House sergeant-at-arms offered to send Secret Service agents to Vermont with Smith, an offer he turned down. "I thought it would look like grandstanding," he says.

The NRA denies any responsibility for the harassment, claiming that the organization doesn't condone violence and that the more inflammatory campaign literature was the work of local gun clubs. But Smith blames the NRA. "They created a climate of fear, a climate of anger, and a climate of hatred," he says. "The national guys ran the offense and the local guys pulled the trigger."

The NRA's claim that it is not responsible for the actions of affiliated gun clubs is made particularly suspect by the national gun lobby's oft-repeated claim to be the official Washington representative of these same groups. "The NRA family extends to nearly 14,000 affiliated clubs and associations," brags one NRA flyer.

On election day, the NRA scored a bull's-eye in the Vermont race. Smith was defeated by Burlington's socialist mayor, Bernie Sanders. While not minimizing the role played by the NRA in his defeat, Smith emphasizes that gun control was only one factor. "Don't forget, there was also a rising tide of anti-incumbency," he says, "and I was running against a classic outsider who was saying that government is screwing you and I'm going to help you. When it all came together it was really hellish—like a tsunami hitting. If gun control had been the only issue, I think I would have been the congressman today."

Many politicians were surprised that the NRA had fought Smith so aggressively, spending $18,000 to defeat him, when his opponent was an avowed socialist who was on record as openly supporting gun control. Some mused that the NRA, its membership declining and its credibility as an electoral and legislative giant-killer eroding, simply wanted to show politicians that it was ready, willing, and able to target and defeat those who crossed it—even if it meant electing an individual with a worse record.

Smith laughs bitterly at this analysis. Even the NRA wouldn't hurt itself legislatively just to make a point, he says. How, then, does he explain the gun lobby's support for his rival? "It's simple," Smith says. "There was a deal."

He claims that in September 1990, members of a local gun group with ties to the NRA met secretly with representatives from the Sanders campaign. At that meeting a deal was struck: The NRA would wage a strong campaign against Smith and, in return, Sanders would vote against gun control. According to Smith, two NRA members who were at the alleged meeting, and who supported Smith, were disgusted by the deal and told his campaign director, Judy Schaeller, about it. But according to Schaeller, neither of the two are willing to talk publicly about the allegations for fear of retribution from other members of the gun group.

No one took the charges seriously when Smith made them two months before the election; most wrote the allegations off to Smith's lagging campaign. Eight months later, when Representative Sanders voted against the Brady bill and the pundits reacted with surprise, Smith was able to say, "I told you so." But as an out-of-office politician, it gave him little satisfaction to do so.

The NRA's Jim Baker today denies that there was ever such a quid pro quo agreement between the NRA and Sanders, although he does say he was aware of Sanders's opposition to the waiting period bill at a time when all others expected the socialist candidate to vote *for* the measure.

"My understanding was that during the campaign, Sanders indicated to gun groups in Vermont that he wasn't in favor of the Brady bill," says Baker, and those groups simply passed the information on to the NRA.

When told about Smith's charges, John Franco, former legislative director for Sanders, just laughs. "Somebody must be having LSD flashbacks," he says. Franco's version of the events of campaign 1990 mirrors Baker's: "All that happened was that gun groups asked what Sanders's position was on several issues, including the Brady bill. He told them that he supported some gun measures but not the Brady bill. There was *never* any agreement with the NRA. Quite the contrary; the NRA offered to endorse him and offered PAC money and he refused either. The NRA on its own campaigned against Smith—with neither an explicit nor implicit agreement with the Sanders campaign."

Whether there was a deal or not, however, the result was the same: Smith—an "aye" vote on Brady and on the assault weapons ban—was out. Sanders—an opponent of both bills—was in. It was also an important PR victory for the NRA. If the election of Tom Andrews in Maine gave opponents of the gun lobby satisfaction, then Smith's defeat in Vermont gave them pause. The NRA might have been injured, but, like a wounded lion, it was still dangerous.

The gun lobby had another important victory in the House and a major loss in the Senate in the 1990 electoral arena. In September, Representative Jolene Unsoeld, a Democrat from Washington State, had surprised many by introducing a bill that would allow U.S. companies to produce clones of banned foreign semiautomatic weapons— whether AK-47s or Uzis—as long as they used only components made in the United States. Jim Brady, his acerbic wit obviously not impaired by Hinckley's bullet, dubbed the Unsoeld bill the "Kill American" campaign (a reference to the popular union advertisement urging consumers to "Buy American"). The bill passed the House easily in October by a vote of 257 to 172.

That Unsoeld should offer such a bill startled many. As a state legislator Unsoeld had earned a reputation for being a liberal activist: prochoice, proenvironment—and pro-gun-control. Unsoeld insisted that she had never *really* been in favor of gun control—she had just voted that way. That explanation was further muddied when she remarked that although she had not changed her views on gun control, as a U.S. representative she had "learned from her constituents."

Others, more cynical minded, claimed Unsoeld's pedagogue was of a baser sort, pointing to the fact that on the morning after she introduced her amendment, Unsoeld's reelection committee received a check from the NRA for $4,950. Unsoeld called the timing "coincidental."

Handgun Control, Inc., decided to use Unsoeld's race to show that it, too, had the ability and determination to go after its political enemies. The organization bought thousands of dollars of radio airtime in Unsoeld's district, running ads charging that Unsoeld had been bought off by the NRA.

"You know the definition of a Washington, D.C., politician," stated the ad. "Someone who takes a stand but then sells out to a special interest . . . for money. That's what happened to your Representative Jolene Unsoeld." When the Unsoeld campaign threatened to sue radio stations airing the ads, many of them dropped the attacks.

The NRA was, of course, happy when Unsoeld squeaked out a victory in November, but its enthusiasm was tainted by the changing battlefield suggested by HCI's willingness to pour money into the electoral arena. That would clearly spell trouble ahead—although HCI's campaign war chest was hardly a match for the NRA's vast resources. Still, in critical races, the NRA was no longer the sole pecuniary voice. And offsetting Unsoeld's win in the House was the loss in the Senate of the NRA's candidate, Rudy Boschwitz of Minnesota. In spite of NRA PAC contributions totaling nearly $20,000, the Republican Boschwitz lost to a progressive—and pro-gun-control—Democrat, Paul Wellstone. It was a particularly embarrassing defeat for the NRA since its candidate was the only Senate incumbent to lose in 1990. What's more, the campaign had clearly been a priority for the gun lobby; the NRA had put more money into the Minnesota race than it had into any other Senate campaign, save one. (It had spent $22,529 in an unsuccessful attempt to unseat the Democratic senator from Iowa, Tom Harkin.)

Of course, the NRA tried to put the best possible face on the year's events. In the December 1990 issue of *American Rifleman*, ILA chief Wayne LaPierre boasted that "the mission we only dared to dream about just months before is now reality. We have achieved total victory! All gun control is dead in the 101st session of Congress."

The NRA trumpeted Unsoeld's victory and Smith's defeat. It

bragged that it had been able to stall the Brady bill, through the efforts of House Speaker Tom Foley. The old song title says "It's So Nice to Have a Man Around the House," and Tom Foley, the NRA's man around the House, had been able to get the assault weapons ban killed in the House-Senate Conference Committee. But despite these victories, the inescapable truth was that, in 1990, the NRA's nose had been bloodied for the first time in the Senate, and that the next year promised to be a pivotal one for the gun lobby. The NRA was determined to score a decisive victory to prove that it was still king of the legislative Hill.

But Sarah and Jim Brady were equally determined to deny the NRA that victory. "Since 1986, we had been laying the groundwork, cultivating working relationships with everyone on the Hill—everyone who would talk with us," says Sarah Brady. "By 1991, we had very close working relationships with everyone. Then it was time to take it to the floor of Congress—and hold our breath."

# 10

# PALACE COUP

THERE ARE FEW things you can count on in the ever-changing environment of the nation's capital: cherry blossoms in the springtime; promises of a tax cut before each presidential election; and a palace coup at the NRA headquarters every few years. As writer Robert Sherrill once pointed out, "Beneath the hearty fraternal exterior of [the] NRA's officialdom, there's bilious intrigue."

No sooner had 1991 begun than the gun lobby's leadership was seized by one of its quasi-regular paroxysms. This time it was Executive Vice President J. Warren Cassidy's turn to be devoured by his own organization.

Cassidy's problems began soon after he took control of the NRA following Ray Arnett's overthrow in 1986. Cassidy had made few friends during his time at the helm of the ILA, and not many more in his first two years in charge of the entire organization. He had proved an inept chief executive as well as a personally unpopular individual. Even worse, to many board members, Cassidy appeared too willing to compromise on gun issues—at least in comparison to hard-core leaders like Harlon Carter, the pugnacious Neal Knox, and ILA director Wayne LaPierre. When, at the end of 1988, Cassidy prepared to fire Wayne LaPierre, the executive vice president's chief rival within the organization, the board of directors made a preemptive strike, passing a series of motions designed to strip Cassidy of his powers and nudge him out the door. But Cassidy refused to leave, and rather than risk the bad publicity sure to follow an actual firing (the Arnett fiasco was still fresh in everyone's mind), the board hoped that their chastised leader would shape up.

Meanwhile, in columns published in a variety of gun magazines, Neal Knox continued sniping at Cassidy's alleged "wimpiness." "The Mont[y] Hall of the gun movement," Knox called him. "He's the guy that plays 'Let's Make a Deal.'"

As NRA membership declined and more battles were lost, Cassidy became the scapegoat, not only for Neal Knox but for all members dissatisfied with the organization. Then, in 1989, rumors about sexual liaisons involving Cassidy and various female NRA employees were whispered around the building. These problems came to a head in the fall of 1990, when a lawsuit alleging sex discrimination was brought against Cassidy by former NRA employee Marsha Beasley. Word soon got around that during the court proceedings Cassidy had admitted to having a number of affairs with NRA workers. The coup de grace came when it was revealed that to settle the lawsuit Beasley and her lawyers had been paid $500,000—from NRA funds.

Cassidy still refused to go quietly. In the January 1991 issue of *American Rifleman*, he penned an open letter to NRA members in which he lashed out at Neal Knox, charging that Knox's attacks on him were lies created to drum up business for Knox's own lobbying group, the Firearms Coalition. Cassidy also wrote a letter saying that, contrary to Knox's claims, all was fine and friendly in the executive suites at NRA headquarters. Cassidy's plan was to get all six top NRA officials to sign his "unity" letter, which would then be published in *Guns & Ammo* magazine. When three of the six refused to do so, Cassidy mailed it anyway, thereby removing any doubt that the officials were indeed split.

The patriarch of the NRA, Harlon Carter, who was battling cancer at his home outside of Tucson, Arizona, now entered the fray, writing in support of Neal Knox, the man he had once fired. "The NRA has now come approximately full circle around to where we were prior to 1977 in Cincinnati," Carter wrote in a sidebar to a Neal Knox *Guns & Ammo* column, "but there is no group now able to move in and remedy the situation as there was then."

Perhaps shamed by Carter's words, the board finally took action. In addition to the discrimination suit itself (and the half-million-dollar settlement), Cassidy's other sexual liaisons with NRA staff, the charges that he wasn't tough enough in defending gun owners' rights, and the drop in membership from 3 million to 2.3 million, there were allegations of corruption involving computer software purchased by the NRA. Although it was not known if Cassidy was linked to the $10 million scandal, the former mayor of Lynn, Massachusetts, had enough strikes against him.

"Cassidy's firing of Beasley was just the straw that broke the camel's back," says one twenty-year veteran of the NRA board. "We were set to fire him. His cronies got the motion tabled, but Cassidy saw the light and resigned."

On February 7, 1991, a solemn Warren Cassidy gathered his staff together and informed them that the stress of his job had tired him out. He would not be running for another term as executive vice president when the board met in San Antonio in April. Rather than stay on as a lame duck, Cassidy added, he was resigning, effective in two weeks. General operations director Gary Anderson would take over his position until a new executive vice president was elected by the board in two months. Then, like Ray Arnett before him, Cassidy packed up his belongings and left.

The resignation came as a surprise to NRA members, who had been told nothing about the controversies involving their leaders. Ironically, unless they read *The Washington Post*—the newspaper considered enemy propaganda—most members were not even aware of the fact that their organization's membership had been dropping steadily for some time. All the perennially warring factions within the NRA realized that Cassidy's exit presented a unique opportunity for change. Faced with declining membership rolls (and, not inconsequentially, the income members provide), unprecedented challenges in Congress, and political isolation from former allies, the group stood at a crossroads.

The NRA could soften its opposition to the milder forms of gun-control legislation before Congress—the Brady bill and the DeConcini ban on assault weapons—and make peace with police groups. Or it could harden its position still further, channel even more resources into lobbying and less into hunting and sporting programs, and go after law enforcement leaders who opposed it.

"If they should get wise and move more toward the center, things would be more difficult," Mike Beard, of the National Coalition to Ban Handguns, said a few weeks before the San Antonio convention where the new board would appoint Cassidy's successor. "If they'd take a more reasonable approach to the issue—at least more reasonable from *my* point of view—start dealing with the police in a rational way, et cetera, then we might be in more difficulty than we are. But so far, the NRA can be counted on to do the wrong thing."

In truth, there was little chance that the gun lobby would become more open to compromise on legislation, or more amenable to working with existing police groups. As always, a host of factors pushed it down the road of obduracy. Since 1977, when Harlon Carter and Neal Knox purged the group of "accommodationists," no faction could come to power under the banner of compromise. Articles in *American Rifleman* and the ILA newspaper, *NRAction*, and countless member letters had for years been linking compromise to another C-word—*Communist*. To support one was to be branded the other.

Members had also been kept in the dark about both the extent of the organization's problems and the reasons for them. What little they knew of the recent setbacks in Congress was blamed on traitors in Congress and, more important, on those *within* the NRA who, like the recently departed Warren Cassidy, lacked the determination to fight hard enough. With its emphasis on gun ownership as a deterrent to communism and its steady stream of hyperpatriotic rhetoric, the NRA was, in many ways, still a creature of the Cold War. It should have surprised no one, therefore, when the NRA took a sharp swing even further to the right, replacing several "moderates" on the board of directors with hard-liners. The big winner was Neal Knox's Second Amendment Action slate, which succeeded in placing eleven of twenty-one candidates on the new board—including Knox himself. To Knox's right, Robert K. Brown, editor/publisher of *Soldier of Fortune* magazine and an incumbent board member, was reelected and joined by eight others on the mercenary's slate of twenty-one.

The hard-liners' victory was complete when the new board named as Cassidy's successor ILA chief Wayne LaPierre—who wears the epithet "hard-liner" like a red badge of courage. "To me 'hard-liner' just means protecting the right of Americans to own firearms in this country," says the forty-one-year-old native of Albany, New York.

LaPierre, a consummate Washington insider, is one of the new breed of NRA legislative workers brought into the fold following the Cincinnati Revolt. Neither a hunter nor a target shooter, LaPierre possesses no particular affinity for firearms. Seated in his comfortable new office on the top floor of the NRA headquarters, everything about LaPierre—from his highly polished black wing tips to his hand-tailored Oxxford Clothes suit and red-striped power tie—testifies to the fact that he is, first and last, a political animal. His pale blue eyes come alive behind the thick lenses of his aviator-frame glasses when he talks about "professionalizing" the NRA staff "to operate in a modern-day world of politics and public relations."

Listening to him talk, it is easy to believe the story whispered within NRA circles about the time a TV news crew took LaPierre to a local gun range to get footage of the NRA lobbyist on the firing line. The event turned into a public relations nightmare when the inexperienced LaPierre almost shot the cameraman by accident.

Fact or fiction, the anecdote is based on an important truth: Wayne LaPierre is no outdoorsman. While most of the NRA hierarchy came to politics because of an interest in firearms, with LaPierre the path was reversed. Before joining the NRA, he had managed political campaigns for five different politicians, and has long served as a board member of the American Association of Political Consultants. His arrival at the NRA in 1978 (starting as a state liaison) coincided with a shift toward legislative activism at the NRA, and his ascension to the office of executive vice president in 1991 made the organization's transition from sporting group to lobby complete. While that pleases one group within the NRA, it will likely drive the membership even lower (and perhaps spark another palace coup a few years down the road) as hunters and target shooters—the groups that make up the NRA's traditional base—are neglected. A LaPierre administration has another disadvantage for the group: Unlike Jim Baker, LaPierre is widely disliked in Congress.

"I'd as soon put a stake through his heart as look at the son of a bitch," says the legislative assistant to a progun congressman. "People generally don't talk to him up here. Any dealing done on legislation is with Baker."

"Wayne LaPierre?" says an experienced Senate aide. "No one likes LaPierre up on the Hill. That's why they don't bring him around. He might go in to meet a member already on the NRA's side. *Maybe.* But to talk to a staffer or to talk to someone who's on the fence—they'll bring Baker in."

LaPierre earned the enmity of Nebraska senator Bob Kerrey during the Senate debate on an assault weapons ban in 1990. Then the head of the ILA, LaPierre sent out a member mailing charging that when Kerrey voted for the DeConcini bill he had "betrayed every honest gun owner in Nebraska. . . ."

> Don't let Bob Kerrey get out of this by pretending this wasn't a gun ban vote. Who is he kidding? Kerrey's anti-gun vote had champagne corks popping at the National Gun Ban lobby. . . . Kerrey has now joined Ted Kennedy and the National Gun Ban lobby in saying that no American has the right to own a gun except for sporting purposes—and they get to tell you what they are. This vote sets America on the road to universal gun confiscation.

If LaPierre thought his blistering attack would force Senator Kerrey to sue quietly for peace with the NRA, he had made a serious miscalculation. Kerrey, a Medal of Honor recipient from the Vietnam War, went on the offensive, entering LaPierre's letter into the *Congressional Record* and ripping into the gun lobby from the Senate floor. He singled out Wayne LaPierre for special reproach.

> Since the enclosed letter was written by Mr. LaPierre, I must say . . . that I was not at all surprised by the misrepresentations of the letter. Mr. LaPierre has been irresponsible in the past. He has been inaccurate in the past and misleading in the past. . . . He has never in the history that he has had with the NRA permitted truth to stand in the way of a powerful appeal. . . .

Kerrey also entered his reply to Wayne LaPierre into the *Congressional Record*. After explaining his vote for the assault weapons ban in detail, the senator from Nebraska closed his letter to the man who would soon become head of the new "tougher" NRA with a prophetic warning. "Allow me to predict," wrote Kerrey, "that your outrageous techniques will, in the end, prove to be counterproductive."

# 11

# OPERATION
# ST. JOSEPH

ALTHOUGH SHE WAS just a child at the time, Rachael Gorlin still remembers everything about the day she saw a man shot in the head not twenty feet in front of her on a nearly empty sidewalk in New York City. She can recall the weather, the clothes the man was wearing, and, later, the nightmares. "Maybe that's why I've always looked at guns differently than Les," she says in a low-timbred voice that makes her sound more like an FM radio announcer than the legislative assistant she is.

"Les" is her boss, a U.S. representative from Oregon, Les AuCoin, and perhaps the best word to describe how *he* had looked at guns during his sixteen years in the House is *obliquely*—when he'd looked at the issue at all. Like most liberals from "gun states" in the far West and deep South, AuCoin knew that facing the issue squarely could be a politically fatal mistake. Although he stopped accepting campaign contributions from the National Rifle Association in 1983, he, like the rest of the Oregon delegation, had remained a faithful—if unexceptional—member of the gun lobby.

Gorlin was not the only member of AuCoin's staff to differ with the boss on the issue. AuCoin's top aide, Bob Crane, had been pushing AuCoin to vote against the NRA for most of the decade the two had been together. In fact, the majority of AuCoin's staff—young, eager

243

liberals attracted to the representative because of his outspoken support for abortion rights, nuclear arms control, and environmental issues—disagreed with his anti-gun-control votes. Eventually, AuCoin laid down the law; there would be no more discussions about gun control in the office. When AuCoin voted against the Brady bill in 1988, many of his staff were disappointed, but none was surprised.

Each February, AuCoin and his legislative aides traveled to the Eastern Shore region of Maryland for a weekend retreat, where they kicked around issues and outlined strategy for the coming year. At the 1991 retreat AuCoin dropped his bombshell: He was going to come out in favor of the Brady bill. Not only that, but he wanted to do it in a high-profile manner that would win votes for the legislation.

"We're so proud of you!" Gorlin cheerfully told her boss, but her euphoria was replaced by anxiety when she was handed the task of mapping out a strategy for the issue. A vote on a controversial question must be handled very carefully to minimize political damage, Gorlin knew—especially if, like AuCoin, the voter is changing his position. And that care must be increased exponentially when the opposition is the National Rifle Association.

Gorlin based her plan on a strategy used in 1989 by New Jersey congressman Frank Pallone, Jr., on another "hot button" issue: abortion. Formerly "prolife," Pallone smoothed his switch to the "prochoice" ranks by first contacting prochoice leaders in Congress and getting their support. Then he made an impassioned speech on the House floor about the reasons for his switch. Gorlin hoped that this formula would also work for AuCoin. HCI was contacted, as were the primary sponsors of the Brady bill in the House: Charles Schumer, Edward Feighan, and James Sensenbrenner. Gorlin decided that the key to AuCoin's campaign should be a *Washington Post* op-ed piece explaining his conversion.

"The title that just leapt into my mind when I thought about a piece was 'Confessions of a Former NRA Supporter,' " says Gorlin. "But when I first saw what Les had written, I thought: 'Confessions of a Former Congressman.' I mean, when it came out of the printer, our fingers got singed! No one does things like that around here."

In his piece, Les AuCoin shifted the focus from the Brady bill onto the NRA's death grip on Congress:

For the past two decades, the entire Oregon House delegation, regardless of party, has voted with the NRA right down the line. For a long time, it seemed like the right thing to do. It doesn't anymore. . . . The conventional wisdom still is: If you cross the gun lobby, they'll have a silver bullet waiting for you at the next election. I'm betting that those days are over. . . . I used to tell myself that gun control isn't crime control and—comforted by that thought—I let my 100 percent NRA rating keep arguments about guns from consuming the time I felt I needed for the issues I came to Congress to advance: jobs, education, family security and social justice. . . . What has been happening in our streets has changed my mind dramatically. . . . What I've heard [from constituents] convinces me that the conventional wisdom about the NRA's clout is hopelessly out of touch—and that the leaders of the NRA are out of touch too. . . . My constituents want policies that reduce violent crime, regardless of whether they are labeled "gun control." The gun lobby guarantees its political irrelevance by denying that. . . . This time, the gun lobby has overplayed its hand. Frankly, I'm sick of it, and I'm sick of gun violence. After too long at the table, I'm ready to do what I can to bust up the game.

"When I read that last line," Gorlin recalls, "I said to Les, 'Bust up the game? Are you sure you want to say this?' He just said, 'Yep,' so I said, 'Oka-a-a-ay,' and we sent it over to the *Post*."

The response to AuCoin's piece, which ran in *The Washington Post* on March 18, 1991, hit like a tidal wave. Although constituent letters and phone calls about AuCoin's switch ran three-to-two in favor of his new position, the negative letters were far more passionate than the positive ones. Many of his rural constituents were outraged not only by his switch but also by the fact that he announced it in the *Post*, the newspaper many Oregonians consider the voice of the "liberal, eastern elite." His office received many letters like the one that read: "You didn't have the courage to show your face back here to tell us."

In fact, AuCoin had wanted to announce his backing for the Brady bill at a district town meeting but felt he didn't have the time for the seven-hour flight home. His integrity questioned, AuCoin now felt he had no choice.

"Okay," he told Gorlin angrily. "They want a town meeting; let's have a town meeting."

His people quickly wrote everyone who had contacted AuCoin's office about his *Washington Post* piece, informing them that an open forum on the issue would be held in the district on the following Saturday. At that meeting, AuCoin found out just how angry gun owners could be when they felt someone was tampering with their rights. He had come face-to-face with the NRA's vaunted Hassle Factor.

"It was amazing," says Gorlin, shaking her head at the memory of the scene. AuCoin had thought that if he explained the details of the Brady bill, people would understand why he was supporting it. "But this was not going to be that kind of meeting," says Gorlin. "There was no dialogue. This was a chance for these guys to vent, and they vented—in a big way."

NRA supporters outnumbered Brady backers at the meeting by about six to one, and opponents of the waiting period were far more vocal about their position than were most of the bill's supporters. For AuCoin, the meeting was a taste of things to come. By taking such a public stand on the issue, he had made himself the lightning rod for the opposition—probably for years to come. "I don't think we'll ever be able to have a town meeting on *any* issue without having to deal with gun control," says Gorlin.

Jim Baker just snorts at AuCoin's self-portrayal as a loyal NRA supporter who had suddenly seen the light and voted his conscience— at great political cost. AuCoin, Baker points out, was *not* an NRA "100 percenter." Although the Oregon representative generally voted with the NRA, he had voted against the Unsoeld amendment in the previous session.

"So I wasn't so surprised when he came out for the Brady bill," says Baker. "And I was even less surprised when a few weeks later he announced he was going to run for the Senate. He had made a *political decision*, that's all."

Gorlin claims Baker's charges are "ludicrous." "Coming out for gun control is the *last* thing you'd do to posture for a Senate race in Oregon," she says. "We had a political consultant tell us, 'Hey, if you vote for the Brady bill, you can just add another two hundred thousand to three hundred thousand dollars to your next race.' But I think for Les it wasn't only about gun control. It was about the fact that the American public thinks politicians are held captive to special interests.

Les's feeling is: 'Not always. Sometimes we can tell these guys to go to hell.' "

But the NRA didn't have time to dwell on AuCoin's "conversion," real or contrived. It seemed that the dike the gun lobby had built over the past decades to contain any gun-control measures was springing leaks everywhere. Each week brought news of another crisis for the NRA, as the momentum to pass the Brady bill grew.

Pro-Brady forces had created a certain amount of this movement, of course. Congressional hearings were timed to give the bill the highest possible profile. Public announcements of new supporters were staggered to maximize their impact. But even the most powerful lobby could not have engineered the slow-building wave of support for the seven-day waiting period that was now sweeping the country. At some indeterminate point, a confluence of forces swirled together to thrust the Brady bill to the forefront of the public stage.

Three days after AuCoin's piece appeared in the *Post*, a congressional committee heard the tearful pleas for gun control from the father of a young shooting victim. "How many tragedies does it take to change political priorities?" asked Edward Prince, father of nineteen-year-old Christian Prince, a Yale student shot and killed during a robbery just weeks before. When it was suggested that the Brady bill would violate the Second Amendment, the elder Prince, tears streaming down his face, demanded: "Was that a well-regulated militia that killed my son? There is only one infringement in this instance—namely, the infringement of Christian Prince's right to life, liberty, and property."

Days later, twelve busloads of residents from East New York— the most dangerous neighborhood in New York City—showed up on Capitol Hill to lobby Congress for the Brady bill. Each wore a hat reading 7 DAYS CAN SAVE A LIFE. In New York City itself, Mayor David Dinkins declared March 27 "Brady Bill Day."

But the biggest setback for the gun lobby was still to come, and the blow was particularly devastating because of its unlikely source. The NRA could, with some degree of truth, explain away Les AuCoin's conversion by saying that he was never the die-hard defender of gun owners' rights he now claimed to be. But there was no denying the credentials of the man who, on March 28, 1991, strode to the lectern at George Washington University Medical Center and told the crowd gathered there (in words that were broadcast across the country that night on the evening news): "With the right to bear arms comes a great responsibility to use caution and common sense on handgun purchases. . . . And it's just plain common sense that there be a waiting period to allow local law enforcement officials to conduct background checks on those who wish to purchase handguns."

The speaker was Ronald Wilson Reagan, the same man who had shared the spotlight with Harlon Carter that electrifying night at the annual NRA convention in 1983, the former president who, more than any other leader in American history, embodied the values the gun lobby proclaimed as its own. And yet, however improbably, there he was, with that familiar half grin and unmistakable halting cadence that had endeared him to mainstream America for the better part of the previous decade, telling the country in words too plain to be twisted by the spin doctors: "You do know that I'm a member of the National Rifle Association, and my position on the right to bear arms is well known. But I want you to know something else, and I am going to say it in clear, unmistakable language: I support the Brady bill and I urge the Congress to enact it without further delay."

It was the NRA's darkest moment. Board member Tanya Metaksa (who had served as the head of Sportsmen for Reagan/Bush in 1980) spoke for many gun lobby officials when she told a reporter that when she heard Reagan's words on television she "felt somebody had stabbed me in the back."

Perhaps the only person not astonished by Reagan's turnaround was Sarah Brady. "I wasn't surprised at all," she states flatly. "I don't think he ever *changed* his heart; I think he *always* felt that way." Sarah had long believed that all Ronald Reagan needed was the right opportunity to make public his feelings about the Brady bill, and that moment came on the tenth anniversary of the assassination attempt that left Reagan gravely wounded and Jim Brady permanently disabled. It was Sarah Brady's idea to use the ceremony honoring the doctors and nurses who had treated the injured men at George Washington University as the dramatic forum for Reagan's announcement. Just after Christmas 1990, she had received a call from Reagan, who had recently read a magazine article about the Bradys' battle for a federal waiting period.

"I just wanted to tell you how supportive Nancy and I both are of your work," Reagan told her.

"I know you are, and I appreciate it," Sarah replied.

She hesitated before continuing. She wanted to ask the former president if she could go public with his endorsement, but Sarah was embarrassed about using their personal conversation for political advantage. On the other hand, she was still kicking herself for not broaching the subject back in 1988 during a similar phone conversation with then-president Reagan. This time she wasn't going to miss her chance; she took a deep breath and said, "You know, I've always been afraid to quote you on your support for our bill."

"Oh, you can quote me anytime you want," Reagan told her.

When, a week later, she read that Reagan was coming to town for the George Washington University ceremony, Sarah realized that that would be the perfect opportunity for him to announce his support. She called her husband's former boss, and he agreed.

Reagan's announcement caused a series of amusing flip-flops inside the Beltway, as politicians—left and right—had to publicly reassess their opinion of the man. As Neal Knox pointed out on his recorded telephone hot line on the day of Reagan's speech, "For more than thirty years, a liberal left has been condemning Ronald Reagan as stupid, lazy, reactionary, and a troglodyte. But for the next few days he's going to be praised as wise, courageous, and visionary, for today Reagan will endorse the Brady seven-day waiting period bill."

On the other side of the ideological fence, those who had once defended Reagan as an astute and nimble-minded statesman now found themselves questioning his mental capacity.

"If you asked Ronald Reagan today what's in [the Brady] bill, he wouldn't have the slightest idea," said Congressman Harold Volkmer.

Spin doctors for the Brady bill, of course, made the most of President Reagan's new support. One called Reagan's endorsement "the nail in the NRA's coffin." Les AuCoin told reporters that Ronald Reagan's support would convince many representatives that it was now safe to vote against the NRA. "If he ain't cover, then there's no such thing." Representative Edward Feighan, a Democrat from Ohio, and a primary sponsor of the bill, claimed, "The Brady bill would have passed this year even without President Reagan's endorsement. With it, our victory is assured."

But these optimistic pronouncements were just part of the Washington PR game. No one was really certain what effect Ronald Reagan's endorsement would have. Speaking on the television show "Meet the Press" three days after Reagan's announcement, Senate Majority Leader George Mitchell confessed, "I don't know a single member of Congress who has changed his mind because President Reagan changed his mind." And, Mitchell added: "I don't think the Brady bill will pass in the form in which it now stands."

Meanwhile, the NRA was working overtime to prove Mitchell right. Its basic strategy was outlined by Jim Baker in an "electronic conversation" held in November 1990 on the CompuServe computer network. As Baker explained to members of the network's "Sportsmen's Forum," the NRA planned on "preempting the inevitable reintroduction of the Brady bill by putting in something having to do with the instantaneous check system. . . . There is a great deal of interest in Congress in having something positive to vote for." In other words, the NRA would introduce another "Brady Buster" bill, as it had done so successfully in 1988 with the McCollum amendment. The killer amendment offered this time—sponsored by West Virginia Democrat Harley Staggers, Jr., a co-sponsor of the McCollum bill— was a near clone of the 1988 legislation, except that instead of directing the Justice Department to first study the feasibility of a telephone "instant-check system" on handgun purchasers, the Staggers bill instructed the department to implement a system within six months.

The fight leading up to the House vote in May was in many ways a replay of the 1988 battle, with both sides arguing that the other's proposal simply would not work. Supporters of Brady leaked a draft copy of a congressional study that concluded that it would take between five and ten years to put the Staggers instant-check system into place.

If the Staggers bill defeated Brady, warned Congressman Charles Schumer of New York, a Brady sponsor, "hundreds, perhaps thousands, of people will die [in the] next year" alone, before the system was up and running.

In full-page advertisements placed in Washington, D.C., newspapers, the NRA countered that a waiting period would prevent honest citizens, not criminals, from purchasing handguns. In that case, the group claimed, unarmed crime victims would be shot down by gun-toting thugs. The gun lobby also hammered away at these points in a television advertisement featuring Charlton Heston. The ad (which cost nearly $100,000 to produce) shows the actor standing in front of a graffiti-covered brick wall at night in dangerous downtown Washington, D.C.

"Three years ago I stood here and called D.C. the murder capital of the nation," says Heston, "and I took some heat for it. Now, three years later, it's still the murder capital of the nation, and you're taking the heat—you, the law-abiding citizens of D.C. They say guns are the problem. But criminals rule your streets, and they disarm you. Guns aren't the problem, criminals are." Heston, who has been walking slowly during these lines, now stands in front of the U.S. Capitol Building. "So when are you going to put the heat on them?" he says, jerking a thumb over his shoulder to indicate the building behind him.

The film crew worked hard to give the advertisement just the right feel. According to an internal NRA memo, "the camera crew had conveniently chalked the brick wall with graffiti to give the scene a 'drug-infested' look, having also sprayed the wall with a water mist for that 'eery feeling.' " The crew was unable, however, to do anything about the lights coming from a nearby office building, which, according to the memo, "jeopardizes the 'drug-infested ambiance.' "

In addition to these advertisements, the NRA quoted United States Attorney General Richard Thornburgh, who called the Brady bill a "17 percent solution"—"since only 17 percent of the handguns acquired by felons are purchased from gun dealers." The solution to crime, repeated the gun lobby—as it had for decades—was "to get tough with criminals, not legitimate gun owners."

But as the days before the House vote went by, momentum for the bill grew like Topsy. One by one, all living former U.S. presidents followed Ronald Reagan's lead in declaring their support for the waiting-period bill.

In a letter to Congressman Schumer, Gerald Ford called the Brady bill "a very reasonable attempt to curtail some of the constant handgun violence plaguing our nation." Then Richard Nixon, visiting Capitol Hill to report on a recent trip to the Soviet Union, told reporters, "I think it [the Brady bill] is necessary and I don't think that anybody who owns guns legitimately . . . should be concerned one bit." Two days later, speaking at a press conference in Iowa, former president

Jimmy Carter was asked if he supported a federal waiting period for purchasing a handgun. "Yes, I do," he answered. "I've long been in favor of the waiting period for handguns, and I've written a letter to Congressman Schumer urging [Congress] to pass the Brady bill, which I think is a very modest approach."

An increasingly desperate NRA stepped up its campaign of intimidation, the tactic that had worked so well for it in the past. When NRA lobbyists dropped in on fence-straddling politicians, they brought with them a videocassette with a sample of the kind of hard-hitting advertisement that would be aired in their districts the next election cycle—should they vote for Brady.

Representative Tom Andrews did his best to counter the NRA's threats by sending a Dear Colleague letter reminding other representatives that he had taken the worst the NRA could dish out—and in Maine, a traditionally progun state—and had gone on to win with more than 60 percent of the vote:

> I know conventional wisdom says you can't cross the National Rifle Association. It also says that a freshman member like myself shouldn't pretend to know everything about conventional wisdom in Washington. My experience has taught me, however, that you can take a stand for what is right on the issue of handgun control and not suffer politically.

Lobbyists from HCI and various police organizations reminded legislators that there was also a political price for voting *against* the Brady bill. Jolene Unsoeld might have won reelection the previous November, but the same HCI media campaign used against her might be more effective somewhere else.

Going into the final days of the legislative battle, House backers of Brady had a large procedural obstacle facing them. Though a majority of the bill's sponsors were Democrats, the House party leader, Speaker Tom Foley, was opposed to the legislation. This meant that the formal party machinery for pushing Democratically-endorsed legislation—called a "whipping organization"—could not be used by Brady proponents. Undeterred, the bill's primary sponsors—Democrats Charles Schumer, Edward Feighan, and Marty Russo, and Republican James Sensenbrenner—formed their own informal "shadow" whipping organization, complete with its own patron saint, St. Joseph, who, according to Feighan, takes on nearly hopeless causes.

The key to "Operation St. Joseph"—as the effort was dubbed—was to convince undecided House members to either vote for Brady or, if they wouldn't do that, then at least to vote no on *both* Brady and Staggers. According to a procedure worked out in the House Rules Committee, Staggers would be voted on first, as a substitute to Brady. If Staggers won, House members would not get a chance to vote on Brady. If Staggers were defeated, Brady backers were virtually certain their bill had enough votes to pass. "Up to the last minute," says HCI spokesperson Susan Whitmore, "the NRA was trying to make representatives think they could have it both ways, that they could vote for both Staggers *and* Brady. So our strategy had to change in the final days. We had been saying we've got to get enough votes to pass Brady, we've got to get enough votes to pass Brady. Suddenly, we had to get enough votes to kill Staggers."

Days before the vote, Representative Schumer called the battle a toss-up. "It's neck and neck," he said. "I would predict if the vote were held today, it would win or lose by no more than four votes. It's that close." The uncertainty of the vote was perhaps the only point on which Schumer and the NRA's Jim Baker agreed. "If anybody is telling you they know what the outcome is," Baker told a reporter, "they're misleading you."

On May 7, one day before the House vote, the Bush administration inadvertently damaged the NRA bill's chances.

For months, the gun lobby had been making the most of Bush's support for Staggers (lukewarm though that support was), while downplaying Bush's hints that he might not veto a waiting period *if* it was part of a larger comprehensive crime package. "The president is not going to take action that is only a partial solution," Attorney General Thornburgh had repeatedly told Congress. "He wants a comprehensive bill to deal with the problem of violent crime."

But on May 7, White House Press Secretary Marlin Fitzwater said, "There are some problems with [Staggers] as well," and added that Bush would veto *either* bill if it wasn't part of a more inclusive crime initiative.

When reporters asked Wayne LaPierre if the administration still supported the Staggers bill, the NRA chief threw up his hands. "It's hard to say *where* they are," he said with barely concealed fury.

With Staggers and Brady running dead even, the withdrawal of presidential support for the NRA alternative was crucial. The message it sent Republicans in Congress was: "Vote however you want. We don't care."

"It was an incredible move," says legislative aide Annelise Hafer, Harley Staggers's principal assistant on gun issues. "Absolutely incredible. I think they were trying to get through this whole thing without having to take a side. That's stupid politics."

"The amount of damage the Bush administration did was incalculable," agrees Don Morrissey, legislative director for Representative Bill McCollum (co-sponsor, with Harley Staggers, of the 1988 amendment).

As for why the administration blindsided Staggers, Morrissey is blunt in his assessment: "The White House just doesn't know what it's doing when it comes to congressional politics. Everybody thinks Bush knows what he's doing because he used to be in the House. But he doesn't know. For chrissake, you don't cave in *before* the vote! When you have the White House giving confused signals, guess what? You have Republicans getting confused."

It was against this tumultuous background of mixed messages, high-running passions, and vigorous arm-twisting on both sides that the debate on the Brady bill and its alternative began in the U.S. House of Representatives at a little after 1:00 P.M. on Wednesday, May 8, 1991.

The debate opened with the by-now-familiar recitation of the advantages and the drawbacks of both bills. The Brady bill would save lives; Staggers was a budget-busting, high-tech pipe dream. The instant-check system was practical and unobtrusive; Brady was feel-good, do-nothing legislation.

But soon a different theme began to emerge in the speeches heard on the House floor. In declaring their support for the Brady bill, member after member spoke out not only against the Staggers bill but against the National Rifle Association itself. Some of the references to the NRA were only obliquely critical: "A vote in support of the National Rifle Association–backed Staggers substitute is clearly a vote to kill the Brady bill," charged Bill Green of New York. But many were openly hostile to the gun lobby:

"The NRA is becoming increasingly out of step with the rest of the nation."

"The NRA is a johnny-come-lately to the gun-control debate and has lost considerable credibility over the issue."

"I am tired of the specious, selfish arguments fostered by the NRA and its allies."

"The NRA doesn't represent what's right for America, they don't represent the opinions of the majority of people in this country, and—in fact—they don't even represent many of their own members on this issue."

"The NRA would rather the members of Congress stick our heads in the sand and ignore this nation's growing crime problem rather than take some positive action by way of passing the Brady bill."

"None of us should believe that the NRA actually speaks for all of its members."

"Mr. Chairman, has the NRA no shame?"

"The NRA has come increasingly to stand for No Rational Argument."

"Stand up to the gun dealers' lobby."

"Thank God for Jim Brady and shame on the NRA!"

During the five long hours of disputation, it became obvious that the NRA itself had become the center of the discussion, a point made quite clearly by Ohio Democrat James Traficant when he told his colleagues, "Today's debate is not about gun laws or waiting periods. Today's debate is: Who in America will write the future gun laws; the U.S. Congress or the National Rifle Association?"

Senator Kerrey's prediction of the previous year—that the NRA's "outrageous techniques will, in the end, prove to be counterproductive"—had been borne out. Angered by the NRA's bullying tactics, the House was using debate over the Brady bill to stick it to the gun lobby. Over one third of all representatives speaking in favor of the Brady bill criticized the NRA by name. "The opposition did a very effective job of painting the NRA as the issue," admits Staggers's aide Annelise Hafer. "They painted the NRA as everything that's evil in America."

Even Jim Baker agrees that the debate on Staggers became a debate on the NRA. "I don't think it *should* have been," he says, "but I think that was true. There was a feeling in some quarters in the House that we want to beat the NRA rather than do something effective about crime control."

But when the time for debate elapsed and voting started at 6:30 P.M., the Staggers forces still felt confident their amendment would prevail. After all, the bill had 100 sponsors, and most of them had been lobbying hard for the measure for two months. They had followed all the procedures, introducing the bill in the Judiciary Committee— even though it stood little chance of passage there—just so the Rules Committee couldn't later block the instant-check proposal from a floor vote by arguing that it had come out of the blue.

And then there was the weight of precedent. No gun-control bill had been passed by the House for years without at least the official sanction of the NRA. Representatives might bellyache about the gun lobby's power, but when the time came to vote, how many would risk incurring the group's wrath? Les AuCoin had put it well just before the vote. Pointing to the House chamber, he had told a reporter, "There are a lot of nervous deers in there right now. They think they're going to get the silver bullet from the NRA."

Staggers's aide Annelise Hafer kept her eyes glued to the electronic tote board above and behind the Speaker's rostrum. For the first several minutes of voting, she noted that the ayes (for Staggers) and nays (against Staggers) were running just about even. Looking at the total number of votes cast, Hafer knew that many members were waiting to commit themselves. She shook her head. In Congress, a bill that is gaining momentum is said to be like a train that is "leaving the station." Since politicians are basically herd animals, they will often wait during votes on controversial bills to see what their colleagues are going to do, and then do likewise. This results in an initial trickle of votes, followed by a last-minute flurry as politicians scramble to climb aboard the departing "train."

With only seven minutes left, the nays column began breaking ahead. Slowly at first, and then, as others noticed what was happening, much faster: 140—146—149—163—177—203.

"It's almost there!" came a shout from the cluster of Operation St. Joseph workers, as the board showed the nays within striking distance of the 218 votes needed to defeat the Staggers bill. And then, to the cheers of Brady supporters, the nays hit the magic number of 218— and kept right on going: 220—226—230.

Hafer was stunned. When the voting finally ended, the numbers showing on the electronic board proved the magnitude of what had just happened. A battle that just hours before had been described as "too close to call" had ended in a rout. In all, 234 representatives voted against the instant-check system and only 193 had sided with it; the NRA's Brady-buster had lost by 41 votes. The House immediately proceeded to vote on the Brady bill—a formality at this stage. The measure passed by a vote of 239 to 186.

At a press conference held in a packed room on the second floor of the Rayburn House Office Building following the vote, Charles Schumer was jubilant. "This marks a turning point," the brash congressman declared. "The stranglehold of the NRA on Congress is now broken."

Sarah Brady was more cautious. Yes, victory was sweet, she said, but she cautioned those gathered in the room that the House vote was only half the battle. Whether or not the Brady bill would become law was now up to the Senate, and what that legislative body would do, said Sarah, was anyone's guess.

Just across Independence Avenue, a weary Jim Baker was stopped by reporters as he was walking out of the Capitol Building. Would he comment on the NRA's loss that day? Baker just glared at his questioner. "It's never over until it's over," he said, and walked off.

# 12

# THE LAST BATTLE

FLANKED BY ENOUGH uniformed police officers to quell a respectable-sized riot, Howard Metzenbaum stared at the scores of reporters jammed into the tiny meeting room just off the Capitol rotunda, and did something quite out of character: He smiled. It was a small smile and a fleeting one—a momentary disruption of the wizened seventy-four-year-old Ohio senator's normally severe features—but he had reason to do so. Sometime in the next few days, the Senate would finally vote on the Brady bill, the legislation he first introduced over four years before. Metzenbaum felt good about the bill's chances. The cause for his optimism stood all around him: Cops were the reason the Brady bill had gotten as far as it had, and if the bill passed, Metzenbaum knew that it would be thanks to the support of cops.

"It is good to be standing up once again with my friends in the law enforcement community," Metzenbaum began. "We have worked together on many a good fight in the past. Without your support we could not have passed bills to ban plastic guns and cop-killer bullets."

As he spoke, Metzenbaum looked at some of the law enforcement officials who surrounded him. To his right was Neil Behan, the white-haired founder and head of the Law Enforcement Steering Committee. To his left was the imposing figure of Lee Brown, the police commissioner of New York City, who had the build of a linebacker. The press

258

conference was supposed to remind Metzenbaum's colleagues that it was the police of America who wanted this bill passed, who were, in fact, demanding that it pass. Metzenbaum had put it succinctly at another press conference, a year earlier: "On the one side we have the NRA. On the other side we have the police officers who risk their lives to protect the public."

It was fitting that Metzenbaum should be the standard-bearer for a bill that, if passed, would represent the gun lobby's greatest defeat. For Howard Metzenbaum was a liberal version of the NRA's persona: cantankerous, opinionated, spoiling for a fight. If you asked Senate staffers their opinion of Howard Metzenbaum, you'd be likely to hear expressions ranging from "aggressive," to "cutthroat," to "rubs people the wrong way," to "a pain in the ass." Republicans are far less laudatory. One thing all agree on, however, is that, like the NRA itself, Metzenbaum is effective in what he does. He is known as an obstructionist par excellence, a master tactician of Senate rules. It is Metzenbaum's willingness to toss the monkey wrenches of parliamentary procedure into the Senate machinery, bringing the entire process to a halt, for even slight political advantage that frustrates and often infuriates his colleagues.

One Senate aide tells a story that illustrates Metzenbaum's style. "At the end of a Congress," says the aide, "people move bills through under unanimous consent—they're called UC bills. You know, they're private relief bills, some piddly-ass favor for a constituent, whatever. UC bills need three signatures: the majority leader, the minority leader, and the chair of the Budget Committee. Anyway, I was down on the floor last year and I was looking at some of these bills, and the signatures read: majority leader, minority leader, Budget chair, Howard Metzenbaum. I look again. *Howard Metzenbaum?* Yep, there he was with a staff of six people, going through all these bills like a fucking gatekeeper!"

Metzenbaum's unpopularity with his colleagues, as well as his standing as an "arch liberal," caused the legislation's other backers to distance the Ohio senator from the Brady bill in most press releases and public discussions of the measure. For the same reason, the NRA never *failed* to remind people that the bill was sponsored by Howard Metzenbaum. More often, the waiting-period legislation was referred to as Biden's bill, for Judiciary chair Joseph Biden, or, more recently, as the Mitchell compromise, for House majority leader George Mitchell—a seemingly surprising choice given that up until a few weeks before Mitchell had been regarded as an *opponent* of the federal waiting period. The pundits had enjoyed the delicious irony of the incident in March when, three days after Ronald Reagan's stunning reversal on gun control, Mitchell, the Senate's top Democrat, had appeared to trash the bill on "Meet the Press."

"It's a very odd position for George Mitchell to be ostensibly to the right of Ronald Reagan on anything," a Republican political consultant had said at the time. "I'm certain that his political gyroscope must have brushed up against a magnet."

Like most politicians from gun states, Maine senator George Mitchell had never taken the lead on gun-control legislation. But Mitchell was just a cautious politician (cautious, that is, even for a politician) who had, on occasion, quietly voted in favor of gun-control bills—most recently, for the DeConcini assault weapons ban in 1990. Sarah Brady maintains that it was merely Mitchell's guarded manner of speaking that caused his words on "Meet the Press" to be misinterpreted. "His statement didn't put a panic into *us* because we had been talking with him all along," says Brady. "It was *how* he said it; he realized later he hadn't stated his position very well."

What Mitchell actually said was that he was against the Brady bill unless it were changed "to have a waiting period that makes sense and accomplishes something." While most took that to be a general indictment of the bill, Mitchell had actually been voicing a specific complaint—about the fact that the Brady bill did not *force* police to run a background check on handgun purchasers, it merely *allowed* them to by granting a seven-day waiting period. Although the NRA now bashed the Brady bill for *not* mandating a check, that provision had been removed from the original legislation to make the bill more palatable to the foes of gun control. When the mandated check had been a part of the bill, the NRA had criticized the measure for "forcing a lot of unnecessary paperwork on our already overworked police."

Having to defend their ever-shifting stand sometimes made life difficult for NRA officials. One such incident occurred following a TV exchange between Senator Metzenbaum and Wayne LaPierre after the Staggers bill had been defeated by the House in May. The new NRA chief had declared the Brady bill useless because it lacked a background check. After the camera was turned off, Metzenbaum turned to LaPierre. "Well, if you want a mandatory check, we'll be glad to put that in our bill," he said impishly.

"We've got other problems with your bill," a nonplussed LaPierre countered, and stalked off.

Mitchell's compromise bill added a mandatory background check to the Brady bill. It was an odd compromise—the result would mean an even tougher gun-control bill. But after arguing so publicly for a forced background check, the NRA could not now back away from this position.

JUNE 21, the longest day of the year, felt exactly that to Jim Baker. He lit up another Vantage filter cigarette and glanced over at the TV sitting in the corner of his spacious office. C-SPAN was announcing its morning lineup. Leading off would be opening remarks on debate over the Brady bill. Baker listened intently as the announcer gave a thumbnail sketch of the bill's provisions, and then snorted and shook his head as he detected a mistake in the announcer's recitation.

"Typical," he said, and stabbed out his cigarette in an ashtray. The tall lobbyist ran a hand through his long, prematurely gray hair and then slowly stroked his drooping mustache. Baker was used to working twelve-hour days, but for weeks it had been rare for his wife to see him before 10:00 P.M. His days were full of strategy sessions on the Hill with the leaders of the opposition to the Brady bill. They included the powerful minority leader, Bob Dole, and Senator Larry Craig of Idaho, an NRA board member; Democratic senator Ted Stevens, the feisty Alaskan who was sponsoring an "instant-check" bill, a souped-up version of the Staggers amendment; and western conservatives Orrin Hatch of Utah and Minority Whip Alan Simpson of Wyoming as well as South Carolina's Strom Thurmond, a Senate fixture since 1956, and ranking Republican member of the Judiciary Committee.

There were several features of the Democratic crime bill that Baker was also fighting, including the semiautomatic ban and limitations on the size of ammunition magazines. But there was no doubt that the Brady bill was politically the most important fight. Baker could imagine the headlines if the NRA lost on the waiting-period bill: NRA DE-STROYED.

Just six weeks before, even after the House vote, most insiders were warning that the Brady bill would face a much tougher time in the Senate because sparsely populated rural states had much more power there, where representation wasn't based on population. That should have worked in the NRA's favor, since those rural states were largely opposed to gun control, but by June 6, Baker was already dropping hints to soften a possible Senate defeat. He remarked to a reporter that the NRA might find "some sort of a waiting period less than seven days and more than one day acceptable."

Since then, the group had lowered its profile on the vote. There were no full-page newspaper advertisements against the Brady bill; no Charlton Heston commercials on TV; and no playing the Ghost of Election Future, standing undecided senators before empty graves with markers bearing their names. Jim Baker was taking pains to ensure that this vote did not become a referendum on the NRA.

BY THE THIRD week of June, the strain of waiting for the vote on Brady had begun taking its toll on legislators and their staffs. Everywhere, tempers were on edge. No one was certain on exactly which day the Senate would finally vote on the bill—or, indeed, on what the final bill would look like. Both sides were constantly huddling, trying to sweeten their proposals *just enough* to lure undecided senators on board. Aides were forced to redraw their ranking grids daily, sometimes hourly, as senators shifted from the Undecided column to the Leaning For column or the Leaning Against list with every change in the bill. Even the bill's name was as ephemeral as a chameleon's markings. One morning it was the Biden-Mitchell bill; by evening it was known as Mitchell-Kohl (for Wisconsin Democrat Herbert Kohl). And by the next morning, the federal waiting-period bill had become the Mitchell-Kohl-Gore-Metzenbaum compromise.

The one name consistently attached to the bill was the most unlikely: Mitchell. The Senate majority leader had put all the weight of his office as well as his personal political influence behind the bill he had so recently seemed to oppose. Many attributed his change of heart to presidential ambitions, for although Mitchell's efforts were unlikely to win many new votes from Maine voters, his strong support for a nationally popular bill was sure to be remembered in 1996. For whatever reason, Mitchell's office now took the lead in the feverish race to craft a compromise that could be supported by fifty-one United States senators.

The Mitchell–(fill in the blank) compromise now offered $40 million to be given to states to upgrade their criminal records, leading Jim Baker to call it "the Brady bill with money." The Republicans responded by shoveling money into their own crime bill: some $3.2 billion to build prisons, train new police officers and federal agents, and fight youth gangs.

When no vote had been scheduled by Monday, June 24, the tension level in the city ratcheted up a notch. The July Fourth holiday recess—set to begin sometime that week—suddenly loomed ahead. Senators wanted to go home to their districts for the long weekend, and the delay on the crime bill, caused mainly by the waiting-period controversy, played havoc with their holiday travel plans. No one wanted to leave with the issue unresolved; the pressure to find a compromise increased.

Lobbyists on both sides played a critical role in attempting to craft legislation that could garner enough votes for passage while still preserving the essence of their positions, and in trying to convince undecided senators to come over to their side. Operating out of the office of Senate Minority Leader Bob Dole, Jim Baker phoned or visited dozens of Senate offices. So did Sarah Brady. Sometimes the two came within minutes of passing each other on the way in or out of an arm-twisting session.

A rumor that the vote would be taken on Tuesday came and went. On Wednesday, June 26, the word was that this was it: The vote was imminent. But evening came and still no vote was taken.

Other sections of the crime bill were debated and voted up or down. The Senate turned back an administration proposal that would have allowed police to make searches without warrants. They agreed to expand the death penalty to include some forty-nine additional crimes. They approved another Bush proposal to place new limits on the right of death row prisoners to have their executions delayed, and accepted an amendment to make drug-related murders in Washington, D.C., a death penalty offense. The Senate worked until past midnight, but it did not vote on the Brady bill.

The following day—Thursday, June 27—dawned warm and hu-

mid. At ten minutes after ten o'clock, the Senate once again took up
the crime bill. But the public's attention was focused not on Congress
but on the Supreme Court building one block east of the Capitol
where Justice Thurgood Marshall was announcing his retirement after
twenty-three years on the Court. There was little occurring on the
Senate floor during the day to interest the public, anyway. The real
action once again took place behind closed doors throughout the Capitol where the two sides were still working to come up with a compromise on the Brady bill.

Sarah Brady was late arriving at the Capitol that day. She first had
to drive her twelve-year-old son, Scott, to National Airport, where he
took a plane to camp. It was his first extended trip away from home
and Sarah was distraught. Although she knew it was silly, she couldn't
shake the feeling that Scott's leaving by himself that day marked a
transition point: Her only child was growing up. As she was driving to
the Capitol she had a sobering thought. What if the Brady bill came
up for a vote that day—and lost? To lose my child and the Brady bill
both on the same day, she thought. That would be difficult to take.

But when she arrived at the Capitol, Sarah went to work, lobbying
undecided senators and firming up those who were leaning toward the
latest version of the waiting-period bill. When the Senate took an
afternoon break, there was still no word on when a vote would take
place. In the early evening, a rumor began circulating that a vote was
scheduled for midnight. Sarah noted the possibility, but was skeptical.


THE SENATE IS known as a "Gentlemen's Club," and, sexist implications aside, that is generally true. During debate on the Senate floor,
even the bitterest enemies always refer to each other as "the distin-
guished senator from ———." In the labyrinthine marble halls surrounding the Senate chamber, a sense of stately decorum is observed.
Even in the press area above the Senate floor where reporters are
seated on a single row of revolving stools, male representatives of the
fourth estate are required to wear jackets.

Traditions are everything in this genteel environment. Crystal
shakers, once full of sand to blot the excess ink left by quill pens, are
still kept on senators' desks. If that seems extreme, consider the several
black-lacquered snuffboxes that rest on ledges by the Senate rostrum

as they have for more than a century. Though no longer used, the boxes are regularly refilled with fresh snuff.

As the night of June 27 wore on, however, a dreamlike, almost hallucinatory atmosphere took hold of the north wing of the Capitol. Perhaps it was the pressure to work out a compromise before the July Fourth recess. Or maybe it was the fact that after so many late-night sessions, senators and their staffs were simply nearing exhaustion. Whatever the reason, with each passing hour the Senate felt and looked less like a "Gentlemen's Club" and more like the men's locker room at an exceptionally ornate YMCA. Ties were loosened; hair was left disheveled. Voices, generally kept in respectful hushed tones in the marble halls surrounding the chamber, were given free rein.

This informal attitude extended to Capitol employees. The guards who normally stood on either side of the massive doors at the Senate chamber's main entrance were now slouched in chairs playing a game of Trivial Pursuit without the board.

"What's the only man-made object visible from the moon?" asked the shorter of the two guards, reading off a card.

"The Taj Mahal?" guessed his companion (incorrectly).

Suddenly, a harried-looking Bob Dole burst from his office (actually, a suite of elegant rooms used by the minority leader) just down the hall from the Senate chamber's main entrance. He marched across the lobby, past the guards—who had now moved on to the science category—to another meeting room. Rounding the corner, Dole brushed by Democrat Patrick Leahy. Like several other senators not involved in negotiations on the Brady bill, Leahy was strolling around the Capitol halls, killing time until the Senate either voted or recessed.

"Hey, Bob," the Democrat called out to the rapidly disappearing figure of the Senate minority leader, "I want to go home to Vermont!"

Without breaking his stride, Dole shrugged, sighed, and then disappeared down the hall.

For hours this pattern continued. The halls around the Senate would be quiet for long periods and then, suddenly, they would be filled with a flurry of activity as the senators involved with the negotiations, or their aides, came tearing through on their way to another meeting. At one point during the long evening, Orrin Hatch came through the lobby, the strain of hard negotiations evident on his face.

"How's it going?" a reporter asked.

"I'm going to get my AK-47," Hatch said and pantomimed shooting the assault rifle from his hip.

Around 10:00 P.M., the rumor that a vote would come at midnight had been replaced by one that said negotiations had deadlocked. According to this information, the Senate would recess within the hour, leaving the Brady bill's fate to be decided after the Fourth of July holiday recess. Sarah Brady heard the rumor, and, exhausted, decided it was probably true. She told her colleagues to call her if anything happened and drove home.

Not much later, a group of weary reporters stood at one end of the main lobby comparing notes on the various rumors and attempting to divine the Senate's intentions from the different sounds of the footsteps of legislative staffers coming through the marble-floored room. "I think we should go home," said one man, rubbing his eyes. "Nothing's going to happen tonight."

Even as he was speaking, there came from behind him and down a long hallway the *tap-tap-tap* of brisk footsteps. The sound grew louder until, around the corner and moving at great speed, came Kevin Burtzlaff, an aide to Howard Metzenbaum. Burtzlaff continued through the room at a fast clip, his briefcase swinging back and forth like a pendulum as he walked with a loose-limbed gait.

"Kevin," called one of the reporters, hurrying to catch up to the aide. "Is there anything you can tell me? Can I go home?"

"I wish you could," said Burtzlaff. "Then I could, too."

The reporter nodded and started to walk off when Burtzlaff called after him, "But I don't think you want to do that just yet." The reporter turned back. Burtzlaff was smiling slightly. Then the aide walked quickly away.

It's been worked out, thought the reporter to himself, suddenly excited. They're going to vote tonight.

Others had reached the same conclusion. A few minutes later, Gail Hoffman, HCI's chief lobbyist, dialed Sarah Brady's home phone number. The phone rang twice before it was picked up.

"Hello?" It was Sarah, her usually deep voice even lower due to fatigue.

"Sarah, get back up here," Hoffman said.

"Why? They're not going to vote, are they? I just opened a beer."

"Sorry, yes. They're going to vote tonight."

"Well, I'm not going *anywhere* until I finish my beer."

Instead, Brady made a thermos of coffee, drank a cup, climbed into her car, and drove back to the Capitol as fast as the speed limit allowed.

At a quarter till midnight, the full Senate gathered in its chamber and, at long last, began debate. It was not, however, debating the Brady bill itself. According to the compromise that had been hammered out over the course of that long evening, the body would debate and vote only on the Stevens substitute bill that night. This was the "instant-check" bill, the Senate version of the Staggers amendment that the House had soundly defeated only weeks before. Howard Metzenbaum tried to emphasize the fact that this was "old wine in a new skin" by continually referring to the Senate bill as the Staggers amendment instead of the Stevens bill. The Senate bill differed from the House version in the length of time it gave the Justice Department to set up an instant-check system: two years under Stevens; six months under Staggers.

If the Stevens substitute passed, that would be the end of the Brady bill for that session. If the Senate defeated Stevens, however, a vote on Brady would still have to be taken the following day. In an effort to win votes for the Brady bill, Democratic sponsors had agreed to drop four other gun-control provisions of lesser importance from their crime bill: a ban on ammunition magazines holding more than fifteen rounds; a requirement that the names of individuals who make multiple firearms purchases in a thirty-day period be reported to federal authorities; a provision that would allow pretrial detention of individuals charged with firearms offenses; and a prohibition on the sale of weapons to people convicted of violent misdemeanors.

After more than four years of controversy over the waiting-period legislation, there was little new to say about it or its substitute. Senators merely repeated their arguments one more time. Orrin Hatch painted the decision over which bill to back as a litmus test on the Second Amendment. "Let nobody make any mistake about it," he said. "If you believe in the Second Amendment and the right to keep and bear arms, which has been time honored in this country, this is your chance to vote for it." Howard Metzenbaum raised the specter of the gun lobby's undue influence in Congress: "The NRA is singing the same old song in an effort to defeat the Brady bill."

Finally, at almost one o'clock in the morning, the roll call vote was taken. Voting in the tradition-bound Senate is done by voice or hand sign; an electronic voting board such as the House uses would seem a bit plebeian. When they are ready to vote, senators merely wave a hand to get the clerk's attention. Then they give a thumbs-up or thumbs-down sign.

The vote in the Senate was straightforward. The roll was called and the votes recorded. Within minutes, the presiding officer announced the total: yeas—forty-four; nays—fifty-four.

The Stevens bill had been defeated.

Sarah Brady, watching from the gallery, was too tired to be elated. While her co-workers at HCI went out to celebrate over champagne, she drove herself home and crawled into bed. She also considered the revelry to be a bit premature. There would be time enough to celebrate when the Brady bill itself passed tomorrow—"*if* it passes," she quickly corrected herself.


SARAH BRADY WAS right not to count the NRA out too quickly. Early the next morning—Friday, June 28—Jim Baker was back on Capitol Hill trying to put together one last plan for derailing the Brady bill. But it was apparent, even to Baker, that such a prospect was now unlikely. The Senate had clearly signaled its intent the previous night when it turned back the Stevens bill by some ten votes. The best the NRA could now reasonably expect was to wring some face-saving concessions in exchange for not having their friends in the Senate throwing in every procedural holdup to block the bill.

The mood in the United States Capitol Building on that Friday was very different from the nearly hysterical tone that had marked the proceedings the night before. It was back to business as usual for the chamber, although, once again, no one was certain exactly when, or even *if*, the vote on Brady would take place. Once again the two sides huddled; but this time they met together, in a bipartisan effort to fashion a bill broadly acceptable to all sides, in an attempt to avoid a divisive floor fight.

At two o'clock in the afternoon, with the scheduled recess threatening, the two sides finally reached a compromise. The bill's official title reflected the extraordinary amount of wheeling and dealing that lay behind it: the Dole-Metzenbaum-Mitchell-Domenici-Kohl-Thurmond-Gore Modification of the Mitchell-Kohl-Gore-Metzenbaum Provision.

Many seemingly arcane provisions had been added; some existing provisions had been tinkered with. Instead of a seven-day waiting period, the Dole-Metzenbaum–et al. compromise called for a waiting period of five working days, in effect, a week. The attorney general was instructed to attempt to get 80 percent of all state criminal records computerized within two and a half years. When the instant-check system was up and running, the waiting period would be automatically repealed. States would each share in a federal kitty of $100 million provided annually to upgrade criminal records.

Despite these changes, the NRA could not escape the fact that beneath all the bells and whistles, beneath the avalanche of sponsors in its new multihyphenated name, what was being presented to the full Senate with the support of both party leaders was the Brady bill—in no meaningful way different from the legislation conceived five years earlier. In an attempt to salvage something—anything—from what appeared to be an overwhelming defeat, the NRA had its supporters in the Senate introduce an amendment stipulating that individual states could not have waiting periods longer than the one provided by the Brady bill. This preemption clause, which would have affected ten states, was defeated on a voice vote. Had the measure been accepted, the NRA would have supported the resulting compromise amendment—waiting period and all. But without even that one shred to claim as a victory, the gun lobby had no choice. The NRA remained opposed to the compromise.

At 2:45 P.M., opponents tried one last parliamentary move to derail the Brady bill, attempting to cut off debate on the amendment. Once again, supporters carried the day, defeating the motion by a vote of fifty-eight to forty-one.

A sense of inevitability concerning the now-imminent vote on the Brady bill pervaded the Senate. Unlike the situation in the House of Representatives in May, no one in this chamber needed to wait until the voting was half over to know which train they should climb on. The certainty that after five years of hard work their side was about to carry the day made the HCI workers giddy. A reporter asked HCI lobbyist Gwen Fitzgerald what she thought would happen next.

"Debate, for an hour," she replied.

"And then?"

"And then we kick the NRA's butt!" shouted Fitzgerald.

Almost exactly an hour later, debate on the Brady bill ended. It had been anticlimactic, a familiar rehashing of all the old arguments.

As the voting was about to begin, Bob Dole walked over to George Mitchell and the two weary legislators shook hands. This time, suspense over the outcome of the vote was replaced by revelry on the part of supporters and fatalistic acceptance on the part of opponents. Even as the roll was being called, colleagues on the Senate floor were congratulating Mitchell (a beaming John Glenn—a leading supporter of gun control since 1968—clasped the majority leader's hand in a soul shake) and offering condolences to Stevens and other NRA supporters.

When the presiding officer announced the results, there was not a single individual in the huge room who was surprised. His voice rang out through the chamber: "Yeas, sixty-seven. Nays, thirty-two. The amendment as amended is agreed to."


ONLY MINUTES LATER, crowded together on the northeast lawn of the Capitol Building, at a spot known as the "swampsite," the victors stood before more than a dozen news crews and reporters. Jim Brady wore a smile as bright as the Day-Glo–green trim on his wheelchair. Standing behind him, weary but elegant in a black dress and large gold earrings, stood Sarah Brady, her eyes red with a combination of emotion and exhaustion. Surrounding the couple was the gaggle of senators who had put together the compromise package: Howard Metzenbaum, Bob Dole, George Mitchell, Herbert Kohl, Joe Biden, and Al Gore.

Pointing to the Bradys, Biden told the reporters, "This day is their day and we salute them. What happened today will save American lives."

When asked why he, a longtime supporter of the NRA, had worked so hard for a compromise that included a waiting period, Bob Dole, who had been gravely wounded in World War II, answered, "When you've felt the sting of a gunshot wound, you can understand how Jim Brady feels and Sarah Brady feels."

After a few minutes, the press conference broke up; news crews had to rush across town to their offices to get video footage edited in time for the evening newscast. Once the cameras were turned off, the group of senators melted away into the humid afternoon. As a tired but ebullient Jim Brady was wheeled off, two reporters caught up with him.

"Mr. Brady," asked one reporter, "are you satisfied with the change from seven days to five working days?"

"Oh, that," said Jim. "There's no sense cutting up bunny rabbits over it."

The reporter just stared blankly at the man in the wheelchair for a few seconds. Cutting up bunny rabbits? Maybe, thought the reporter, Jim Brady was having problems with his thought processes.

Then Jim Brady smiled and said, gently, "Splitting hares? Bunny rabbits?" Brady continued: "There was a great deal of disinformation out on this bill. The first red herring that came up, we were able to go: 'Pull!' "

Brady swung his cane up to his shoulder and sighted along it, as if it were a shotgun. Tracing a sweeping semicircle across the Capitol dome, Brady squeezed an imaginary trigger.

"Pow!" he said, jerking the cane to simulate the shotgun's kick. "No more red herring."

Sarah Brady walked over.

"I'm sorry," she said as she grasped the handles on the back of Jim's wheelchair, "but we have to get going."

Jim Brady gave the reporters a "she's-the-boss" smile.

As the couple was leaving, one reporter called out a final question.

"Mr. Brady, you once referred to the NRA as the 'Evil Empire,' " he said. "How would you characterize it today?"

Jim Brady turned slightly in his wheelchair and looked back at the reporter. "The Defeated Empire," he said, smiling. "I'd call it the Defeated Empire."

# EPILOGUE

"WELL," DRAWLS Jim Baker, "we lost that one. Nobody likes to lose. Hell, I *hate* to lose. But you win some and lose some. You just have to try to win more than you lose. And when you look at the voting records on specific issues relating to firearms, our record is pretty darn good. I don't think the NRA—or Handgun Control, for that matter—rises or falls on one particular vote."

Several months after both houses of Congress passed the Brady bill, Jim Baker could afford to be philosophical about the losses. The crime bill, to which the waiting period was attached, was dead in the water. Although the larger package narrowly passed the House on November 27, 1991, Senate Republicans managed to block the bill in the Senate the following day, after President Bush promised to veto the legislation (which was, claimed Bush, "too soft on criminals").

"The real reason the president and the Republicans oppose this bill can be summed up in three letters," countered an angry Senator Joseph Biden. "N-R-A."

The NRA's other "defeat," the passage of a Senate ban on assault weapons, proved as chimerical as the vote on Brady. Gun-control advocates thought they had a chance to pass such a ban in the House when, on the day before the vote, a deranged man armed with a semiautomatic pistol opened fire in a cafeteria in the town of Killeen,

Texas. By the time the gunman finished shooting, twenty-two people were dead; it was the single worst gun massacre in the nation's history. Although the gun used in the killings (a Glock 17, the infamous "plastic gun" of earlier congressional debate) would not have been banned by the assault weapons legislation, the seventeen-round ammunition clip in the weapon would have. Such a proscription "would have slowed him down," said Representative Charles Schumer, "so that his bullets could not be sprayed and sprayed and sprayed. It's very clear he was not using a six-shot revolver."

But the killings influenced only one vote—that of Texas representative Chet Edwards, whose home district included Killeen. The bill was soundly defeated, 247 to 177.

"We cleaned their clocks on that one," boasted Jim Baker after the vote. "It just goes to show what I've been saying all along: It's never over until it's over."

Sarah Brady shares that philosophy. She promises to intensify her efforts to get the Brady bill passed—with or without a comprehensive crime bill. "This is just one more frustrating step in the saga of getting this thing into law," she says. "I don't want it to be held hostage anymore to a crime bill. I'd like to see it go on its own. We made the decision that since the president said he'd sign it as part of the crime bill, we had to use that vehicle, although we didn't particularly like it. We married ourselves to it. But not anymore."

In the meantime, the NRA is making an effort to regain police support, going about the task not by conciliation but by stepping up attacks on police leadership and by supporting alternative police organizations. The NRA's Division of Law Enforcement Relations (LER), which was started in July 1988, has a budget of $1 million a year. Its political orientation is seen in the fact that the LER is a subdivision of the ILA, the NRA's lobbying wing. The department publishes a tabloid newspaper, called *The Badge*, with a circulation of over 150,000. Articles in the paper include product information on new sidearms, pieces about police problems (STRESS: LAW ENFORCEMENT'S HIDDEN ASSAILANT), and a healthy dose of anti-gun-control propaganda. The division also offers a number of programs, including a speakers' lobby, a death benefits program (for survivors of officers killed in the line of duty), a scholarship program, and a discount buying program for soft body armor.

But the LER is only part of the NRA's fight to undo, or at least ameliorate, the damage done by the schism with law enforcement that began during the battles over armor-piercing bullets and "plastic guns."

In the summer of 1991, the NRA went after one of the top names on its "hit list": Dewey Stokes, the tough-talking national president of the Fraternal Order of Police. With 225,000 members, the FOP is the largest police organization of its kind in the nation, and Stokes, a twenty-three-year police veteran from Columbus, Ohio, was a long-time backer of the Brady bill. Worse yet, from the NRA's standpoint, he had been willing to travel around the country speaking at campaign rallies for politicians who had "crossed the line" and voted for gun control. Stokes's presence lent politicians the "tough-on-crime" image they needed to survive NRA attacks, for despite his stand on gun control, no one could mistake Stokes for a weak-kneed liberal.

Ironically, Stokes is politically to the right of many NRA members. He fumes over what he sees as modern society's tendency to coddle criminals. The purpose of prison, says Stokes, should be to punish—not reform. "I'm for permanent and total incarceration without rehabilitation for repeat offenders," he says. "It used to be in baseball, three strikes and you're out. Why should we turn these people loose to prey on society? Now we're seeing three or four percent of the population incarcerating the rest of us." Stokes even accuses the NRA of harboring liberals. "The only thing that bothers me about the NRA," he says, "is when I see how many people within the group are directly affiliated with the American Civil Liberties Union. That bothers me. That's the old Stalin theory, we'll destroy you from within."

With the bulldog face of a street cop straight from central casting, the political convictions of a John Bircher, and the fiery oratorical skills of a Baptist preacher, Stokes's support has been even more important to politicians than Sarah Brady's.

"There were firearms on this country's doorstep when we were founded and I believe there will be firearms on the doorstep when the good Lord comes to make us null and void," says Stokes. "But what person would leave his wife or children a fully loaded Uzi for home protection? There's a commonsense approach to this. And when the NRA tells me that the Brady bill will only save ten percent of the twenty-three thousand people who are killed each year, I want to ask

'Who in the NRA is going to pick the twenty-three hundred out of the twenty-three thousand who's going to die?' "

When Stokes ran for reelection in August 1991, the NRA supported his challenger, New Jersey detective Tom Possumato, Jr. (an opponent of gun control), with favorable articles in *The Badge*, and, according to Stokes, with under-the-table contributions totaling almost $100,000. The money, charged Stokes, was funneled through an NRA group called the Law Enforcement Alliance of America (LEAA). With that help, Possumato was able to buy advertisements for his candidacy in several magazines, including *Soldier of Fortune* and the NRA's *American Hunter*.

The NRA denies Stokes's charges, including the assertion that the LEAA has anything to do with the gun lobby.

"They're not a front for us," says Sam Cross, head of the NRA's Law Enforcement Relations division, adding with a laugh, "I wish they were. We could certainly use them. We support them and they would probably support us."

But when pressed on the issue, Cross admits that the gun lobby "may have given them [the LEAA] some start-up money" when the group was formed in early 1991. Cross fails to mention that the head of the LEAA, a former San Jose police officer named Leroy Pyle, is a member of the NRA's board of directors.

"I'm proud to be affiliated with the NRA," says Pyle. "Just like I was proud to be affiliated with law enforcement for twenty-seven years. I'm proud of the people who share my values, and one of them happens to be the NRA. The only people who would consider us a front for the NRA are those people who are very, very strongly antigun." Pyle tosses the charge that he is merely a front for special interests back at Stokes, who, Pyle claims, takes money from Handgun Control, Inc., a group the LEAA head detests. Of Sarah Brady herself, Pyle was quoted in *The San Francisco Chronicle* as saying, "That ugly cackler. She pulls her husband around like a pull-toy on a string. My friends and I say if that ever happened to one of us and our wife did that, somebody would slip into the house one night and slit her throat."

Regardless of where Possumato's money came from, in the end it was not enough to help him unseat Stokes, as members of the FOP cast their votes more than two to one for the incumbent. Organized law enforcement remains estranged from the NRA.

If the NRA couldn't convince America's cops that it was the guys in the white hats, then perhaps it could at least win back some of the American public—as it had with its "We Are the NRA" campaign of the previous decade. This time, however, according to a plan devised by the NRA's PR agency, Ackerman McQueen, and a New York marketing firm, the gun lobby would use the latest technology in its battle for American hearts and minds. The NRA would use a satellite TV network to beam its progun messages across the country. The centerpiece of the NRA Network would be an hour-long video magazine called "The GuNRAck." Each show would be hosted by a pair of anchors and feature several segments, each lasting one to four minutes long. An internal document describes the segments as follows:

- CAPITOL PATROL: Legislative issues and discussions with ILA federal, state and local lobbyists.
- CLEAN SHOTS: Hard-hitting three-minute commentaries by leaders . . .
- THE BADGE: Includes what NRA is doing for/with law enforcement . . .
- SAFETY FIRST: Features the "Eddie the Eagle" program and how the NRA is educating children about safe and responsible gun use.
- BETCHA DIDN'T KNOW: Brief, graphics-only bites about little-known services of, or facts about, the NRA . . .

According to a document prepared by the New York marketing firm Wunderman Worldwide, the show was necessary because "Our voices, and our *truthful unbiased* story are being drowned out by a hysterical and sensational press. . . . The public and the press all too readily see the NRA as fanatical bad guys." The NRA Network would, it was hoped, act as a force to counteract such negative publicity. Another Wunderman Worldwide internal memo stated that reaction to the concept from sixteen gun manufacturers had been positive. Sigarms was said to be "very enthusiastic"; Colt was "very interested"; Mossberg was "very excited"—but thought a more neutral name, such as the Outdoor Network, "might be more appealing." The Smith & Wesson representative expressed interest in the project, but warned that his company wouldn't advertise on a show that featured "two guys sitting in a bass boat for an hour."

Despite these early optimistic pronouncements, plans for "The GuNRAck" and the Outdoor Network are still on hold, for reasons the NRA declines to discuss. The NRA continues to rely on the tried-and-true methods of direct-mail campaigns to "get the word out."

And so the Great American Gun War continues—the opposing factions as bitterly divided and the issue as emotionally charged as ever. It doesn't help that both sides operate under a political imperative that prevents them from giving any credence to the claims of the other. As a result, ambiguity and nuance survive in this debate about as long as a wingless duck on the opening day of hunting season. Where facts are needed, the NRA offers bumper sticker slogans: GUNS DON'T KILL PEOPLE, PEOPLE KILL PEOPLE; WHEN GUNS ARE OUT-LAWED, ONLY OUTLAWS WILL HAVE GUNS.

Where reasoned discussion is required, pro-gun-control advocates often fall back on insulting the opposition. NRA members are painted as dangerous kooks or, at best, witless bumpkins. While these tactics may work well for each side *organizationally*, inflating their member-ship rolls, it is the American public that suffers most as a result, for the deadlock resulting from this polarization ensures that gun fatalities and injuries will continue to plague our country.

Even the most basic questions involving the gun-control issue are more complex than either side allows. For example: What role do handguns play in self-defense? Procontrol activists cite studies indicat-ing that the owners of handguns are far more likely to kill themselves or a family member with their guns (through suicide, during a family argument, or by accident) than to kill an intruder. But the effectiveness of handguns as a means of self-defense isn't measured by merely counting the number of bodies lying on the front doorstep, say NRA members, and they point to a study that emphasizes the number of times gun owners scare intruders off by merely *displaying* their weapons.

The Stockton lesson—which holds that both sides will seize upon the same incident to prove their diametrically opposed arguments—makes the issue even more confusing. This form of radical spin-doctoring was seen once again following the Killeen, Texas, massacre.

To those who favor a ban on handguns, the massacre at the Luby's Cafeteria was a clear-cut and compelling example of why such a prohi-bition is needed: twenty-two innocent people of all ages shot to death while eating lunch at a neighborhood cafeteria by a madman with a handgun. Survivors of the tragedy were seen weeping on TV, imploring *someone* to "do *something* about all these guns."

But NRA supporters looked at the same scene of devastation and came away with a different conclusion. These anticontrollers even had their own Killeen survivor to quote: a young woman named Suzanna Gratia. Gratia escaped the carnage at Luby's by crawling out a broken window. Her parents, however, weren't so lucky. Her father died trying to overpower the killer; her mother was shot dead as she cradled her dying husband in her arms. According to Suzanna Gratia, many of those who died that day could have survived—if she had been armed.

"I *used* to carry a gun in my purse," she said in a TV interview only days after the shootings, "and I immediately reached for my purse, went to open it, and realized that I didn't have the gun. And then it was like, *now what?* . . . My only regret is that myself or some other person, a reasonably sane person, didn't have a gun. You cannot take away my right to protect myself!"

*And what about a woman whose life has been threatened by a former boyfriend or ex-husband?* ask NRA supporters. *Should she be denied the right to protect herself with a handgun?*

*But what about all the children who are killed each year by "toy" guns that turn out to be real ones?* counter procontrol activists. *Don't you care about them?*

There are, thankfully, a few voices of moderation on the subject of gun control—although they are rarely heard over the roar of partisans—and if progress is to be made in the seemingly endless Great American Gun War, it will come when enough people heed these voices. Professor James Wright, a sociologist at Tulane University and co-author of the first comprehensive study of felons and their guns, *Armed and Considered Dangerous*, is one such voice.

Wright's findings support the NRA's contention that measures such as waiting periods and restrictive licensing procedures will have only limited effect on the ability of criminals to obtain arms. Wright also points out the flaw in the argument that cutting down on the number of guns sold will result in a safer society since there will be fewer guns around to be stolen.

"As of today there are guns in half of all U.S. households," he says.

"Even if you started right now to make it more difficult for citizens to purchase new guns, it would be decades—if not centuries—before the total supply out there to be stolen would be affected. The obvious counter would be 'You've got to start sometime and you've got to start somewhere, so why not here and now?' I have no response to that, other than to say: Just don't expect to see positive results in our lifetimes."

The gun lobby often quotes Wright—when it's to its advantage. But don't look in NRA publications to find out what the Tulane professor thinks of the gun lobby's oft-repeated contention that the answer to crime is to "get tough on criminals."

"Their view is simplistic in the extreme," says Wright.

> The U.S. is already the toughest of the advanced industrial societies on crime and criminals. We lock up a larger fraction of our population for longer periods of time than any other advanced Western nation. And yet we have overwhelmingly the largest crime rate. So this notion that you can just "turn down the screws" and get tough on criminals . . . well, hell, we've been doing that for 70 years, not to any noticeably positive effect. That line of argument generally overlooks the price of building new prisons, the cost of keeping them there, what happens to men in prisons—which generally is that they get meaner and tougher and get to be better criminals. The argument "Let's get tough" is a cheap cop-out.

Or listen to the voice of Edward Ezell, curator of the Smithsonian Institution's national firearms collection. Many on the procontrol side consider Ezell an NRA patsy because he has spoken out against many gun-control measures, even testifying before Congress against the ban on assault weapons (as part of a panel that included an NRA board member, no less). But during the Senate hearing the gun expert surprised many—including the NRA—when he said that instead of the ban on assault weapons, he supported a registration and licensing procedure for *all* gun owners, a program that could include a mandatory safety training course. Ezell's proposal was far more radical than what professional gun-control advocates were recommending.

> When I was testifying before the Senate, I was trying to tell those guys—Look, you have to impose some rationality on this discourse

because right now it's all emotion; it's all anecdote; it's all people trying to score points. And that's a hell of a way to do public policy decision making.

We have a social problem with firearms. There's no question about that. But we have to develop some kind of reasonable social compromise that will allow us to address that problem in such a way that we're not dividing this society into those who really favor it and those who don't favor it. Because that just means that a lot of people are going to go underground with guns, a lot of people are going to become even more disrespectful of the governmental process than they already are and we'll still have the social problem of guns on the street that we have now.

Look, I don't think the Russians will come pouring in if we prohibit guns tomorrow. But I also don't think it'll stop crime either. Somehow we have to look this issue more squarely in the face and I don't see either the NRA or any anti-gun people doing that.

If gun-control activists are surprised by Ezell's moderate views, gun enthusiasts are just as unsure about what to make of Eric Sterling, a name familiar to those who followed the great legislative battles of the 1980s over gun control. As an aide to Democratic representative William Hughes of New Jersey (a prominent member of the House Crime Subcommittee), Sterling helped craft some of the key gun-control bills of that period—bills the NRA loathed. Today, as head of a Washington think tank devoted to criminal justice issues, Sterling's views on gun control have mellowed.

It's a cultural, urban versus rural thing. There's this feeling that there's something a bit funny about people who own guns. We make fun of them. "It's a penis substitute. It's a fetish. They're sickos."

The flip side—from the NRA point of view—is of these urban socialist reformers who are unrealistic. "They want to take all guns away. They're siding with lefties who are tolerant of big government and high taxes. They're willing to sacrifice the Constitution for their one-world, UN, commie-pinko stuff."

But can we look at guns in a nonjudgmental way? Can we say: These things are in the environment and they're dangerous. How do we minimize the harm without blaming people—without saying: you're evil, you're perverted, you're a gun nut? The debate shouldn't be about blaming people or calling them immoral or bad. We should be figuring out a strategy to reduce some of the lethality involved and trying to build a consensus around that.

In an attempt to build that consensus, researchers at the Centers for Disease Control are doing pioneering work in treating gun violence as a public health issue—like drugs or sexually transmitted diseases—rather than as a political/legal/moral question. This approach has produced a number of policy options. For example, our society could require that guns be manufactured with built-in combination locks (like the ones on many briefcases) so that only the owner could use them; limit the muzzle sizes of guns to reduce their lethality; provide for mandatory gun safety courses for all gun owners; require childproof safeties and indicators to show if a gun is loaded. These changes would have only a minor impact on the number of gun injuries and fatalities, but they do represent a starting point for discussing "gun control" in a new way—one that may prove less divisive than traditional approaches to the issue.

Recent changes within the NRA make such a rapprochement seem unlikely for the time being, however. The organization's response to its troubles has been to circle the wagons, to become even *more* intransigent and even *less* willing to consider anything that smacks of compromise. "We are at the dawn of a new NRA," promised Wayne LaPierre in a 1992 fund-raising appeal. "Starting immediately, the NRA is going to be a strong, dynamic, vibrant organization."

The view that any losses suffered by the gun lobby are attributable solely to a lack of "toughness" is one of the NRA's defining characteristics. The primary spokesperson for this point of view is Neal Knox, now back on the NRA's board and more influential than ever. According to Knox, the NRA's problems began when the organization "helped pass the armor-piercing-bullet and plastic gun bills in a misguided effort to appear more 'reasonable'—which only resulted in [the] NRA appearing weak." Knox has nothing but disdain for "wimps" who argue that the NRA should be trying to win back friends in Congress, who advocate mending fences with normally progun legislators alienated by the NRA's strong-arm attacks directed at all who fail to toe the gun lobby line. Like the doomed warriors in Tennyson's poem "The Charge of the Light Brigade," the NRA's foot soldiers in Congress had their orders, and "Theirs not to reason why, Theirs but to do and die." Knox's solution to any problems in Congress is vintage NRA: "Take out a few turncoats. Slap down a few and the rest will get the message not to mess with our gun rights."

The new NRA board (which includes not only Neal Knox and several of his hard-core allies but the even more extreme members of the *Soldier of Fortune* slate) will undoubtedly support all efforts by Executive Vice President Wayne LaPierre to make the gun lobby even tougher and less open to compromise.

It's hard for most Americans to understand today's NRA apart from the many myths about it—both pro and con. The gun lobby is neither the Evil Empire its foes claim nor the superpatriotic defender of the most cherished American values it claims to be. At one level, the NRA is simply a very effective single-interest pressure group. While it's true that the group defends its interests more zealously and attacks its opponents with more venom than do most of its peers, these are differences of style, not substance. The NRA wears no velvet glove over *its* iron fist.

Still, there *is* one important difference between the NRA and most other lobbies, and that difference has to do with the cause the NRA defends: the cause of guns. Stripped of all hyperbole on both sides of the issue, the essential facts about guns in America today are these: There are a lot of them out there, and great harm is done by or with them. The word *epidemic* may be overused, but surely it applies to the gun violence that claims nearly 30,000 American lives each year. When lobbyists for most other groups get their way with Congress, the result is usually that consumers pay a few pennies more—or even a few dollars more—than they should for a product. But when the gun lobby's leaders prevent consideration of even the mildest gun-control measures the results are very often tragic: Large numbers of people are shot, maimed, and killed.

It is undeniable that the gun lobby's power has declined recently, and it is likely to continue to drop as Americans—sick of the war in our streets and tired of the NRA's unwillingness to compromise in order to stem that plague—demand that their elected representatives enact gun-control laws. But it is too soon to sound the death knell for the NRA. And the group's membership, which had declined to 2.3

million, began growing again in late 1991. Several months later, the NRA could claim 2.6 million members. No matter how you feel about the National Rifle Association (and nobody is neutral about it), and despite its current problems, there is no denying that the NRA— cantankerous and cranky, splintered by bitter infighting and as uncompromising as ever—remains a powerful force in American politics.

# SELECTED BIBLIOGRAPHY

## PART I: THE RISE OF THE NRA

### CHAPTER 1: THE STOCKTON LESSON

*Articles*

Caputo, Philip. "Death Goes to School." *Esquire*, December 1989, pp. 137–155.

*Los Angeles Times*. "Rifleman Kills 5 at Stockton School." 18 January 1989, p. A1.

———. "Drifter Had a Fondness for Firearms." 18 January 1989, p. A1.

———. "Rifle Used in Carnage 'Easier to Buy than Handguns.' " 18 January 1989, p. A3.

———. "Gunman Had Attended School He Assaulted." 19 January 1989, p. A1.

———. "Somber Students and Teachers Wrestle with the Horror." 19 January 1989, p. A20.

———. "Outrage in Stockton." 19 January 1989, p. B6.

———. "Stockton—Tending to the Psyche." 20 January 1989, p. A1.

———. "Escalating Hate Reportedly Consumed Gunman." 20 January 1989, p. A3.

———. "Grieving Stockton Starts Healing Process." 22 January 1989, p. A3.

———. "Mourners Seek Solace at Rites for Slain Children." 22 January 1989, p. A3.

———. "Stockton Bids Goodby to Slain Schoolchildren." 24 January 1989, p. A3.


### Government Reports and Hearings

Kempsky, Nelson, et al. "A Report to Attorney General John K. Van de Kamp on Patrick Edward Purdy and the Cleveland School Killings." October 1989. Office of the Attorney General, California Department of Justice.

U.S. Congress. Senate. Committee on the Judiciary. Subcommittee on the Constitution. *Assault Weapons.* Hearings. 101st Cong., 1st sess. Washington, D.C.: U.S. Government Printing Office, 1990.


## CHAPTER 2: THE EARLY YEARS

### Books

Bigelow, Donald N. *William Conant Church & The Army and Navy Journal.* New York: Columbia University Press, 1952.

Leddy, Edward. *Magnum Force Lobby.* Lanham, Md.: University Press of America, 1987.

Sherrill, Robert. *The Saturday Night Special.* New York: Charterhouse, 1973.

Trefethen, James, and Serven, James. *Americans and Their Guns: The National Rifle Association's Story Through Nearly a Century of Service to the Nation.* Harrisburg, Pa.: Stackpole Books, 1967.


### Articles

*American Rifleman.* "Concerned NRA Members Redirect Their Association." July 1977, pp. 16–17.

Carmichel, Jim. "The NRA Revolution." *Outdoor Life,* September 1977, pp. 102–08.

Mitchell, John. "God, Guns, and Guts Made America Free." *American Heritage,* February 1978, pp. 4–17.

*New York Times.* "The Rifle Association." 13 December 1873, p. A1.

———. "A Victory for America." 27 September 1874, p. A1.

———. "Rifle Group Ousts Most Leaders in Move to Bolster Stand on Guns." 23 May 1977, p. 16.

———. "Hard-Line Opponent of Gun Laws Wins New Term at Helm of Rifle Association." 4 May 1981, p. B11.

Wingate, George. "Early Days of the NRA." *American Rifleman,* May/June 1951.

*Government Reports and Hearings*

U.S. Congress. Senate. Committee on the District of Columbia. "Dangerous Weapons." Unpublished hearing. File (71) SD-T 41 (Box K), 6 June 1930.

*Miscellaneous Documents*

Ackerman, Hood, & McQueen. *A Tribute to Harlon Carter*, videotape, 1985.
Gilmore, Russell S. "Crack Shots and Patriots: The National Rifle Association and America's Military-Sporting Tradition, 1871–1929." Ph.D. dissertation, University of Wisconsin, 1975.


CHAPTER 3: ONE OF THE GREAT RELIGIONS OF THE WORLD

*Books*

Leddy, Edward. *Magnum Force Lobby*. Lanham, Md.: University Press of America, 1987.
Sorauf, Frank. *Money in American Elections*. Glenview, Ill.: Scott, Foresman/ Little, Brown College Division, 1988.

*Articles*

*American Rifleman*. "Four Years of the Carter Administration: An Affront to the Rights of Gun Owners." October 1980, p. 59.
———. "President Reagan's Speech Elicits Vigorous Applause." July 1983, pp. 40–41.
Bruce-Briggs, B. "The Great American Gun War." *The Public Interest*, Fall 1976, pp. 37–62.
Cohodas, Nadine. "Senate Approves Bill Easing Gun Control Law." *Congressional Quarterly*, 13 July 1985, pp. 1391–92.
———. "House Votes to Weaken U.S. Gun Control Law." *Congressional Quarterly*, 12 April 1986, pp. 783–85.
Freund, C. P. "The NRA's Friendly Fire." *Regardie's*, December-January 1984, pp. 66–70.
Graves, Florence. "The Fastest Gun in Town Draws a Blank." *Common Cause*, February 1982, pp. 14–21.
Keller, Bill. "NRA, Liquor Industry Seek to Save BATF." *Congressional Quarterly*, 3 April 1982, p. 720.
*New York Times*. "White House Planning to Kill Firearms Enforcement Unit." 19 September 1981, p. A1.

*Government Reports and Hearings*

*Congressional Record.* 99th Cong., 2d sess., 9 April 1986. H1645-H1651. Washington, D.C.

————. 99th Cong., 2d sess., 10 April 1986. H1741-H1757. Washington, D.C.

Congressional Research Service. *Federal Regulation of Firearms.* Report prepared for the Committee on the Judiciary, U.S. Senate. Washington, D.C.: U.S. Government Printing Office, 1982.

U.S. Congress. House. Committee on the Judiciary. Subcommittee on Crime. *Legislation to Modify the 1968 Gun Control Act.* Hearings. 99th Cong., 1st and 2d sess. Washington, D.C.: U.S. Government Printing Office, 1986.

## PART II: CRACKS IN THE EMPIRE

### CHAPTER 4: THE BULLET AND THE BADGE

*Articles*

*American Rifleman.* "Here We Stand." November 1986, p. 7.

————. "The Facts About 'Plastic' Guns." September 1987, pp. 42–43.

Anderson, Jack. "Lawmaker Seeks to Ban Plastic Pistols." *Washington Post,* 14 March 1986, p. D13.

————. "Plastic Handgun Fools Airport Sensors." *Washington Post,* 18 April 1986, p. C21.

Aquilino, John. *Insider Gun News,* August 1988, p. 3.

*Washington Post.* "NRA Gets Meese to Withdraw Proposal to Ban 'Plastic Guns.' " 22 October 1987, p. A1.

*Government Reports and Hearings*

*Congressional Record.* 99th Cong., 1st sess., 17 December 1985. H12229. Washington, D.C.

U.S. Congress. House. Committee on the Judiciary. Subcommittee on Crime. *Armor-Piercing Ammunition and the Criminal Misuse and Availability of Machineguns and Silencers.* Hearings. 98th Cong., 2d sess. Washington, D.C.: U.S. Government Printing Office, 1984.

U.S. Congress. House. Committee on the Judiciary. Subcommittee on Crime. *Firearms Which Escape Detection at Airport Security Checkpoints.* Hearings. 100th Cong., 1st sess. Washington, D.C.: U.S. Government Printing Office, 1987.

*Miscellaneous Documents*

Battema, John. Letter to Representative Mario Biaggi. 27 March 1986.

Boyd, Thomas. Letter to Senator James McClure. 16 March 1988.

Feighan, Edward. Letter to Attorney General Edwin Meese. 16 November 1987.

International Association of Chiefs of Police. Special Bulletin. "IACP President Joe Casey Under Attack from NRA." Undated.

Vaughn, Jerald. Letter to G. Ray Arnett. 13 February 1986.

National Rifle Association. Emergency alert. 8 December 1987.


CHAPTER 5: A WAR IN THE STREETS

*Books*

Wright, James, et al. *Under the Gun: Weapons, Crime, and Violence in America.* New York: Aldine, 1983. Rev. ed. of *Weapons, Crime, and Violence in America.* 1981.

Wright, James, and Rossi, Peter. *Armed and Considered Dangerous.* New York: Aldine, 1986.


*Articles*

*Public Health Reports.* "Firearms Injuries and Deaths: A Critical Public Health Issue." March–April 1989, pp. 111–20.


*Government Reports and Hearings*

Fingerhut, Lois, et al. "Firearm Mortality Among Children, Youth, and Young Adults 1–34 Years of Age, Trends and Current Status: United States, 1979–88." *Monthly Vital Statistics Report,* 14 March 1991, pp. 1–15.

*Statistical Abstract of the United States.* Tables 123, 124, 283, 286, 287, 290, 306. Washington, D.C.: U.S. Government Printing Office, 1990.

U.S. Congress. House. Select Committee on Children, Youth, and Families. "Children and Guns." Hearings. 100th Cong., 1st sess. Washington, D.C.: U.S. Government Printing Office, 1989.


CHAPTER 6: HOLDING ACTIONS

*Books*

Alderman, Ellen, and Kennedy, Caroline. *In Our Defense.* New York: William Morrow and Company, Inc., 1991.

Trefethen, James, and Serven, James. *Americans and Their Guns: The Na-*

*tional Rifle Association's Story Through Nearly a Century of Service to the Nation.* Harrisburg, Pa.: Stackpole Books, 1967.

## Articles

Aquilino, John. *Insider Gun News*, February 1991, p. 1.

*Broadcasting.* "Dukakis Campaign Responds to NRA Ads with Warning of Legal Action." 17 October 1988, pp. 28–29.

Burger, Warren. "The Right to Bear Arms." *Parade Magazine*, 14 January 1990.

Hofstadter, Richard. "America as a Gun Culture." *American Heritage*, October 1970, pp. 3–85.

*Malden Massachusetts News.* "Ask Turn-In of Handguns." 25 October 1976, p. 1.

*The New Gun Week.* "Dukakis Out to Disarm Massachusetts." 4 July 1986.

Wingate, George. "Early Days of the NRA." *American Rifleman*, May/June 1951.

## Government Reports and Hearings

U.S. Congress. Senate. Committee on the District of Columbia. "Dangerous Weapons." Unpublished hearing. File (71) SD-T 41 (Box K), 6 June 1930.

## Miscellaneous Documents

Abrams, Robert. "Assurance of Discontinuance." Office of the Attorney General of the State of New York, 28 June 1991.

*American Rifleman.* Cover. October 1988.

Bush, George. Letter to the National Rifle Association. 2 September 1988.

Cooper, Charles. Letter to Daniel Taylor, General Counsel, Dukakis-Bentsen Campaign. 14 October 1988.

Dukakis, Michael. Letter to Senator Stanley Zarod. 22 March 1976.

Handgun Control, Inc. "PAC Expenditures to U.S. Senate Candidates by the National Rifle Association, 1983–1990." Washington, D.C., 1991.

LaPierre, Wayne. Statement at news conference. Dallas, Texas, 17 October 1988.

Morrissey, Moira. Letter to Stephen Shulman. 17 June 1988.

National Coalition to Ban Handguns. "Study of NRA Campaign Funding." Washington, D.C., 1982.

National Rifle Association. "Computer Processing: January 2–July 31, 1990." Internal document, 1990.

———. Member letter. 21 October 1981.

———. Illinois Legislative Alert. 12 June 1981.

———. Member letter. 4 October 1983.

Powell, Lewis. Speech before the American Bar Association. Cited in Brady, Sarah. "The 2nd Amendment: What It Really Means." *San Francisco Barrister*, December 1989, pp. 6–7.

Shulman, Stephen. Letter to Moira Morrissey, Assistant Attorney General, State of New York. 30 March 1988.

## CHAPTER 7: ENEMIES WITHIN AND WITHOUT

### Books

Dickenson, Mollie. *Thumbs Up*. New York: William Morrow and Company, Inc., 1987.

Shields, Pete. *Guns Don't Die—People Do*. New York: Arbor House, 1981.

### Articles

*American Rifleman*. "Here We Stand." January 1990, p. 7.

*Congressional Quarterly*. "NRA–Ad Agency Battle." 4 October 1968, p. 2676.

McGuigan, Patrick. "Loose Cannons." *Policy Review*, Summer 1989, pp. 54–56.

Moldea, Dan. "Shootout on 16th Street." *Regardie's*, April 1987, pp. 105–24.

### Miscellaneous Documents

*Handgun Control, Inc.* "Campaign '88, Blueprint for Action." Supporter packet. Washington, D.C., 1987.

Nauser, Deborah. Letter to author. 1991.

## PART III: GUN WARS

## CHAPTER 8: DRUMS ALONG THE POTOMAC

### Books

Ezell, Edward. *The AK47 Story*. Harrisburg, Pa.: Stackpole Books, 1986.

### Articles

Fackler, Martin, et al. "Wounding Effects of the AK-47 Rifle Used by Patrick Purdy in the Stockton, California, Schoolyard Shooting of January 17, 1989." *The American Journal of Forensic Medicine and Pathology*, vol. 11, no. 3, pp. 185–89.

*New York Times*. "Epidemic in Urban Hospitals: Wounds from Assault Rifles." 21 February 1989, p. A1.

———. "The Search for an Issue." 16 March 1989, p. A1.

### Government Reports and Hearings

Bureau of Alcohol, Tobacco and Firearms. *Report and Recommendation of the ATF Working Group on the Importability of Certain Semiautomatic Rifles.* Washington, D.C., 1989.

*Congressional Record.* 100th Cong., 1st sess., 11 April 1989. Washington, D.C.

Federal Election Commission. "Committee Index of Candidates Supported/Opposed (Index D), 1979–1990." Washington, D.C.

*Federal Register.* "Draft Report on Systems for Identifying Felons Who Attempt to Purchase Firearms." 26 June 1989, 26902-26940.

U.S. Congress. Senate. Committee on the Judiciary. Subcommittee on the Constitution. *Assault Weapons.* Hearings. 101st Cong., 1st sess. Washington, D.C.: U.S. Government Printing Office, 1990.

U.S. Congress. Senate. Committee on the Judiciary. Subcommittee on the Constitution. *The Brady Handgun Violence Prevention Act.* Hearings. 101st Cong., 1st sess. Washington, D.C.: U.S. Government Printing Office, 1989.

### Miscellaneous Documents

Bennett, William. Memorandum to Edwin Meese on drug policy. 14 March 1988.

———. Press statement. 14 March 1989.

Sensenbrenner, F. James, Jr. "Dear Colleague" letter. 11 August 1988.

Thornburgh, Richard. Letter to Vice President Dan Quayle. 20 November 1989.

Warner, James. Letter to William Bennett. 10 August 1989.

## CHAPTER 9: FIRST BLOOD

### Articles

LaPierre, Wayne. "The 101st Congress Has Ended . . . and Victory Is Ours!" *American Rifleman*, December 1990, p. 46.

*Maine Sunday Telegram.* "Democrats Back 7-Day Handgun Waiting Period." 3 June 1990, p. Al.

Stewart, Jim, and Alexander, Andrew. "Firepower: Assault Weapons in America." Cox Newspapers series, 21 May–2 November 1989.

### Government Reports and Hearings

*Congressional Record.* 101st Cong., 2d sess., 23 May 1990. S6789-S6801. Washington, D.C.

U.S. Congress. Senate. Committee on the Judiciary. *Review of the Second National Drug Control Strategy.* Hearings. 101st Cong., 1st and 2d sess. Washington, D.C.: U.S. Government Printing Office, 1990.

### Miscellaneous Documents

DeConcini, Dennis. Letter to President George Bush. 22 May 1990.
National Rifle Association. Member letter. 4 October 1990.

## CHAPTER 10: PALACE COUP

### Articles

Cassidy, J. Warren. "Open Letter to NRA Members." *American Rifleman,* January 1991, p. 51.
Knox, Neal. "The NRA Needs Your Vote." *Guns & Ammo,* February 1991, p. 24.
*Washington Post.* "Vice President of NRA Board Resigns Post." 10 February 1991, p. A6.

### Government Reports and Hearings

*Congressional Record.* 101st Cong., 2d sess., 5 June 1990. S7132-S7133. Washington, D.C.

## CHAPTER 11: OPERATION ST. JOSEPH

### Articles

AuCoin, Les. "Confessions of a Former NRA Supporter." *Washington Post,* 18 March 1991.
*New York Times.* "Gun Control Bill Backed by Reagan in Appeal to Bush." 29 March 1991, p. A1.

### Government Reports and Hearings

*Congressional Record.* 102d Cong., 1st sess., 8 May 1991. H2821-H2876. Washington, D.C.

### Miscellaneous Documents

Andrews, Thomas. "Dear Colleague" letter. 19 March 1991.
Baker, James. Transcript of "Sportsmen's Forum." CompuServe Information Service, 15 November 1990.
Carter, Jimmy. Author interview. 26 April 1991. Iowa City, Iowa.
Ford, Gerald. Letter to Congressman Charles Schumer. 18 April 1991.

National Rifle Association. Internal memo. "Texts of NRA's Two Upcoming TV Ads, One for DC Market & One for VA Market." 20 February 1991.
Reagan, Ronald. 1991. Remarks at the George Washington University Convocation. 28 March 1991.


CHAPTER 12: THE LAST BATTLE

*Articles*

*New York Times.* "Senate Approves Handgun Controls." 29 June 1991, p. A1.

*Government Reports and Hearings*

*Congressional Record.* 102d Cong., 1st sess., 27 June 1991. S8927-S8947. Washington, D.C.
*Congressional Record.* 102d Cong., 1st sess., 28 June 1991. S9039-S9087. Washington, D.C.


EPILOGUE

*Books*

Wright, James, and Rossi, Peter. *Armed and Considered Dangerous.* New York: Aldine, 1986.


*Articles*

*The Badge.* "New Jersey Officer Challenges Stokes for Top FOP Post, Promises Heated Race." July 1991, p. 3. Washington, D.C.: National Rifle Association.
Baker, Susan. "Without Guns, Do People Kill People?" *American Journal of Public Health,* June 1985, pp. 587–88.
Kellermann, Arthur, and Reay, Donald. "Protection or Peril? An Analysis of Firearm-Related Deaths in the Home." *The New England Journal of Medicine,* 12 June 1986, pp. 1557–60.
Kellermann, Arthur, et al. "The Epidemiologic Basis for the Prevention of Firearm Injuries." *Annual Review of Public Health,* 1991, pp. 17–40.
Kleck, Gary. "Crime Control Through the Private Use of Armed Force." *Social Problems,* February 1988.
Lee, Robert, and Sacks, Jeffrey. "Latchkey Children and Guns at Home." *Journal of the American Medical Association,* 7 November 1990, p. 2210.
Lee, Robert, et al. "Incidence Rates of Firearm Injuries in Galveston, Texas, 1979–1981." *American Journal of Epidemiology,* vol. 134, no. 5, pp. 511–21.
*National Journal.* "NRA Aids New Gun Group." 18 May 1991, pp. 1185–86.

*NRAction.* "House Strikes Gun Ban from 'Crime' Bill." November 1991, p. 1. Washington, D.C.: NRA Institute for Legislative Action.

*San Francisco Chronicle.* "A Police Shootout Over Gun Control." 10 August 1990, p. B3.

*Washington Post.* "Police Group's Leadership Election Seen as Showdown Over Gun Control." 11 August 1991, p. A3.

### Government Reports and Hearings

U.S. General Accounting Office. Program Evaluation and Methodology Division. *Accidental Shootings.* Washington, D.C.: GAO, March 1991.

### Miscellaneous Documents

Ackerman, Hood, & McQueen. "Content and Treatment Recommendations for the NRA TV Network." Internal document, 19 September 1990.

Compass Entertainment, Inc. "Sales and Marketing Research Calls for the OUTDOOR NETWORK." Memorandum to Wunderman Worldwide, 22 August 1990.

Kates, Don, Jr. "Guns, Murder, and the Constitution." Policy briefing paper. San Francisco: Pacific Research Institute for Public Policy, February 1990.

Kopel, David. "Why Gun Waiting Periods Threaten Public Safety." Issue paper. Golden, Colo.: Independence Institute, 1991.

Wunderman Worldwide. "NRA Network Status." Office memorandum, 23 August 1990.

# INDEX